07/22

$2.0]

SNOW BOUND

SNOW BOUND

LADD HAMILTON

WSU
PRESS

Washington State University Press
Pullman, Washington

Washington State University Press, PO Box 645910, Pullman, Washington 99164-5910
Phone: 800-354-7360   Fax: 509-335-8568
© 1997 by the Board of Regents of Washington State University
All rights reserved
First printing 1997

Unless otherwise noted, the drawings and photographs in this book are from *In the Heart of the Bitter Root Mountains: The Story of "The Carlin Hunting Party"* by Heclawa (Abe Himmelwright), New York: G.P. Putnam's Sons, 1895.

Library of Congress Cataloging-in-Publication Data
Hamilton, Ladd.
    Snowbound / Ladd Hamilton.
       p. cm.
    Includes bibliographical references (p. 0.
    ISBN 0-87422-153-6 (cloth) : acid-free paper).—
    ISBN 0-87433-154-4 (paper : acid-free paper)
      1. Hunter—Bitterroot Range (Idaho and Mont.)—History—19th century. 2. Winter storms—Bitterroot Range (Idaho and Mont.)—History—19th century. 3. Hunting—Bitterroot Range (Idaho and Mont.)—History—19th century. I. Title.
SK 15.H34 1997
813'.54—dc21   97-18694
                                         CIP

Contents

For my brother, Deane

Author's Note

This is the true story of a tragic incident that prompted an outburst of ethical and moral argument in the winter of 1893-94, not only in the region where it occurred—in the mountainous country between Spokane, Washington, and Missoula, Montana—but also in places as far east as New York.

With two exceptions, all the characters are real, although I have given a few of them greater roles in the drama than the documentation supports. I also have imagined what might have happened in Spokane as the Carlin party prepared to depart for the Bitterroot Mountains and at several points on the trail. In every case, however, the narrative is consistent with the facts as they were recorded in William E. Carlin's diary, in A.L.A. Himmelwright's book, *In the Heart of the Bitterroot Mountains*, and in the reports of officers of the U.S. 4th Cavalry and 25th Infantry.

The fictional characters are the sheriff's deputy who operated the feed store in Kendrick where Martin Spencer went for weather information, and Roberts, the *Spokane Review* reporter. I have had to imagine how Fannie Colegate and her son, Charles, must have responded to the first indication that something had gone seriously wrong. Thus the material concerning them in the early chapters is rooted in my assumptions rather than in documented fact. Charles's participation in the search for his father, near the end of the book, *is* documented by several sources.

Descriptions of the military units' activities are based primarily upon the official reports of First Lieutenant Charles Elliott, 4th Cavalry, and Captain George Andrews, 25th Infantry, and letters of Brigadier General William P. Carlin, commander of the Department of the Columbia at Vancouver Barracks. These reports and other military correspondence are housed in the National Archives in Washington, D.C.

In many places I created dialogue based upon fragments from Carlin's diary, as reproduced in Himmelwright's book. For example, Ben Keeley's complaints that the party was taking too long to work down the Lochsa River, and the discussions that ensued, are based on this sentence from Himmelwright's chapter eleven: "Keeley was anxious to turn the rafts loose and trust to luck in running through, but the others did not consider it safe at all, as we didn't know what was below us." I have quoted indirectly the conversations that I imagined took place; that is, without quotation marks. Where quotation marks appear, the reader can assume that those were the words actually written or spoken.

The *Spokane Review* of November 25, 1893, in a story reprinted in the *Lewiston Teller* on November 30, said that "Himmelwright had agreed to meet his mother in Chicago October 20, more than a month ago." That is the basis for the references to Mrs. Himmelwright in this book.

Readers familiar with the story of the Carlin hunting party may be surprised by my spelling of the name of the camp cook. The usual spelling is George *Colgate*. That is the spelling used by the U.S. Forest Service on the grave site it maintains in the Clearwater National Forest, by all the newspapers reporting on the adventure, by the U.S. Army, and even by the men who were with him on that hunting expedition. I have found only one reference to the affair in which that spelling is not used, and that is in an article written for *The Pacific Northwesterner* in 1975 by George Cerveny, a relative, who said the family spelled it *Colegate*. Cerveny was right. The census records of Kootenai County, Idaho, where the family lived, list the name as *Colegate,* as does the obituary of Charles Colegate in the Rathdrum, Idaho, *Silver Blade*. I saw no reason to give the cook the wrong name, simply for the sake of historical consistency.

The Nez Perce Indian name for the Clearwater River was Kooskooskee, and that was the name that appeared on many maps in the 1890s. At the time of the Carlin party's expedition, the part of the river now known by whites as the Lochsa (LOCK-saw), a Flathead Indian word meaning "rough water," was called the North Fork of the Middle Fork of the Kooskooskee, or Clearwater, and the river now known as the Selway was called the South Fork of the Middle Fork. To use those names in this narrative would have been confusing since different streams now bear them. So I have in most instances referred to the rivers by the names they have now. From the Selway east to its headwaters, the river is the Lochsa.

From the Selway west to Kooskia (KOOS-key), it is the Middle Fork of the Clearwater. From Kooskia west to Lewiston, where the Kooskooskee pours into the Snake, it is simply the Clearwater.

The river Himmelwright calls the St. Joseph does not exist. The river is the St. Joe.

The Indian names that abound in the region also may be confusing to many readers. Here is a guide to the pronunciation of some of them:

Kamiah (CAM-ee-eye).

Kootenai (COOT-en-ee)

Nez Perce (Nezz-PURSE). The French NAY-pair-SAY is never heard here.

Weippe (WEE-ipe).

The local pronunciation of Coeur d'Alene (cur-duh-LAIN) is much like the French, although most residents say CORE-duh-LAIN.

St. Maries (Saint Mary's).

Except where noted, the illustrations are from Himmelwright's book, *In the Heart of the Bitterroot Mountains*. Both Himmelwright and Carlin, the expedition's leader, had cameras, and most of the engravings were made from photos they took.

Ladd Hamilton
Lewiston, Idaho
May 1997

Headquarters Department of the Columbia
Vancouver Barracks, Wash.

November 14th, 1893

To the
Adjutant General of the Army,
Washington, D. C.

Sir:-

I have the honor to report to the Major General Commanding the Army that a party of six citizens has been snow-bound, or lost, in the mountains of Clearwater River, Idaho, since about October 20th, and I have sent three different parties of men under officers to search for them. At my request the General Commanding the Department of Dakota kindly sent a force from Fort Missoula, Mont., to aid in the search.

It is possible that no results will be accomplished before the date of my retirement, November 24th, instant. It is for this reason I respectfully request the Major General Commanding to instruct the Commander of this Department to continue the search until the lost party shall have been found or their fate known . . .

Very respectfully,
William P. Carlin
Brigadier General, Commanding.

Spokane, Washington
September 15, 1893

1 Martin P. Spencer, newly arrived by train from Missoula, found the Hotel Spokane without much trouble and set his bags down in front of the desk. He was twenty-seven years old, of medium build, with deep-set, piercing eyes and a dark mustache. He told the clerk that a room had been reserved for him and he would be staying for two nights. When the clerk pushed the hotel register toward him, he noticed that the others already had signed in:

William E. Carlin, of Buffalo, New York; A.L.A. (for Abraham Lincoln Artman) Himmelwright, of New York City; John Harvey Pierce, of White Plains, New York; and George T. Colegate, of Post Falls, Idaho. Also there was a name he had not expected to see: Brigadier General William P. Carlin, of Vancouver Barracks, Washington.

The general, Spencer surmised, had come to see his son and companions off. Other officers apparently had come with him, for the register also carried the names of Lieutenant Clough Overton, 4th Cavalry, and Lieutenant Charles P. Elliott, 4th Cavalry, both of Vancouver Barracks; and Lieutenant Gordon Voorhies, 4th Cavalry, of Fort Walla Walla. The register did not yet bear the names of two Cavalry officers from Fort Sherman, at Coeur d'Alene, Idaho, who would arrive later in the day. Spencer signed the register, and a bellboy picked up the key and the bags and led Spencer briskly up the stairs.

The Carlin hunting party, whose venture into the Bitterroot Mountains would be remembered for a hundred years, was now complete.

The general rose unsteadily from his chair and raised his glass—for the last toast, he said, because it was time this party broke up.

Thank God, Himmelwright thought. He had eaten too much dinner and drunk too many brandies, and all he wanted now was to get to his room and into bed. But since the general wanted it, there would have to be one more toast.

To the young gentlemen who are off on this great adventure, the general was saying, God bless them all; if he were not chained to a desk in Vancouver, he would surely be going too. As indeed he would. Although the general was only two months from retirement, he was fit, tough, and still able to rough it. Furthermore, he had been divorced for several years, and was free to indulge his taste for action. He had seen a good deal of frontier duty during the Indian wars, had fought at Stone River, Liberty Gap, Chattanooga, and Missionary Ridge in the Civil War, and would be remembered as one of the Army's best fighters. He raised his glass and drank, then pushed back his chair and went around the table, shaking hands with each of the young gentlemen in turn. First the younger Carlin, then Himmelwright, then Pierce, and finally Colegate, the cook, and the guide, Spencer. Following the general's lead, the fellow officers who had come with him all passed through the group, shaking hands. Voorhies was here because he was a friend of Will Carlin, Overton because he was a friend of Abe Himmelwright; Elliott and the officers from Fort Sherman were here because the general had invited them to come. They then joined their commander, who was waiting at the door, and the 4th U.S. Cavalry Regiment left the private dining room of the Hotel Spokane.

Himmelwright headed for his room, but there would be no sleep for him yet. Young Carlin went with him, wanting to talk. It had been a great party, Carlin said, much pleased with the evening, and he could hardly wait until he was up there on that wilderness trail with a good horse under him. Carlin often talked like that, in boisterous clichés, and Himmelwright usually found his bright enthusiasm amusing. But tonight he was too tired. Why didn't Will go to bed?

Inside Himmelwright's room, Carlin slumped into a chair and said he hoped Abe wasn't too disappointed about the mountain goats. Of course he was disappointed, Abe said, but there would be other hunts.

Himmelwright had set his heart on a hunt for mountain goat, the elusive creature of the high places. But Spencer had told them there would be no hunting for mountain goats this time. He had seen the weather reports, and all signs pointed to an early winter. If they got trapped by snow in the high country, they might not get out until spring. Himmelwright said he couldn't complain if they had to settle for less than they'd hoped for, since it was his fault. They had planned to begin this hunt in August, which would have given them plenty of time to get into the high country. But he had been held up in New York by business and couldn't join the others until the middle of September. In the meantime, waiting for Himmelwright, Carlin had asked Colegate to go to a mutual friend on northern Idaho's St. Joe River and if possible borrow a couple of bear dogs. And he and Pierce spent much of their time hunting for grouse on the Palouse prairie southeast of Spokane.

They had done most of their hunting in the rain. The Palouse prairie, like the rest of the region between the Cascades and the Bitterroots, had endured one of the wettest summers on record. Lewiston, Idaho, at the junction of the Snake and Clearwater rivers, got 19.43 inches of rain in 1893, compared to a normal rainfall of about 11 inches. In September, October, and November, the area got 9.12 inches. This heavy autumn rainfall had prompted the fears of an early, hard winter in the mountains—where much of that rain fell as snow.

Carlin now reminded Himmelwright that Spencer had promised them good hunting in the river bottoms. They would see elk, bear, moose, and black-tailed deer—maybe even grizzlies.

A grizzly would be wonderful, Himmelwright said, hoping that Carlin would now leave. Instead, Carlin changed the subject. What was Abe's impression of Colegate, he wanted to know. Carlin and Himmelwright had used the cook's services on a hunting trip five years earlier on the upper St. Joe River.

Himmelwright said he thought Colegate had looked tired. Worse than tired, was Carlin's impression. They both remembered Colegate as a hearty, outgoing little fellow full of jokes, a fair harmonica player, and a fine cook, handy around camp. Now he looked worn out, and he had said hardly anything during this evening's dinner.

Carlin said he would talk to Colegate about that tomorrow, and he left for his own room.

The next morning Himmelwright slept longer than he should have, ate a quick breakfast, and went shopping for boots and gloves. Pierce remained in the hotel, busy with correspondence, and Carlin hastened to see Colegate before the cook got involved with Spencer in provisioning the outfit.

How was George feeling today? Carlin asked the cook. He felt fine, Colegate said, and it seemed to Carlin that the old fellow did look a little less drawn. Then Colegate reminded Carlin that he had brought two bear dogs with him yesterday from Post Falls but had forgotten to give Carlin the note that came with them.

The note was from Fred Palmer, who had sent the dogs down with Colegate from his place on the upper St. Joe, and who had entertained Carlin and Himmelwright on their earlier hunt in that region.

Dear Carlin,
I send you two terrier dogs, which we have used with success on bear, etc., on condition that you come up and pay us a visit on your return. Hoping they may be of service to you, I am most cordially yours,
Fred Palmer

This was really good of Fred, Carlin said to Colegate, as he put the note in a shirt pocket. And he thanked Colegate again for bringing along his own spaniel, Daisy, for hunting grouse.

Daisy's name reminded him of something and he pulled Palmer's note from his pocket. He read it again. Sure enough, Fred had forgotten to mention the names of his two terriers. Well, Carlin said to Colegate, they would have to call them something. But that could wait.

What they had to think about now, Carlin said, was Colegate's health. Was he absolutely certain he was up to this trip? He wasn't a young man any more.

He was only fifty-two, Colegate said, and he considered himself very spry for his age.

Had he been to a doctor lately?

He had, Colegate confessed, but only for the usual little things—a sore throat a month ago, a touch of the flu in April. As a matter of fact, Colegate said, he had gone to his doctor after receiving Carlin's invitation to join the expedition, just to make sure there would be no problems. Dr. Webb had told him that a wilderness trip would probably do him good.

Carlin said he wanted to hear that from the doctor, and Colegate promised he would have the doctor get in touch with him before they left Spokane.

There was a knock on the door and Spencer came in carrying a writing tablet and pencils. That ended Carlin's talk with Colegate, but he wanted a word now with Spencer.

They would need horses, and he wanted Spencer's advice on how many they should buy. Spencer said he would let Carlin know after he and Colegate had decided how much food and equipment they'd be carrying.

That would be fine, Carlin said, but he didn't want to scrimp. Think of everything they might need and then some, he advised Spencer and Colegate. They would buy enough horses to carry it all.

Carlin left, saying he had to pick up a few things.

So while Carlin and Himmelwright were out doing some shopping of their own, and Pierce was writing the last letters their families would receive for more than five weeks, Spencer huddled with Colegate in the cook's hotel room to decide on the provisioning. After much writing and erasing, they produced a list of necessities:

125 lbs. flour	30 lbs. sugar
30 lbs. breakfast bacon	1 lb. tea
40 lbs. salt pork	8 lbs. coffee
20 lbs. beans	2 doz. cans cond. milk
10 lbs. oatmeal	3 lbs. baking powder
40 lbs. salt	citron, sage, mace, thyme
10 lbs. cornmeal	10 lbs. alum
5 lbs. dried apples	5 lbs. raisins
5 lbs. dried apricots	½ lb. pepper
1 gal. maple syrup	½ gal. vinegar
2 doz. tallow candles	block matches
3 lbs. laundry soap	1 gal. brandy
6 cakes toilet soap	40 lbs. potatoes

Spencer later met with Carlin and Himmelwright, and the three drew up a list of needed camp equipment:

1 10 x 12 ft. wall tent	½ doz. knives and forks
1 7 x 7 ft A-tent	9 tin plates
1 large fly	9 tin cups
10 double blankets	2 butcher knives
2 heavy quilts	2 large spoons
½ doz. towels	1 large meat knife
3 canvas pack covers 4 x 6	1 4-lb. ax
5 yards crash	1 2-lb. ax
5 yards heavy muslin	1 8-inch flat file
3 camp kettles (nested)	1 box copper wire rivets
2 gold pans (for dishpans)	2 lbs. wire nails
1 granite stew pan	1 ball coarse twine
2 frying pans	1 ball light twine
1 reflector	50 ft. extra rope
(for baking bread)	1 coffee pot
1 rubber airbed	1 doz. extra cloth sacks

That list of camp gear did not include oats for the horses or the personal equipment of the three hunters. They all had fishing tackle and guns and Carlin and Himmelwright both were taking good cameras.

Carlin's primary firearm was a three-barrel combination rifle and shotgun handmade for him by a gunsmith who had spent fourteen months on the project. The two 12-gauge shotgun barrels, side by side, were paradox bored—that is, with a few inches of rifling near the muzzle so they could accurately shoot bullets as well as shot. Below and centered between these two was the .32-caliber rifle barrel. Of all Carlin's possessions, he prized this gun most.

Himmelwright had a 12-gauge repeating shotgun fitted with a paradox barrel, making it both a shotgun and a repeating rifle. Like Carlin's, this gun was handmade and one of a kind. Carlin and Himmelwright had spent a good deal of time, shortly after Abe's arrival, displaying and comparing their new guns. There was nothing wrong with Himmelwright's handmade paradox, but he had to agree that Carlin's was a marvel. It weighed under eight pounds, had excellent balance, a silky smooth mechanism, and a stock made of the finest Italian walnut. Carlin showed Himmelwright one of the ball cartridges for which the two shot barrels had been designed. He had cut the paper shell open, exposing a conical bullet with a single groove and five wads of cardboard between the bullet and the powder. Himmelwright said he presumed the barrels and shells had been properly tested. Carlin unrolled a heavy paper target punctured by ten shots, all of them within a circle eleven and three-quarters inches in diameter. The shots had been fired alternately from each barrel, he said, at a distance of two hundred yards.

Carlin and Himmelwright also took Smith & Wesson revolvers. Pierce had brought a .45-caliber Winchester repeating rifle and a Smith & Wesson revolver, and Spencer had a .40-caliber single-shot rifle. In addition to these arms, the party had in reserve a .40-caliber Winchester repeating rifle.

That afternoon, Spencer met with Carlin and Himmelwright to talk about horses. They would need ten, he said: five riding horses with saddles and five pack horses to carry the camp. They decided that Spencer and Carlin would pick out the horses while Himmelwright bought the equipment on the list Spencer and the others had drawn up. Colegate by now was out rounding up the groceries while Pierce arranged for a freight car to carry the horses, dogs, food, and equipment to Kendrick, Idaho, the end of the Northern Pacific line from Spokane into the Clearwater country.

That freight car would leave for Kendrick early the next day, and the Carlin party would follow on the passenger train. There was so much to do in so little time that Carlin became distracted. He didn't notice until it was too late that he had not heard from W. Q. Webb, M.D., George Colegate's doctor.

2 Who were these New York men, as they would become known? Will Carlin was born in 1866 at Fort Yates, North Dakota, where his father, the general, was stationed. He was educated there, at the U.S. Military Academy at West Point—like his father—and at Rensselaer Polytechnical Institute at Troy, New York—like Abe Himmelwright. As a young man, he spent much time in the field with Army units and developed a liking for the outdoor life. He was an authority on firearms, especially the revolver, and an expert marksman, as was his wife, Cora, who often went shooting with him. He had explored many wild parts of the Pacific Northwest before his venture into the Bitterroots. Four years earlier, for example, he had accompanied Army Lieutenant James A. Leyden on

a mapping expedition into British Columbia, serving as the party's photographer. Twenty-seven years old and a seasoned outdoorsman when he organized this hunting party, he was well built and tanned, with dark hair and eyes, a carefully trimmed mustache, and an outgoing, bright personality that exuded self-confidence.

Abe Himmelwright, a year older, quieter, and more reflective, was a civil engineer with a business of his own in New York. A longtime friend of young Carlin he, like Carlin, had spent much time in the wilderness, some of it as a railroad surveyor. He prided himself on his woodsmanship and his engineering skills. He was clean-shaven and brown-haired, of medium height, and a bit overweight.

John Pierce was Carlin's brother-in-law. He was twenty years old and still suffering from the after-effects of a bad bout with malaria, which he had caught during a tour of the Caribbean. He hoped this hunting excursion would alleviate his symptoms. He was a slender, attractive man with a subdued and introspective personality. He was strong for family; for a living, he managed his father's investments, and when not engaged in such matters his correspondence kept the relatives in touch with one another. From his physician father, Dr. H.M. Pierce, he had picked up a general knowledge of medicine, another reason why he may have been invited along on this expedition. An avid shooter who enjoyed bird hunting, he had little interest in bigger game, and his ability to rough it must have surprised even himself.

⟨⟩

The passenger train arrived at Kendrick in the early afternoon of September 17, about an hour behind the train carrying the horses, dogs, and provisions. Carlin and the others checked in at the St. Elmo Hotel and then went to check on the freight car. The air was damp and chilly with a suggestion of rain to come.

Kendrick itself was not a pretty sight. A bad fire a month ago had taken out three dozen businesses, leveled the building that housed the *Kendrick Gazette*, and reduced a dozen square blocks to charred ruin. The town was laid out at the bottom of a narrow canyon beside a river prone to flooding and the six hundred or so people who lived there had got used to flood and fire. The St. Elmo Hotel, a wooden structure originally, had been burned earlier and rebuilt with brick. It was a two-storey building with a flat roof and a verandah on the main-street side. The August fire had destroyed the buildings across the street and the empty space had become a playing field. On both sides of the city the mostly bare hills came down steeply to the valley floor, leaving room only for the river, a railroad track, and the town's two parallel streets of houses and shops. The recent cold rains had muddied the ground, keeping most of the residents indoors. Spencer, walking from the train to the hotel, peered at the sky and said he did not like the looks of this weather.

There was nothing to worry about, Colegate insisted. It was a typical September. October was almost always warm and dry, and of course after the first frost there would be a pleasant Indian summer that could last well into November.

This was what the others wanted to hear. Carlin, Himmelwright, and Pierce, with Colegate's help, got the horses unloaded, led them into a small corral next to the hotel, and saw that they were settled for the night. They left the three dogs in the corral also, on leashes. The time had come, Carlin said, to give names to the two bear dogs from northern Idaho. Were there any suggestions? Pierce said Idaho would be a good name for one of the terriers and Himmelwright, agreeing, said Montana would be right for the other one. They would be hunting close to the border between the two states, he pointed out, and those names made sense geographically. It certainly made sense to him, Carlin said, and so it was done. The mostly black terrier with the white chest and forelegs became Idaho for the purposes of this trip, and the white one with the splotches on his back became Montana. Then the hunters checked again on the freight car to make sure everything there was secured before returning to the hotel.

Meanwhile, Spencer had found a feed store on Kendrick's main street where he thought he might learn in some detail what the weather had been like in the region this summer.

Awful, agreed the several farmers gathered there.

Rain, rain, rain, one of them said. So much rain that he lost most of his corn. Not that it mattered much. The financial panic that plunged the country into gloom that summer also was affecting farmers on the ridges around Kendrick. There may have been no market for that corn anyhow, one of them said.

Well, it was just too bad, another declared, and the proprietor of the feed store, a middle-aged German with side whiskers and a mild paunch, couldn't recall a summer this wet.

And cold, added another.

Damn cold, the proprietor said. He'd never had to fire up the stove this early in the fall but here they all were, he observed, standing not far away from the warmth.

Spencer bought a sack of tobacco and walked back down the street to the hotel, thinking this might not be the most pleasant hunting trip of his career. All he had heard confirmed his prediction that this was likely to be a nasty winter. He found the other four in the St. Elmo bar and joined them for brandies and an early supper.

That night, after Colegate had gone to his room, Spencer gathered the other three in his. Colegate should not be going on this trip, he said bluntly. He might say he was well, but he didn't look it.

Carlin agreed with the guide, but said he had Colegate's word that his doctor had approved.

But they hadn't heard from the doctor, Spencer said, and Carlin said that was his fault. He should have got in touch with the doctor and didn't do it. He said he would have another talk with Colegate in the morning. He would offer the cook a month's wages if he agreed to return to Post Falls.

Well, Spencer said, that was certainly more than generous. And on that note the other three went to their rooms.

Shortly after dawn on the 18th, Pierce and Himmelwright took the horses to the blacksmith to be shod and the other three returned to the freight car to get the food and equipment ready for packing.

But first Carlin took Colegate aside and told him that he was clearly in no shape to spend the next few weeks in the mountains. Carlin said he would pay him a month's wages if he would just go back to Post Falls, and no hard feelings.

Colegate said he couldn't do that. He had signed on for this job, and he intended to finish it.

Carlin said there would be other expeditions when they could join forces; he had other hunts planned and would like to use Colegate again. But not this time.

Colegate said he was in good shape, feeling great, and eager to start.

Himmelwright joined the conversation, saying Colegate was probably the best judge of his physical condition. If Colegate said he was fine, Himmelwright told Carlin, maybe they should believe him.

All right, Carlin said. He would believe him, and he could be their cook through thick and thin. But he ought to remember that if he ever got sick and couldn't keep up, he shouldn't expect the others to go out of their way to help him.

That was just the way he wanted it, Colegate said.

They walked across the street to the freight car and began packing the provisions. They arranged everything in convenient portions under Colegate's direction and packed them in cloth bags. As Pierce and Himmelwright brought the horses back to the corral, Spencer and Colegate threw on the wooden pack saddles and loaded them. Colegate suggested that he buy some fresh meat and vegetables for their first couple of days on the trail, and Carlin agreed. He gave Colegate some money and the cook went looking for a grocery store.

The party of Easterners had acquired some notoriety in Kendrick, where such visitors were rare, and a number of people had come to see the departure. At about 1 p.m. the hunters were ready to leave, and as the five horsemen and five pack animals milled in the mud in front of the hotel, somebody shouted that he wanted a picture. Carlin, glancing around, saw a man on the hotel's second floor verandah waving a camera and signaled the group to stop and hold still. The man on the verandah snapped the picture and waved the camera again. Carlin waved back, then formed a line and led the party down the muddy street and out of town, heading east.

The night's rain had turned to a light drizzle in the morning and by noon had stopped altogether. The sun came out as the riders followed a wagon road through a narrow valley and then across rolling farm country toward their first destination, a place some fourteen miles away known as Snell's mill.

In the bright September sunshine, with the great adventure ahead of them and provisions for five weeks coming along behind, their spirits soared, and even Spencer shared in the exhilaration. He told of other hunting parties he had guided into the mountains and the babying he'd had to do with some of them. Carlin sang snatches of ditties popular at the time, and Himmelwright and

Colegate traded jokes about their earlier hunting trip on the St. Joe. Pierce, the accountant, got some kidding because now that he was this far away from White Plains, there was no one to manage his father's money and the family would be broke when he got home.

The three dogs, Daisy, Idaho, and Montana, trotted happily along, darting frequently into roadside bushes to sniff and explore, then running ahead to scout the way.

All agreed it was wonderful to be on the road at last. It would be even better, Carlin declared, when the road ran out and they were finally in true wilderness. They would drink to that, the others said.

They reached Snell's mill at sundown, unpacked the horses, and built a cooking fire. A man named Gainer, the owner of the farm and tiny sawmill, came down to the roadside where they were unpacking to meet the travelers and pass the time of day. After a brief visit, he told them they were welcome to sleep in his barn if they wished. Carlin said they would like to very much and thanked him for his generosity. Gainer went back to his house and Colegate started supper. He got a metal grill, a kettle, and a folding reflector oven out of the kitchen box. When the water started to boil he put the kettle aside and got out a frying pan and rubbed the inside with a piece of bacon fat. He had bought a chunk of fresh beef that morning in Kendrick, and he cut this into small pieces, dipped them in flour, and browned them in the pan. Then he put the kettle back on the fire, dropped in the meat, and got the water to boiling again. He poured the grease from the pan into the kettle and used the pan to make his bread dough, mixing flour, baking powder, salt, water and condensed milk. He put the pan of dough in the reflector oven facing the fire, then he cut up two potatoes and dropped them into the stew pot along with a half dozen carrots and an onion. By the time the stew was ready to eat, so was the bread.

It was plain fare, Colegate said, almost apologetically, but the others declared that it was as good as any meal they'd ever eaten on the trail. Colegate was like other cooks: He could practically live on compliments and he had received many in the course of his part-time career as a camp cook. A short, wiry man, he had been born in England and had lived in San Francisco and Washington state before moving to Idaho. In Post Falls he operated a shingle mill and served as justice of the peace, a position of prominence.

He enjoyed camp life and could handle not only the cooking but also the packing and the skinning and curing of hides—an all-around handy fellow, as Himmelwright described him.

Colegate could also be stern: After this meal, he warned the others, there would be no meat unless they killed it. Don't worry about that, Carlin said. They would bring him plenty of game.

They washed the tin cooking utensils with water from the farm well, then sat around the fire drinking black coffee and talking until well after dark. Finally tired, they picked their way across the road to the barn and went to sleep on the hay.

At noon the next day, still on the wagon road, they entered the Nez Perce Indian reservation and shortly thereafter crossed the North Fork of the Clearwater on a ferry operated by Indians. It took three trips to move the five men, three dogs, and ten horses. From the ferry, the wagon road took them above and parallel to the main Clearwater for several miles and then turned to the left and up to the Weippe prairie.

The weather remained good, the scenery delightful. The bunchgrass had turned a pale yellow, and the brushy glades were a rich blend of orange, red, and green. As the party gained altitude above the Clearwater the signs of autumn became more distinct; by late afternoon, when it came time to camp, the air had a nip in it—a sign that the hunting would be good, Carlin said.

After the horses were unpacked, Himmelwright took Colegate's dog, Daisy, and went hunting for grouse. Daisy seemed to know where to look, for they returned to camp with several birds, which Colegate cleaned and cooked whole on a spit over the fire. Carlin, lifting his cup of coffee, proposed a toast to Abe, who had provided the party's first wild meat—and of course to Daisy, who helped. This had been their first full day on the road, and they agreed that it couldn't have been better. That evening before getting into his blankets, Colegate put some beans to soaking in the kettle.

When the hunters awoke the next morning, September 20, the sky was gray and the air damp. After a breakfast of bread, bacon, beans, and coffee, the party reloaded the horses and set out in a light drizzle toward the small farm town of Weippe. There they looked up a man named John Gaffney, whom Spencer knew, and from him they bought the forty pounds of potatoes on Colegate's list. From Weippe they proceeded on, up the diminishing wagon

The cabin at Brown's Creek. The terrier in the foreground is one of Fred Parker's bear dogs—the one the hunters named Idaho.

road through alternating meadows and timber, gaining altitude. The rain was falling harder by now. Carlin, trying to recoup the high spirits of the day before, broke into song, a popular melody they all knew, and Colegate pulled a harmonica out of his pocket and joined in. But nobody else seemed in the mood for gaiety. Carlin gave up and fell quiet, Colegate pocketed his harmonica, and the party moved in silence through the cold rain until reaching Brown's Creek.

There was a log cabin here, empty and apparently abandoned. Although it was still early, Spencer suggested they halt for the night and take advantage of the shelter. They did, unpacking the horses in the rain and hauling the packs inside. The cabin was in decent condition, although a previous visitor evidently had pulled up part of the plank floor to use as firewood—probably on a day like this one, Pierce said. Spencer collected enough dry twigs and forest duff under the trees to build a small cooking fire in the stone fireplace and Colegate prepared supper.

Rain continued falling outside. But inside, where Spencer's fire painted a glow on their faces, the travelers were drying out and feeling happier. The three dogs, tired and still muddy, sprawled out on the floor and quickly went to sleep. As the potatoes boiled and the coffee percolated, Himmelwright declared that brandy was meant for weather like this. Carlin agreed wholeheartedly. Pierce fetched a jug from one of the packs and they drank a round from tin cups, reminding Himmelwright of the endless toasts they had drunk that night at the Hotel Spokane. So he proposed a toast to the first two days on the road, and they drank another round. Pierce returned the brandy to its pack. The travelers, now dry and warm both inside and out, enjoyed their supper as the daylight faded and the rain continued to rattle on the cabin roof.

Colegate poured some red beans into a kettle of water to soak overnight and crawled into his blankets. The other four soon followed and all were asleep before the fire burned itself out.

It was still raining when Spencer awoke in the pre-dawn dark, thinking he had heard footsteps on what was left of the wood floor. Evidently not, he decided; he could now hear only the breathing of his sleeping companions—and, of course, the rain. He lay in his blankets for some time, thinking and listening to the rain, a discouraging sound. It meant the traveling would be even more difficult today than yesterday. And he remembered that soon they would be without the wagon road, which ended not far from here. If the rain continued into the morning, it might be a good idea to spend the day here at the cabin, he thought. They could shoot some grouse, maybe catch some fish, have a good rest, and hope for better weather to come. He was wondering what the others would think of that plan when he heard the door open. A little burst of cold, damp air passed over him, then he heard the door close and those steps on the floor again. He now understood that he had been awakened by someone going outside, presumably to relieve himself. Whoever it was had spent quite a while out there in the rain, Spencer thought. Spencer could hear him settling back into his blankets, and when he heard the fellow muttering softly to himself he realized it was Colegate. He also realized that he had better make that same trip. He pulled on his boots, got into his hat and slicker, stepped quietly outside, and was back into bed in no time at all.

3 At daybreak it was still raining hard. Carlin and Himmelwright, no longer warmed and soothed by their brandies, swore at the weather and gave a heartfelt "amen" to Spencer's suggestion that this day's travel be canceled. Pierce and Colegate agreed, and the

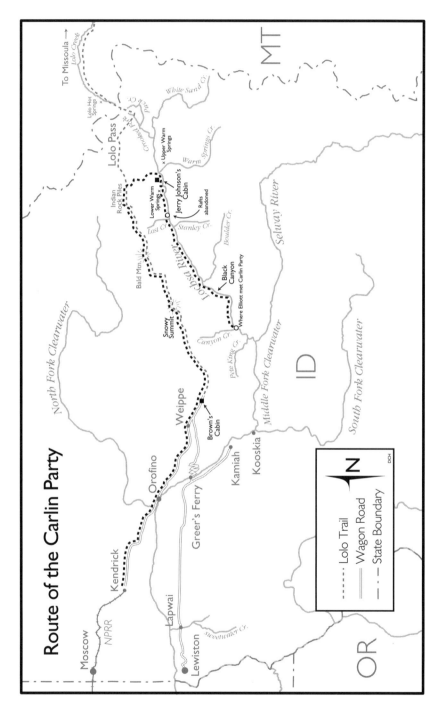

Route of the Carlin Party

five ate a leisurely breakfast in the cabin, listening to the rain and discussing plans for the day.

Spencer and Colegate washed the dishes, carrying water from Brown's Creek and heating it in the fireplace. Pierce took care of the horses and dogs, and Carlin and Himmelwright played rummy on the cabin's ancient table.

By mid-morning the card players were bored and looking for something else to do. Himmelwright decided he would take Daisy and look for grouse. Carlin got out his tackle kit and took some line and a book of flies down to the creek. Pierce got his revolver out of the pack and went grouse hunting with Himmelwright, thinking more of target practice than meat for the camp.

Carlin cut a willow switch some seven feet long, tied a few feet of line to the small end of it, and attached one of his flies. He cast into the middle of the creek and had a trout on his line as soon as the fly touched the water. He guessed the trout to weigh about a pound and a half. He cast again, and again a fish hit the fly immediately. Carlin continued to cast his fly upon the creek, and when he returned to the cabin after about an hour he had fifty-three fish weighing between a half pound and a pound and a half.

Himmelwright and Pierce came back at noon, not so lucky, with two grouse each.

Himmelwright said he wished his gun were half as lucky as Carlin's fly. But it wasn't any particular fly, Carlin said. He had tried several flies, just for fun, and they all had the same effect; the creek simply teemed with trout, all of them apparently too hungry to care what they struck at. And he added that the rain might have had something to do with it. He always seemed to have better luck when he fished in the rain.

Company came in the afternoon, an old-timer in a yellow slicker and a big hat, riding a pony through the rain. Spencer, outside gathering wood when he arrived, walked over to meet him. There was something familiar about the old fellow, Spencer thought, but he couldn't place him. As the visitor dismounted, Spencer noticed that the horse was packing a good week's worth of provisions plus a rifle and an ax.

After an exchange of greetings, the horseman observed that Spencer and his party had found a good camp for a rainy day. There was an even better cabin not far from here, he said; it also was empty, and he was sure the owner wouldn't mind if they used it.

Spencer felt some relief at these words. He had feared for a moment that this cabin might belong to the old man, and that he and his party might not be welcome here. But the other explained that he was here only to round up some of his cattle and move them down to the river valley before winter. They were pretty badly scattered, he said, and he was prepared to spend some time at the chore.

Then he startled Spencer by saying he remembered him. Wasn't he the guide who had taken a party of hunters into the Bitterroots at about this season a year ago?

He was, Spencer told him, also remembering that encounter. And now he was guiding another hunting party, this time some people from the state of New York.

By now the others had become aware they had company, and they came out of the cabin. Spencer explained that he had met the old rancher a year ago near here as he guided a party up to the Lolo Trail.

The rancher said he didn't suppose they would be going in very far this time since it was so late in the season. Spencer said it was at least this late in September last year when he and his party went in, and they had no trouble

Well, the rancher said, that was a different kind of September. They could be trapped in those mountains by snow if they weren't careful.

He wasn't much worried, Spencer said. He pointed out that he and his party had come out last year on the 20th of October, and this year he planned to be out on the 15th. Spencer felt a bit defensive, as though he had to justify his party's presence here and its itinerary. He realized his optimistic talk was mainly for the benefit of his traveling companions; his own opinion was that the rancher had the logic of the mountains on his side.

Well, the old man said, they could suit themselves. But everyone he knew, including the Indians, expected a hard, early winter, and he was pretty sure they were right. He glanced toward the New York men and said to Spencer that this was no time for a tenderfoot to be heading into the Bitterroots.

Did Spencer think they could stand the trip? he asked, casting his eye again on Himmelwright, Carlin, and Pierce.

Carlin said he was pretty sure they could pull through. The rancher's "tenderfoot" reference riled him, and he decided to change the subject before one of the others said something in anger. Carlin asked the old man about the hunting they might find in the Bitterroots and such matters, and the conversation continued politely for half an hour. Then the visitor announced that he had to be on his way and mounted his pony. Carlin offered him a dozen trout in a cloth sack, which the old man accepted with thanks and tied onto his saddle bag. He tipped his hat and nudged his pony down the mud-slick wagon road.

Himmelwright, watching the old man go, muttered that he didn't appreciate the insult, and wished Carlin hadn't given him the fish. They may be from New York, he said, but they probably were as experienced in the woods as he was. As a former railroad surveyor, Himmelwright was well used to life in the wild. He had spent one winter in northern Idaho with a survey crew, forty miles from civilization. Carlin had bivouacked with his father's troops many times, in many kinds of weather, and was just as irked as Himmelwright.

Spencer, aware that Carlin and Himmelwright were seething over the "tenderfoot" insult, told them they should calm down and forget it. If they felt they had been demeaned, he said, they should blame him, since he had been foolish enough to mention that they came from the state of New York. The old man had no way of knowing they had any mountaineering experience, and out here anybody from New York was bound to be considered a tenderfoot. Look at it this way, he told them: The old man was simply expressing his concern for their safety, in his own rather crude manner.

Spencer was right, Pierce said. The rancher meant no disrespect and he, for one, took no offense. Pierce's statement struck Spencer as both helpful and wise, since Pierce was the tenderfoot in that group.

It also occurred to Spencer that the old rancher's warning may have been both well meant and justified. He stared at the mountains to the east, hardly visible through the cold rain, shrugged his shoulders, and went inside.

Making camp at Snowy Summit.

Late that afternoon the rain eased to a stop, and by dusk the sky was almost clear. The men spent that night in the cabin and shortly after dawn on September 21 they were on the wagon road again. It took them as far as Musselshell Creek, which they reached at about 10 that morning, and there it disappeared.

From here on, Spencer told the others, the going would not be so easy. They would be traveling single file, over an Indian trail, and they would have to rearrange the outfit. They interspersed the pack horses among the riders so that they could be more easily controlled. Himmelwright objected that with the riders separated in this way they would be too far apart to talk to one another. It would spoil some of the fun, he told Spencer. But Spencer said Himmelwright should look at the bright side. This way, Carlin's singing wouldn't bother anybody.

The party plodded on, still gaining altitude above the Clearwater. The day was warm and mostly sunny, with a light breeze pushing occasional clouds across the sun. Carlin began to yodel, a sign to Spencer that he could still sing loudly enough to be heard. He stopped after Spencer shouted to him, half seriously, that he might stampede the horses.

At midday the travelers were winding up a steep trail through dense timber, in relative silence. There wasn't much shouting back and forth now; horses and riders were working hard. They began to encounter patches of snow. In the middle of the afternoon they reached the top of a high ridge, a place called Snowy Summit, where the snow lay six inches deep. Spencer remembered a good camping spot near a brook in a small ravine to the right of the trail, and there on the bare ground under a big cedar the Carlin party spent the night of the 21st.

Fannie Colegate opened the top drawer of a chiffonier she shared with her husband, looking for a measuring tape. The tape was there, but she didn't see it. All her eyes could comprehend was a familiar white cardboard box lying in one corner. What was it doing here? She stared at it for a moment, then lifted it out and opened it. She quickly closed it again, put it back in the drawer, and rushed out of the house in search of her oldest boy, Charles. She found him in the woodshed stooped near a pile of sawmill waste, splitting kindling.

He had to go find Doctor Webb in Spokane, she told him, and then, changing her mind, said that would take too long. She would go into Post Falls and telegraph the doctor from there. She told Charles to hitch up the pony while she got ready, and plan to go with her. They would wait in Post Falls for an answer. Fannie was afraid she knew what the answer would be.

For God's sake, she asked herself again, what were the catheters doing in that drawer?

She threw off her apron, grabbed a coat and her purse, and rushed out the door to the buggy. She climbed up beside Charles and the two drove the couple of miles to Post Falls, a little town on the railroad between Spokane and Coeur d'Alene. At the telegraph office, Fannie got down, telling Charles to take care of the horse, and went inside. She took a sheet of paper and a pencil from the counter and wrote down the message she wished to send to Dr. W.Q. Webb of Spokane: George left without catheters, it said, and he had now been gone for five days. What should she do?

She gave the paper to the operator, paid him, and told him she expected a reply momentarily. Then she went outside to sit with Charles on a bench on the wooden sidewalk.

They waited and worried.

At age sixteen, Charles was old enough to know about illness and something about medicine, and he knew that the catheters were crucial to his father's good health. (The so-called "French" catheter widely used in 1893 consisted of a rubber tube about fifteen inches long and half as thick as a pencil, tapered at one end and fluted at the other. The user inserted it in the penis and pushed it through the urethra and into the bladder, creating a channel for the discharge of urine. People in those days usually cleaned it, if camping out, by splashing some whiskey or brandy on it.)

Charles didn't know exactly what was wrong with George Colegate's elimination system, but he knew that the catheters made it possible for his father to urinate. And since the Colegates were a church-going family, Charles also knew what it was like to endure a full bladder without relief. Along with his mother, he wondered why the catheters were in the bureau drawer. And he thought, as he waited, that he might soon be hurrying to Kendrick with the instruments his father had for some strange reason left behind.

Fannie would have been even more concerned had she understood the doctor's gut reaction to her news. Webb was furious. He had told George Colegate that he could not go into the mountains unless he took along his catheters and used one every day. And George had promised that he would. As far as he knew, the three catheters Fannie had found in the bureau drawer were the only ones George owned. Without them he was in grave trouble and could be suffering already.

Webb didn't think Colegate would be well enough now to continue the hunt; in that case, the others in the party might bring him back out, at least to Kendrick, and continue the hunt without him. Webb didn't know these men. Colegate had told him only that a party of Easterners had hired him. Webb hoped they would know enough to do the right thing.

Although Fannie couldn't understand why those catheters were still lying in the bureau drawer, the doctor had a pretty good idea. He'd had other patients like George Colegate, suffering from enlargement of the prostate over a long period. In George's case it had been some twenty years since the swelling gland had begun to squeeze the urethra, the canal that carried urine from the bladder. In those years of poking thin rubber hoses up into the bladder, the tube had become scarred and the bladder inflamed. The process, always awkward, no doubt had become painful. The doctor guessed that George Colegate, looking forward to five weeks free of oversight by doctor and family, had decided to hell with it; he would leave the damned things in the bureau drawer and take his chances. Or he could have forgotten to pack them in the confusion of preparing for departure. But nature would surely by now have reminded him that he had better not go on without them.

Once into the mountains, his chances would be slim. If he was lucky, Webb thought, Colegate would get too sick to travel soon enough that his companions could bring him out while there was still time. Otherwise, God help him.

The doctor sent an errand boy to the telegraph office with this message for Fannie Colegate: Send someone to Kendrick with catheters immediately, it said, and find George at all cost. And the doctor added that there was no time to waste.

The next morning Charles was on the train to Kendrick with some money in his pocket and the three catheters in the cardboard box in his suitcase. He had no idea what he would find when he got to Kendrick or where he should go for news of the Carlin party. Another passenger told him that nobody went through Kendrick without stopping at the St. Elmo Hotel; he should check there first.

He did, and learned that the hunters had left Kendrick on the 18th. It was now the 22nd. He inquired whether anybody might be going in that direction soon; nobody seemed to be. There was a sheriff's deputy in town, working out of a feed store on Main Street, and Charles went to see him. The deputy, a rotund German of middle age, knew of the party and in fact had talked with its guide.

The guide had been concerned about the weather, he said, and the thinking around here was that it was going to be a bad winter. He said he doubted the hunters would spend much time in those mountains once the snow started to fall.

Charles by now had decided he would have to rent a horse, buy some supplies, and ride after them. But it would take him another day to get ready, and they would by then have had a six-day lead. There were several people in the hotel lobby who knew that country well, and they told him to forget it; he would never catch up with the hunters now, and if he tried he would probably get lost. One old-timer told him that once the hunters got beyond the Musselshell only they would know where they were going. If you can't find them, you can't catch them, he said. And several others sitting around the stove agreed.

Charles, disheartened and bewildered, decided he had better take the advice of his elders since they seemed to know what they were talking about. But what should he do with the catheters?

Leave them at the hotel desk with a note on the box, one said, and go home to your Ma. That way, they will be here if the Carlin party comes back or if someone goes into the mountains in their direction.

Someone else thought it would make more sense to leave the instruments at the doctor's office on Main Street, since that's where a person would naturally look for something like that. He was overruled on the grounds that the doctor's office was frequently closed, whereas the St. Elmo never was. And nobody passed through Kendrick without stopping here.

That was good enough for Charles. He took a piece of hotel stationery and wrote on it that this was the property of George Colegate and should be given to him or anyone representing him as soon as possible. He gave the note and the cardboard box to the desk clerk, who put them on a shelf under the counter.

Charles got a room for the night and took the next train back to Post Falls, wishing he had better news for his mother.

4 The three New York hunters, the guide, and the cook awoke on the 23rd after a fairly comfortable night—except for chunks of snow that occasionally dropped on them from the cedar branches above. It was dry and bare here, but all around them the ground was white. A cold wind blew through the trees, there was dampness in the air, and Spencer had the feeling as he lay in his blankets that this would not be an easy day.

On the trail near Rocky Ridge.

Nor was it. Colegate, moving slowly and silently, made break-fast and the other four got the camp packed and the horses loaded. While they ate, Carlin noticed that Colegate, who had drifted off into the trees, had been gone quite some time. When he returned, Carlin asked him if he felt all right.

Oh sure, Colegate said. He sometimes got these stomach cramps but they never lasted very long.

Spencer, overhearing this conversation, prayed that Colegate was right, that his problem was simply stomach cramps.

Colegate had some difficulty getting into his saddle, but he managed it without help and the five were under way again before sunup. Yesterday's high spirits had been dampened by gloomy weather and the cook's discomfort. But neither of these discour-agements proved as devastating as what they found after a couple of miles on the trail.

The Lolo proved to be hardly a trail at all. Trees had blown down across it in many places, requiring the riders to maneuver their horses through heavy brush to get around obstacles. They frequently had to cross steep slopes, some covered with loose rock, or scree, as the mountaineers called it. At one point, while crossing a scree slope covered by six inches of snow, a pack horse stumbled, went down on its knees, struggled to its feet, and started sliding toward the rocks below. As the riders watched helplessly, the horse managed to halt the slide and slowly make its way back to its position in the line.

It was not the only horse whose legs had been bloodied by this morning's travel; the others had been cut also by whipping brush, sharp boulders, and splintered tree branches. Himmelwright's pant leg was badly ripped. He expected the leg itself had been cut, but he was not about to dismount in order to find out. The pack horses, which normally followed the leader, sometimes became confused in the tangle of downed trees and brush and wandered off in various directions. Each time the riders went after them, cursing furiously, and after much heaving and tugging got them back into line.

By early afternoon, both horses and riders were bruised and exhausted. Himmelwright, recalling the Nez Perce War sixteen years earlier, and the Indians' famed retreat from the Weippe Prairie over this trail to Montana, with their women and children, wondered how in the world they did it. Spencer, who had taken a hunting party through this country in the previous year, didn't remember the trail as being this bad. When they came to a glade near a couple of streams, Spencer told the others that this was far enough. The next decent camping spot, he said, was another five miles up the trail, and he didn't think the horses could make it.

He looked sharply at Colegate and added that it wasn't only the horses that needed the rest.

Colegate, slumped in his saddle in quiet misery, had to be helped down.

Within an hour they had the horses unpacked and fed and the camp set up. Spencer washed the horses' bruised backs and legs with soothing alum water before turning them loose to graze. It was a clear, cool afternoon, with enough daylight left for fishing, and Carlin tried his luck in both streams. After half an hour he had enough trout for this night's supper and tomorrow's breakfast. Himmelwright and Pierce, in the meantime, took Daisy to look for grouse. The hunting was good and their bag, added to the number shot on the trail during the day, came to eight birds. Spencer volunteered to cook. He fried the trout in bacon fat and roasted the birds over the fire. Four of the group enjoyed a hearty meal, but Colegate, saying he wasn't hungry, refused to eat and spent the late afternoon and evening sitting wretchedly on a log.

Charles got off the train at Post Falls and walked the two miles home, carrying his suitcase and a burden of woe. He would have to tell his mother that he had failed in his mission. She would be distraught and she was somewhat dependent on him, since he was the oldest of Fannie's seven children. His younger brothers and sisters would want to know what was wrong. Fannie would expect him to tell them because she would not know how to. Even though Fannie was no prude, she would not know how to explain to her young children—the girls, especially—what a catheter was and how it was used, and why the discovery of these three had put her in such a panic. So Charles would do it. That was the easy part. Not so easy was his elder-son obligation to take care of his mother, to give her what comfort he could, and try to find some tiny raft of hope for her to cling to in her distress.

Charles was about half way home when his neighbors, the Benjamins, caught up with him in a team and wagon carrying a load of coal. They stopped and offered him a ride, that is if he wouldn't mind riding in the wagon with the coal; there wasn't enough room for three on the seat.

Charles not only didn't mind, he was grateful. The wagon had boards on three sides only. He could sit on the open back and dangle his legs over the edge, and he would be far enough from the Benjamins that there could be no conversation. Charles wouldn't have to explain where he had been with his suitcase and why. If Mr. Benjamin had come alone, it would have been all right. But at the age of sixteen, he couldn't talk about such things as his father's problem in the presence of a woman.

The sun had gone down when the wagon reached the Colegate place. Charles got off, pulled down his suitcase, and thanked the

Benjamins for the ride, hoping they would drive on and not stop to visit.

They wished they could stop and say hello to Fannie, Mrs. Benjamin said, but it was getting late and they had best go on. Perhaps he would say hello for them.

He would do that, Charles said, and hurried gratefully across the road toward the house where his mother awaited him.

Fannie Colegate was dismayed at his news, but not surprised. She had known there was only a wild chance that Charles could reach the hunting party before it disappeared into the wilderness. She had clung to that wild chance, even so, and now that it was gone she fumbled around for someone or something to blame. There was George, the most prominent candidate for her anger. And there was Charles, whom she had trusted (unwisely, perhaps?) with this crucial errand. Charles had the bad luck to be the one who was there, a handy coat rack for her to hang her troubles on. He thereby suffered twice—once for his own self-admitted failure and again for his mother's unspoken but unmistakable disappointment in him.

Charles told his brother George, Jr., the next oldest, what had happened and what it probably meant, describing to him the business of the catheter. And he told young George to let the others know. Fannie would say only that their father had failed to take his medicine with him into the mountains, counting on the children to get the facts by one route or another from Charles.

By the next morning Fannie at first thought that she would go to Spokane and have a talk with Doctor Webb. She wanted to know what was happening to her husband now and what was likely to happen in the days ahead. How long could he go without medical attention?

But in the two days following her discovery of the catheters in the bureau drawer, Fannie's panic had ebbed and her first feelings of despair had diminished. She would not go to Spokane after all; she had a pretty good idea what the doctor would say. George had been living with this prostate problem for twenty years, and the doctor had told them both many times what would happen if George ever strayed far from his catheters for too long.

She hoped that when George got sick, the others would bring him back to Kendrick, and he would be taken care of there. George had traveled with young Carlin before, on the St. Maries, and he had great respect for the general's son. Carlin would know what to do, she felt, and therefore there was no need to get all heated up.

Fannie assured Charles that he had done all he could and she was pleased with him. Everything would turn out all right, she said. And she had to believe that, because there was nothing she could do now to make a difference for George.

Charles, as eager as Fannie to hope for the best, shared her new attitude, basking in her approval of his efforts.

5 The next morning, September 24, Colegate felt well enough to cook breakfast, much to Spencer's relief. The guide had about decided that they would have to give up on Colegate. Spencer had even thought the day before that he should talk to Carlin about it, but Carlin was off fishing and the thought was gone by the time Carlin returned with his catch. Now, on another crisp, clear day, the cook was bustling about the fire baking bread and making coffee, and Spencer felt things were back to normal. The others seemed to share his pleasure on this fine morning as they ate what was left of the birds and the trout, saving enough breast of grouse for noonday sandwiches.

The traveling was even worse than it had been the day before. The goal was the top of Bald Mountain, a high point on the main ridge between the Lochsa and the North Fork of the Clearwater. The trail traversed steep slopes, some of them strewn with small rock and boulders, fallen trees, heavy brush, and whipping branches. Now and then a horse, trying to squeeze between boulders, would get stuck and one of the riders would have to dismount and pull or push the horse free. Packs came loose as they knocked against trees and had to be replaced and secured. It was slow going and dangerous. No songs came from Carlin now, only grunts and curses. Even the three dogs seemed to have lost their appetite for this adventure; they moved wearily along behind the train, taking advantage of the packed snow, making no sounds and leaving the trail only when it became impassable even to them.

At noon, for want of a better place, the party took its lunch break at a spot so eroded by a swift-running stream that the horses had no comfortable place to stand. They shifted about uneasily for the ten minutes it took the men to eat the sandwiches packed in the saddlebags.

Finally, in late afternoon, Spencer located a reasonably level camping spot in eight inches of snow a short distance from the summit. There was no bare ground because there was no timber on the upper third of Bald Mountain, so the campers laid tarpaulins on the snow. They wouldn't need tents, Spencer said, because he expected the weather to remain clear at least until tomorrow.

Tired and torn as they were, the riders had to agree it was a beautiful afternoon. After they had unpacked the horses and washed them with alum water they hobbled two of them, as usual, and left most of the others to move about freely; they would not go far and would return for the morning feeding. Spencer tied his big white mare, Molly, to a stump with a rope some thirty feet long, then started a small cooking fire. All but Colegate then walked up to the top of the mountain to look at the country around them.

To the north and northwest lay the basins of the St. Joe and St. Maries rivers, hidden in the folds of forested ridges rising from the deep shadows etched by the lowering sun. More near at hand was the North Fork of the Clearwater, out of sight in its own deep blue-green basin. To the south and west they could see the basins of the main Clearwater, the South Fork, and the Kooskooskee, or Lochsa. And in the hazy distance far to the south rose five of the Seven Devils, their snow-tipped, rocky outlines glistening in the sun.

Carlin lit a pipe, noisily sucked the tobacco into life, then declared that in his opinion none of them would ever see a sight like this again. Pierce, sitting on a rock, nodded his head in respectful silence. Himmelwright swore that the view surrounding them was worth every step of the way up this mountain and every ache in his body. Even Spencer, who had been this way before, was impressed. But he told the others they had better not linger, since the afternoon was about gone.

When they got back to camp, expecting to find supper started, they found instead that Colegate had sickened again. He had kept the fire going, and he had got out a kettle and the coffee pot, but now he was sitting on the kitchen box in obvious pain. The day's hard ride had been too much for him, he said, but he would be all right in the morning. And he would be able to get the supper if he could just rest for a little bit.

Spencer's heart sank. The relief he had felt this morning, when Colegate had seemed so much better, now was swept away.

Carlin walked to where Colegate sat, drew close to him, and touched his forehead. It felt hot and damp. What was the matter? Carlin wanted to know. Colegate said again that it was only stomach cramps, that he had suffered these bouts before, and that they always went away. Carlin said it didn't look like stomach cramps to him. Was there something Colegate wasn't telling them?

Colegate swore that he would be all right. He would be all right now, he said, if it hadn't been for that rough day's ride. It had taken too much out of him.

Well, Spencer said, they were over the worst of it. The trail would not be so bad from here on. If the hard riding was the cook's chief problem, and if he was only having temporary stomach cramps, maybe he would be OK. But if his ailment was more serious, as it looked to him to be, they probably should give up any thought of continuing into the mountains.

This observation seemed to take Carlin by surprise. It had not occurred to him that this adventure, this once-in-a-lifetime hunting trip, might have to be called off because of illness. He looked steadily at Colegate, and demanded that he tell them the truth: How sick was he and what was the problem? He turned to Spencer and said that maybe he and Himmelwright should get the supper started. Colegate pulled his hat down on his forehead and stared into the snow.

Pierce, having said nothing to this point, continued to watch and listen in silence, wondering what wild and dreadful thoughts might be whirling through Colegate's mind. There was something different about the cook in the last couple of days, he thought. He didn't just look weary and uncomfortable; his skin had an odd sheen and tightness, and Colegate's movements were now slow and awkward. Suppose he was really sick, Pierce thought. What might he be thinking now as Carlin confronted him, demanding the answer no one wanted to hear? And Pierce imagined what he himself, in that position, might be thinking: That if he admitted he was in bad shape, requiring them to take him out, it would mean the end of the hunt and he would never get another job in the woods. On the other hand, if he said nothing more than he had, they could go on, and he might shake this ailment and save the enterprise.

Pierce asked himself what he would do, and couldn't find the answer.

Himmelwright found himself wishing that Carlin would not press Colegate too hard for the words that could curdle the cream of this grand adventure, and leave the fruits of their planning and spending to spoil here in the snows of Bald Mountain.

Pierce joined Himmelwright in peeling potatoes, and Spencer and Carlin walked some distance from camp and out of sight of Colegate. Carlin wanted Spencer's judgment as to what they should do.

Spencer said that in his opinion Colegate was sicker than he claimed to be. If that was the case, they should seriously consider taking him back to Kendrick, where he could get medical care. Carlin bent down and picked up a handful of snow. He pressed it into a snowball and tossed it languidly down the slope. Yes, he said, rubbing his wet hands on his pants. Spencer was probably right. But how could they tell for sure and when should they make the decision?

Spencer, kicking the snow with a boot, told Carlin he'd been thinking about that. In his opinion, they had come to decision time. They should not push on beyond this point, he said, if they were eventually going to have to turn back.

Carlin sighed. He respected Spencer's judgment, he said, but he hated to turn back unless it was absolutely necessary. If Colegate said he was going to be OK, maybe they should take his word for it.

Colegate could be lying, Spencer said.

Carlin felt a slow fury mounting in him.

God damn him! Carlin muttered, kicking the ground. If they had to take him back to Kendrick, they would all have to go. To separate would be a mistake this time of year in these mountains. And that would mean the end of the expedition since it would be too late in the season to try again.

Spencer suggested they make no decision until tomorrow. Colegate had been feeling pretty good this morning, and God knows this day's ride could take the shine off anybody. From here on it should not be so bad. If Colegate seemed all right tomorrow morning, Spencer said, and if he was sure he would be OK, then maybe they should chance it and push on up the trail.

That idea pleased Carlin, and the two walked back to camp, retracing their footsteps through the snow.

After supper, as Colegate lay in his blankets, the other four sat around the fire and Carlin told Himmelwright and Pierce that he and Spencer had come to a decision that might not please them. And he explained it. Pierce said it sounded reasonable to him. He would not have objected at any rate since he was the tenderfoot in this group and was not even sure why he had been invited along. Himmelwright, however, was not at all pleased. Why should the whole expedition hang on Colegate's demeanor in the morning? he wanted to know. Why not the morning after tomorrow?

Spencer said the farther into the mountains they went, the farther they would have to come out with a sick man—if Colegate should be really sick. And the less their chance of getting him to a doctor in time. The decision had to be made at some point, and some point soon, Carlin said, and he didn't like it any better than Himmelwright did. Carlin reminded the others that he had more money invested in this adventure than any of them, and the most to lose by cutting it short. Then Himmelwright wanted to know which one of them would decide whether Colegate looked sick or well in the morning. Or were they going to take a vote?

They would know, Carlin said.

Spencer said they should consider the possibility that Colegate's so-called "stomach cramps" were really appendicitis. For if they were, they could have a dead man on their hands just as they arrived at the hunting grounds.

At that point, as Carlin was suggesting the subject be changed, there was a loud whinnying and the tramping of hooves in the snow.

The horses! someone shouted, and all four leaped to their feet. Were they stampeding? someone else asked, and another answered, Maybe.

But the horses weren't stampeding.

Spencer's big mare had run to the end of her thirty-foot rope, crashed against the temporarily immovable object, and pulled the rotting stump out of the ground. She thundered past them, the stump bouncing along behind her through the snow, then turned down the hill and disappeared in the dark.

Spencer, frozen with fear, listened to the crashing around in the blackness below, realizing the horse could kill herself among those boulders and cliffs.

Carlin, mistaking the stump for a cougar, had grabbed his rifle but he had no chance to fire.

Spencer hurried down the slope, followed by Carlin, both aware that if they lost the horse the expedition was probably doomed. But they found Molly, standing quietly and breathing hard, apparently unhurt. The stump had come loose, and the horse now was dragging only the rope. Spencer took the rope in his hand, and he and Carlin led the animal back to camp.

It had been a bad scare, but everything was all right. Colegate had been forgotten, and for the rest of the evening, as the fire crackled and the four men joked about wild horses and flying tree trunks, they never mentioned the cook.

Later, though, as Spencer lay staring at the sky, Colegate returned to his musings like a troublesome wraith. Had he given Carlin the right advice? Spencer wondered. What if tomorrow was like today, and Colegate went from good to miserable? Would that mean turning back for sure, or it would it be too late by then? He tried not to think what might lie ahead of them if Colegate turned out to be as sick as he looked this afternoon. If he let his thoughts wander down that road he might never get to sleep, and he was dead tired. He would think about warm springs and good hunting, he told himself, and he drifted off to sleep.

Carlin sat on a rock with his pipe and a tin cup of coffee balanced on his knee, gazing into the dying fire. It was going to be a cold, clear night; some stars were coming out already. Damn, he said to himself, almost aloud. Why had he not remembered to get in touch with Dr. Webb?

The doctor had been wondering the same thing. He assumed that Colegate had told Carlin that he had his doctor's permission to take this job—as indeed he had—and he assumed also that Colegate had told Carlin why his doctor's permission was desirable: Because his ailment, if not carefully controlled, could be debilitating at best and probably fatal.

Dr. Webb had told Colegate that he would like to explain to Carlin just what Colegate's problem was and how it should be handled. And Colegate had told the doctor that he would have Carlin get in touch with him. Then he had told Carlin that he would ask the doctor to call *him*. And Carlin, in his haste to get packed for the trail, had failed to notice that the doctor had not called.

It had never occurred to Dr. Webb that his patient would wander off into the deep woods without the instruments he needed to stay alive. But he had. Now what was happening out there? he wondered. After taking down several of his medical books, and scouring the chapters on uremia, he consulted the calendar. It had been a full week since Colegate left for Kendrick with the rest of the hunting party. By now, according to his medical authorities and his knowledge of this case, Colegate should be a sick man.

On the other hand, he thought, Colegate might have told his employer that he could not go on, in which case he might already have been brought out of the woods. He could be back in Kendrick, or even in Post Falls. Or he could be suffering the tortures of the damned somewhere in the wilderness of the Clearwater.

Dr. Webb was feeling the irritation of mixed anger, ignorance and helplessness, and he had to do something about it. He sent a wire to Kendrick, asking if there had been any word of the Carlin party. The telegrapher in Kendrick took it down and gave the message to a boy who ran with it to the St. Elmo Hotel. The hotel clerk, after consulting several people in the lobby, told the boy that as far as anyone knew, the party was still out in the woods to the east. He said a rancher had come in from Brown's Creek and reported talking with the hunters there. They had shown no sign of turning back and appeared to be in good spirits.

The boy carried this word back to the telegraph office, and the operator dispatched the message to Spokane.

Dr. Webb had no desire to talk with Fannie Colegate, but he felt an obligation. He sent a wire to her in Post Falls asking if she had heard anything of her husband since her last message to him. Her reply to Webb, carried to the telegraph office by Charles, was that there was no word from anybody, and she felt helpless.

Fannie also had counted the days and understood that unless her husband had been blessed by a miraculous recovery, he must by now be woefully sick. She thought of sending Charles once again to Kendrick and then decided against it. If George got sick, the others would surely get him back to civilization. She had met both Mr. Carlin and Mr. Himmelwright on their earlier visit to the region, and she had a good impression of them both. They would take care of George; she felt certain of it.

Then why was there no word?

Charles, hurrying home on his pony from the telegraph office, made a decision of his own: He would take the next train to Kendrick. He would try to find someone to go with him in pursuit of the Carlin party. He couldn't go into those woods alone because he didn't know the country. He would pick up his father's catheters at the St. Elmo Hotel and deliver them. And if necessary he would bring his father home, and the hunters could cook for themselves.

His decision gave a lift to his spirits, and he nudged the pony ahead. He could hardly wait to tell his mother what he planned to do.

⌁

When Spencer awoke on the morning of September 25 he looked first at the sky, which appeared in the half-light of dawn to be clear or mostly so. Then he turned toward the site of last night's gathering and found himself staring at the back of a man kneeling on the ground and fussing with the tiny beginnings of a fire. Spencer was able to determine that the man was Colegate. He turned onto his back, put an arm over his eyes, and allowed himself a long sigh of relief. Then he sat up and threw off the blankets, pulled on his boots, and got to his feet.

Colegate glanced up as Spencer approached the fire, and asked the guide if he had slept well. He had, Spencer said. And Colegate? How was he feeling this morning? Better, Colegate said, thanks to a good night's sleep. As the fire gained strength, the cook pulled a small reflector oven out of the kitchen box and arranged it on some rocks beside the fire. He shook some flour into a pan, poured a bit of baking powder into it, added some condensed milk diluted with water, and began to mix the dough. Spencer watched Colegate at work and tried to read his face for signs of his condition. There was not yet enough daylight for that, and the firelight dancing on Colegate's features gave him a grotesque appearance that was no help at all. So Spencer, feeling reassured by Colegate's words, went to look after the horses.

The party after the rescue, photographed in Spokane. From the left: John Pierce, Ben Keeley, Will Carlin, Martin Spencer, and Abe Himmelwright.

A pack train waits on the main street of Kendrick for the order to move out. The photo was taken in 1894, one year after the Carlin party made a similar departure. Kendrick served as the staging area for many groups venturing into the Clearwater country. *Courtesy Latah County Historical Society, #10-2-14.*

Kendrick, Idaho, in about 1893. The St. Elmo Hotel is near the center of the photo, just to the left of the flag. *Courtesy Latah County Historical Society, #10-2-15.*

The party's first elk, shot by Carlin at the lower salt lick.

Returning to the Lochsa after trying in vain to reach the Lolo Trail.

Building the rafts. The man sitting on the log is probably Colegate.

At this place the river became impassable, and the rafts were abandoned.

The party crossed the river at this point, to continue the journey on foot.

The St. Elmo Hotel on the party's return to Kendrick.

In the summer of 1894 a detachment under Lieutenant Charles P. Elliott discovered Charles Colegate's remains, transported them back up the river to near where the Carlin party had constructed it's rafts, and buried them under a pile of rocks. George Ritchey took this photo of the grave in the early 1900s. *Courtesy Washington State University Library Manuscripts, Archives, and Special Collections, Neg. # 88-391.*

On the divide between the Lochsa and the north fork of the Clearwater, September 25.

6 Spencer had been right: Once past Bald Mountain the going got better, although the horsemen continued to encounter fallen trees that forced them off the path. By mid-morning they were on the divide between the two main branches of the Clearwater, in relatively flat terrain. The old Indian trail meandered along this ridge, weaving at times to the north, where they could see far beyond the valley of the North Fork, and at times to the other side of the divide looking south to the main Clearwater and beyond that to the drainages of the South Fork and the Salmon.

The scenery was spectacular, but a change in the weather drew their horizons much closer. A cloud bank appeared in the west and by noon it had obscured the sun. At a place called Indian Post Office, two rock piles that served as a sort of message center for the Nez Perces, Spencer called a halt. He dismounted long enough to measure snow depths in the immediate area and found the average to be still only about eight inches. That was not a serious problem, but it suggested to the guide that they had gone about as high into the Bitterroots as they should go. Spencer told the others they should proceed on this route for a few more miles and then turn off on another ancient trail that led down to the Lochsa fork of the Clearwater. They would find hot springs and salt licks there, he said, and excellent hunting.

Carlin and Himmelwright had got used to the idea that they would see no mountain goats on this expedition. But since leaving Bald Mountain they had come across numerous signs of bear, elk, and deer, and their excitement grew. When Spencer mentioned hot springs and salt licks, even Pierce became eager for the Lochsa. He rose up in his saddle, waved his hat in the air, and shouted his pleasure—an outburst of enthusiasm that startled the other four and caused Himmelwright's horse to shy.

❧

When Charles reached home he put the pony in the barn, unbridled it, and went in search of his mother. Fannie was in the kitchen, as usual this time of day, and Charles told her of his plan to take the next train to Kendrick. He would find out whether anyone had seen the hunting party, he said, and if no one had, he would rent a horse, buy some provisions, and go in search of his father.

Fannie heard him out, with great patience, and then asked Charles what he would do if he found the Carlin party.

He would take his father's catheters to him, he said, and remind him that the doctor had ordered him to use them. Then he would return to Kendrick and take the train back to Post Falls.

Fannie hesitated for a long moment, looking past Charles through a window now streaming with rain, and finally told the boy that his plan might have worked a week ago but that it was too late now. The hunters had gone so far into the mountains that Charles would never catch them even if he could follow their trail.

That wasn't what Fannie wanted to say to the boy. She wanted to tell him to go, by all means, find his father, and bring him home without wasting a second. But Charles was only sixteen. He had spent time in the wilds with his father and done his share of camping and trail riding in rough weather, but this was not the job for him. Fannie realized that Charles was too eager for this duty, too determined to be the good son at all costs. That would color his judgment, and in those unforgiving mountains she might lose not only her husband but also her son.

Fannie knew what the rain on her window meant. Rain at Post Falls meant snow in the Bitterroots, and she had weathered too much rain in this cold and clammy summer. She had one man plodding through that high country snow, if indeed he was able. She wouldn't send another.

No, she told Charles, she needed him here. And his father was not in the mountains alone; there were four able-bodied men with him, and they could get him out far easier than Charles could. Her mind would not be changed, she said. If Charles wanted to make himself useful, he could fill the wood box.

Charles, aching with disappointment, turned, and without another word, left for the woodshed.

Fannie pulled out a chair and sat down at the kitchen table. When Charles returned to the kitchen carrying an armload of mill ends for the wood box, he found his mother smoothing the shiny table covering with nervous fingers and staring across the oilcloth at the kitchen wall and its faded pink and yellow wallpaper. He felt a need to speak to her, but he didn't know what to say, so he dumped the wood into the box and went out for another load.

꧁ ꧂

On the Lolo Trail, the gathering clouds had produced a light drizzle that turned to snow by mid-afternoon. Spencer remembered a spring that would make a good camping spot in a small ravine a short way off the south side of the trail, and he suggested they halt there for the night. In the morning, he said, they would make their way down to the river and set up their hunting camp. Colegate seemed no worse than the day before, although he moved slowly, and while the others took care of the horses, he found a dry spot under some firs and started a cooking fire.

Colegate's dog, Daisy, remained with him while the two bear dogs, Idaho and Montana, followed the horses and hung around as they were being unpacked and fed. All three dogs had grown used to life on the trail. Their excited romping of the first couple of days had worn itself out by now and they spent most of the daylight hours padding quietly along where the going was easy—on the packed snow that the horses left behind. Colegate had brought Daisy along as a grouse hunter, and Daisy did the job well. But the others noticed that Colegate seemed to enjoy the dog's company more than he did theirs. Pierce told Carlin that this was probably because the dog didn't expect to be talked to or joked with. Carlin agreed.

He and Himmelwright remembered Colegate from the previous expedition as full of talk and good humor. They remembered that in the evenings, while Carlin sang the popular songs of the day, Colegate would join him on the harmonica he carried in his pocket. There was no harmonica music now, and none of the cook's old jokes and laughter. Carlin wondered if Colegate might pull the harmonica out one of these days when he felt better. Spencer said that just hearing a few notes from that mouth organ now would make *him* feel better.

The snow stopped falling in the late afternoon, and by evening a few stars were out. As the sky cleared, the temperature dropped—a bad sign, Spencer said, because if it got cold enough tonight they would find a hard crust on the snow in the morning, and that could make traveling difficult.

Spencer needn't have worried. He awoke during the night to the sound of light rain falling on fir branches, and happily went back to sleep. The worst they would have underfoot tomorrow, he told himself, would be mushy snow, and they could handle that.

By morning the rain had stopped and the sky was clearing again. As Colegate cooked breakfast, with Spencer's help, the other three men walked up out of the ravine to get a look at the country around them. From the main Lolo Trail they saw a vast sea of rumpled gray stretching from just below them to the high ridge far to the south that separated the drainages of the Salmon and Clearwater rivers. All of the land between was out of sight below the fog bank that had settled over the rivers and the lower mountains. To Himmelwright, Carlin, and Pierce, it was a revelation of the height they had reached since leaving Kendrick. Standing here above the clouds, they could look from the northern Nez Perce Trail, better known now as the Lolo, to the southern Nez Perce Trail, which followed that high ridge in the distance and once had carried the Indians to and from the buffalo hunting grounds beyond the Rockies.

Later today they would descend through those clouds to the Lochsa below. And Pierce, who had been so eager for the Lochsa the day before, now said he found the prospect depressing.

The remark surprised Carlin. Depressing? There were hot springs there, and salt licks, and excellent hunting, he reminded Pierce, and he couldn't wait to get there.

It wasn't just going through the fog that bothered him, Pierce said; it was going downhill. It was losing this splendid altitude and the exhilaration he felt standing here.

But down there is where the good hunting is, Himmelwright pointed out. And there probably is no snow down there, he said.

Pierce said he was sure he'd feel better about it once they were on the trail. They all would, Carlin said, as the three started back to the spring and a platter of Colegate's biscuits and beans.

The five riders, their ten horses and three dogs were already strung out on the Lolo Trail, heading east, when a glaring September sun rose up from behind the mountains ahead of them. As it rose, it touched the tops of the cloud layer below, painting the billows in brilliant shades of gold and purple. Every day, it seemed to Pierce, the scenery grew more wonderful. He had thought the views from Bald Mountain were awesome, and now there was this, a more striking sight than anything he could remember. Carlin and Himmelwright, who kept their cameras with them, had paused to take photographs of the view across the dappled cloud bank to the snowy ridge far to the south.

A couple of hours later, when they reached the old trail going down to the river, the fog lifted and they could see the opposite bank of the Lochsa fork. It was densely timbered over there, while on this side an old burn had left much of the slope bare except for scattered firs and some heavy brush and grass. The trail zigzagged down the face of a steep bluff. Spencer, in the lead, had some trouble following it because of the snow, and each switchback required careful maneuvering. But the snow diminished as the trail descended, and by the time they reached the halfway point there was no snow at all.

As they approached the river, the riders began to encounter groves of old cedars as well as fir and some pine, and the trail became less steep. Himmelwright, the first to notice the sound of the river, shouted ahead to Spencer that they must be getting close. The trail meandered through trees and clearings, much of the time in deep shade, and in one of the glades Spencer pointed out the steam rising from a group of several pools of hot water. But they shouldn't linger here, he said; there would be other hot springs closer to camp.

The trail ended at a level spot on a bench above the river, and when the riders got there they found two men building a log cabin and two others sitting on boxes beside a wall tent cleaning their rifles—hunters like themselves, apparently.

To Carlin, this was a disturbing sight. He had not expected to find all these people in this wilderness, and he turned to Spencer, as if Spencer could straighten it all out. Spencer did. He recognized the older of the two men building the cabin, called out his name, and slid down from his horse.

Jerome Johnson put down the ax he was using to notch logs and held out his hand. Spencer took it, gave it a shake, and introduced Carlin, Himmelwright, and Pierce as they dismounted. This was Jerry Johnson, he told them, an old acquaintance who apparently was planning to spend the winter here. He nodded toward the cabin. They all shook hands, and Johnson introduced his partner, Ben Keeley, who he said would be spending the winter also.

Johnson, a big, robust man with a white beard, looked to be about sixty. Keeley had the look of an athlete in training: lithe and springy. He wore a black mustache and a short beard (which he later shaved off), and appeared to be in his thirties.

The two hunters wandered over to say hello and to explain that they would be on their way back to Missoula in a couple of days. They had been using their gold pans in the creeks nearby and doing some hunting. The hunting had been good, they said, but it was about time to get out. And one of them, pointing up the slope, said the snow level was dropping too fast to suit him.

Spencer, suddenly remembering Colegate, turned and saw the cook trying to get off his horse, having trouble. Spencer ran to him,

Jerry Johnson.

calling out to Carlin for help, and both men—one on each side of the horse—helped get Colegate to the ground. But he couldn't stand, and they set him down on a log with his back against a fir tree.

Spencer told Carlin they had better stop socializing and get their own camp set up before it got dark. He didn't want to camp this close to Johnson, he said, and spoil the old man's privacy; he knew a good spot about a quarter of a mile down the river from here, and he suggested that they should get going quickly. Then Spencer glanced at Colegate, on the log under the fir tree, and shook

A meal in camp.

his head. They should never have taken Colegate off his horse, he told Carlin. Now they would have to put him back on, and Colegate wouldn't like that.

Carlin reminded Spencer that Colegate himself had tried to get off the horse; they had only helped him. He walked over to where Colegate sat and told him they had to move on down the river a ways. Would he need any help getting mounted again?

He didn't think so, the cook said. He stood up, walked to the horse, took hold of the saddle, and tried to lift his left foot into the stirrup. He couldn't quite get it up that far, and Carlin grabbed Colegate's leg behind the knee and helped him lift. Colegate, with much effort, was then able to mount, and was ready to go. The other four bade the two hunters fair traveling on their way to Missoula, waved good-bye to Jerry Johnson, and moved with their pack string down the river, followed by the three dogs.

Spencer had picked a good spot, near the end of the flat they shared with Johnson and Keeley, but out of sight of Johnson's cabin and about six feet above the river. A fairly good trail ran along the flat parallel with the river, providing easy access to the lower salt licks just downstream as well as the upper licks above Johnson's cabin and across the Lochsa. In a clearing amongst a stand of cedar, pine, and fir they erected one large wall tent supported by poles and one smaller tent. They hung a tarp between two poles attached to firs, which would keep rain off the cooking fire. They laid the horses' packs on the ground under two large cedar trees.

Spencer said he and Pierce would cook supper if Carlin and Himmelwright would get Colegate's bed made and Colegate into it. The cook had again been unable to dismount without help, and it was clear that he was in no shape to be of any use. He could barely move, and Daisy's efforts to protect her master made matters even worse. But Carlin and Himmelwright managed, and when they left the tent Daisy was lying on one corner of the sick man's outer blanket.

Since they would be established here for a while, the men could afford to make themselves comfortable. They chopped down several small firs and used the branches to soften the ground under their bedrolls. They used the trunks to build a crude table supported by wooden packing boxes. And they carried rocks up from the river to encircle the cooking fire and provide a base for the reflecting oven. When darkness fell, Carlin declared it as fine a camp as he had ever slept in. And Himmelwright observed that they had the sound of the river to lull them to sleep at night—as if they needed it, Pierce added.

Spencer promised to lead them all down to the lower hot springs in the morning and show them the salt licks. And they should take their rifles, he said, because these woods were full of game.

Before turning in, Spencer pulled a note pad and pencil out of his pack and wrote a brief message which he would give tomorrow to the pair of hunters camped above. It was addressed to Spencer's friend and former partner, William Wright, in Missoula, telling him where he and his party were camped and when he expected to come out. He wrote that the trip might be cut short because of threatening weather and the illness of the camp cook. Spencer planned to ask the two departing hunters to take the note to Wright when they reached Missoula.

⁕

Colegate, apparently refreshed by a night's sleep, already had the fire going when the others emerged from their tents the next morning before dawn. After a breakfast of hotcakes and syrup, the guide and the three hunters left on foot for the hot springs.

It was raining lightly and the brush beside the narrow trail was so wet that the hikers were soaked to the skin within half an hour. This did not affect their high spirits, however, and Spencer had to warn them several times to be quiet. His warnings did little good, and as they approached the licks they frightened a deer, which bounded out of sight before anyone could get off a shot.

By now it was full daylight. They should separate, Carlin said, and take positions behind trees or boulders facing the licks and watch quietly for game. They did, in high anticipation. They remained in their cramped positions for about a quarter of an hour, rifles at the ready, but no game appeared. No deer, no elk, no bear. Carlin broke the silence. He stood up, leaned his rifle against the tree that had been shielding him, and announced that since he was already wet, he might as well get wetter. He wanted to get into the warm water and soak.

Himmelwright, irritated, then stood up also. They had come here to hunt, he told Carlin, and if Carlin didn't want to hunt he should have stayed in camp.

Carlin paid no heed to Himmelwright, fastening his attention on the hot springs, which he began to explore, one by one, dipping his hands into the waters. Finally he shouted to the others that he had found what he wanted; he took off his coat and shirt. Then, sitting on a rock, he took off his boots and pants. His stockings and wool underwear came off last, and he slipped into the steaming water and sat down, wearing only his hat. He started to sing. When he began to yodel, Himmelwright lost his temper and demanded that Carlin shut up before he scared off all the game this side of Spokane.

Carlin did, for the moment. But he soon urged the others to try the springs. The water was great, he said, and in fact the pool where he sat was just right—neither too hot nor too cold.

Pierce succumbed next to temptation. He went among the rocks, probing the pools until he found one that felt right, and got undressed. He soon was sitting in the water and conversing with Carlin, whose pool was about twenty feet away.

Spencer told Himmelwright they might as well join the other two, since hunting was out of the question now. Before long, all four were comfortably bathing in the warm mineral waters and trying not to think about the damp clothes that sooner or later they would have to put back on.

They returned to camp, and that afternoon Carlin asked Spencer to show them the way to the upper springs, on the south side of the Lochsa. Spencer said he'd be glad to, but Pierce decided he would stay put with Colegate. Himmelwright and Carlin thought they might want to spend the night, and told Spencer that if he would lead them there, they would be able to find their own way back. Since they would have to ford the river, they saddled three horses, packed food and blankets, and set out in the rain.

These pools were some three miles upriver from the camp, and to reach them Spencer's group would pass Jerry Johnson's place, where the other two hunters were camped. This was working out fine for Spencer, who planned now to leave the note on his way up the river. But when he and the other two reached Johnson's cabin the visitors already had packed up and gone.

Decided not to wait around, Johnson said, approvingly. He suggested that the Carlin party would be wise to pack out pretty soon also.

Spencer assured Johnson that he was keeping an eye on the weather, and the three moved on up the Lochsa.

Once out of earshot, Carlin repeated what he had said before: The old man wanted everybody else out of these woods so he could have the game to himself.

Could be, Spencer said, but the old prospector knew these mountains better than any of them.

The upriver salt licks were on the opposite side of the Lochsa, and the crossing was hard. The current was strong here and the bottom rocky, and the horses had to pick their way slowly from one bank to the other. After reaching the south side, Spencer led the way through groves of pine and cedar to the warm pools, explaining that the place was so attractive to animals because the steaming waters left their mineral salts on the rocks. The salt licks are a kind of bait, he said. Just hang around there long enough, out of sight, and the deer and elk will come to you.

Spencer returned to the main camp, leaving Carlin and Himmelwright in a temporary bivouac under a large white cedar just out of sight of the hot springs. They planned to remain there quietly for the time being and take up positions downwind of the salt licks just before dusk. They did so, but no deer came, and no elk. When it got so dark that Carlin could no longer see the sight on his rifle barrel, he said he'd had enough of this sitting in the rain. They returned to their temporary camp, built a fire, and tried to dry their clothes while chewing on sandwiches. They turned in early, spent an uncomfortable night listening to the rain and the river, and rode back to the main camp next morning.

⁂

The hunting was no better there, as they discovered in the next few days. It continued to rain, and Carlin and Himmelwright continued to hunt, but the game proved elusive. They saw elk and deer sign everywhere, but the critters evidently moved about only at night. The rain, drumming relentlessly on tents and forever dripping from trees and bushes, cast a pall over the camp. It shortened tempers and it silenced Carlin, who lost the impulse to sing. Pierce, who had a tendency to colds, kept mainly to camp, and yet when he ventured out with Daisy and his shotgun, he and the dog almost always returned with grouse. For the next five days, this was their only fresh meat, and Himmelwright swore that once out of this place he would never touch grouse again.

The men fell into a rain-driven routine. They would hunt or gather firewood during the day, and in the evening build a blazing fire and try to dry their clothes and blankets. They cooked in the rain, ate in the rain, moved about in the rain to keep the blood circulating, and one afternoon walked in the rain to Jerry Johnson's place just for something to do, leaving Himmelwright in camp with Colegate.

Was Johnson keeping dry? Carlin asked him.

Jerry Johnson's cabin.

Pretty well, Johnson said. He and Ben Keeley had got the log walls up and some rafters, and they had covered the rafters partially with tarpaulins. So half of the cabin was dry, at least. But Johnson and Keeley agreed that it had been too wet for comfort for too long.

He'd almost rather see the snow than any more of this rain, Johnson said.

That was easy for him to say, Spencer thought; he was spending the winter here. Spencer had been worrying more than the others about this rain because he realized that the rain here below could mean snow on the ridges above. He decided that he would do tomorrow what he had been thinking about for several days. He would take one of the horses and make an exploratory trip out of the river bottom to check snow levels.

Carlin was complimenting Johnson and Keeley on their progress with the cabin when Keeley said they could use a little help. It would be nice to get the whole place under a sturdy roof, he said, but Johnson broke in with the remark that he and Keeley could handle it. Wasn't much left to do, he said, now that the walls were up, and he and his partner needed something to keep them busy.

Carlin pointed out that house building didn't leave much time for hunting. Would Johnson and Keeley like to have some fresh meat—in case he and his friends got lucky?

Johnson, giving Keeley no time to respond, said the offer was appreciated, but no thanks. They were well provided for, he said.

As the hunters returned to their own camp, Pierce remarked that Johnson didn't strike him as a neighborly type. He didn't want any help with the cabin, and he didn't want any fresh meat.

Spencer agreed that the older man was a bit standoffish, and he supposed that was because he wasn't much used to company. Spencer had been acquainted with Johnson for several years, but he still didn't know much about him. He had been born in Prussia and had spent time in New Zealand, where he developed an interest in mining. Since coming to this country he had prospected in the Cascades and the Rockies as well as other wild parts of the Pacific Northwest. He supported himself mostly by trapping, as far as Spencer knew; he had never struck gold in any amount, and probably never would.

Pierce wondered if there were any gold strikes still to be made.

Probably not, Spencer said. The last gold rush in this part of the country was a good thirty years ago. Still some people kept hoping, and you couldn't blame them. You can find flakes of color in these mountain streams, he said—including the Lochsa—and you know those flakes had to be washed down from some place. But where?

Pierce was intrigued. How would a person go about looking? he asked Spencer. What would you look *for*?

It usually didn't make any difference what you were looking *for*, Spencer said. Most sizable gold strikes were made by accident when someone was looking for something else. And he told a story that Jerry Johnson had told him.

One winter, according to this story, a sick and starving Indian had wandered into his camp, and Johnson had fed and taken care of him. In gratitude, the Indian told Johnson that he knew where there was a great deal of gold. He said that several Indians had been gathering rocks for a sweat bath and in digging up some white stones they had found gold. They didn't want a bunch of whites moving in and spoiling the hunting and fishing, so they kept the information to themselves. But since Johnson had been kind to him, he would direct him to the spot. The Indian didn't know enough English to tell Johnson where the place was, but he would take him there.

They started out but the Indian, not well enough to go far, collapsed. Johnson picked him up, carried him in his arms to the top of a high ridge, and asked him to point in the direction of the gold. The dying Indian raised an arm, pointed toward a distant snow-covered peak, and uttered the one word, "sun." Then he passed out and within a couple of hours he was dead.

It wasn't much to go on, but Johnson had told Spencer that he meant to find that gold. He had visited the peak and the area beyond it, looking for the spot where some rocks had been disturbed to make a sweat bath. He had found nothing, but he was going back in the spring.

That would be in the coming spring, the spring of ninety-four? Pierce asked.

Correct, Spencer said.

Pierce pressed on: Was there a chance he might find it?

Doubtful, Spencer said. Very doubtful. But that was what Johnson and people like him did. They kept looking, and figuring, and sitting out the winters in places like this so they could go looking again in the spring.

Wouldn't it be great if he found it, Carlin said, after all these years of looking.

Maybe and maybe not, Spencer remarked as they walked into their own camp on the flat. Johnson's life, he said, was in the looking; not necessarily in the finding. If he ever found it, there would be nothing left to look for.

That was all very interesting, Carlin said, but he wished that as long as they were camping this close together the old prospector could be a little more friendly.

He also wished, without saying so, that it would stop raining.

7 After a week of hunting in the rain, the Carlin party still had provided no fresh meat for the camp aside from Carlin's trout and the grouse bagged by Pierce. Carlin and Himmelwright had decided that the deer and elk were moving about only by night, when hunting was impossible. But in the afternoon of the seventh day on the Lochsa, Carlin noticed a lot of elk sign in places where he hadn't seen it before. He told the others that this could mean only one thing: The elk had begun to come down from the heights to their winter range. If he was right, the hunting would be good from now on, and he intended to be in place at the lower salt licks by daylight tomorrow.

He left camp at dawn, alone and in the rain, and was wet to the skin by the time he reached the warm springs. There appeared to be no game there, but he told himself he had plenty of time, and he would wait. Before long he heard the whistle of a cow elk below him near the river, and he began walking quietly in that direction. As he emerged from the cedar grove the cow came into view and trotted past him at a distance of some thirty yards. He ducked behind a tree and waited, assuming the cow would be followed by a bull.

Less than a minute later, he saw a huge set of antlers moving slowly above the rim of a small gully eighty yards away. As he watched, the antlers came to a stop and turned one way and then the other. After a few seconds the bull vaulted out of the gully into plain view and paused in an open clump of trees. Its neck and head were hidden by foliage, but Carlin decided he had better shoot before it dashed into the timber. He aimed for the liver and fired. The bull bounded over the brow of the hill out of sight, and Carlin hurried after it. He found the tracks and followed them down a well-used game trail for half a mile into a little thicket. There he spotted the elk. The big bull was lying down behind a log some seventy-five yards away, looking directly at him.

Carlin eased himself into a sitting position, took careful aim at the neck, and fired. The bull staggered to its feet and headed toward the river. Carlin quickly reloaded and fired again, this time at the shoulder, and the elk went down on its breast. It struggled to its feet and continued on three legs toward the river. Carlin's next shot hit the bull in the neck and it collapsed into a heap on the ground. It was still alive, however, and Carlin worried that it might start thrashing around and damage an antler on the rocks. So he finished it with another shot to the neck.

Then, as he later described the episode to the others, he sat down and for a full five minutes admired "the fallen monarch: his magnificent curving antlers; his splendid form and sleek, yellowish sides; the fine, long, reddish-black hair of his scalp and neck." Unfortunately, when Carlin prepared to bleed and dress the bull, he found he would have to do it with a pocket knife because he had left his long-bladed hunting knife in his tent.

He cut out the heart and carried it back to camp as a sign to the others that they would now have fresh meat aplenty. There was quite a celebration when he arrived, and Carlin sent Pierce to Jerry Johnson's place to tell Keeley that he and Johnson could have some of this meat if he would help them pack it out. Then all but Colegate and Pierce started out with horses, accompanied by Keeley. Well before they got to where the carcass lay, they could hear the tumult of dozens of magpies and ravens fighting over the entrails. When they reached the spot, the birds flew up into the trees and waited there while the men photographed the bull, then skinned it and cut it up. The moment they moved out the birds descended on the offal, and as the hunters continued toward camp they could hear behind them the pandemonium of the magpies' raucous feeding.

It was now four o'clock; they had gone only half a mile when darkness overtook them. It was difficult traveling in the gathering dark over wet and sometimes steep terrain. At one point Keeley's horse slipped and rolled down a side hill, but he brought it back to the trail uninjured. When they were still a mile from camp they had to stop. It was now completely dark, and they could not see the trail. They used all the matches they had trying to keep a fire going in the rain with wet fuel, but Keeley managed to make a torch out of cedar shavings. By its light they unloaded the horses and stowed the meat and antlers under a tree, to be retrieved in the morning. Then, with Keeley and his torch in the lead, they slowly made their way back to camp, arriving there at eight o'clock. It had taken them four hours to go less than four miles.

The next day Carlin, Himmelwright, and Spencer took a couple of horses down to pick up the antlers and meat. Himmelwright continued on to the lower salt lick, determined to get his elk. It was raining as usual, and Himmelwright returned to camp at noon, wet and disappointed. He had waited in the rain all morning and seen nothing to shoot at.

Carlin told him to cheer up. He had a wonderful idea, he said: The two of them would ride to the upper warm springs that afternoon, spend the night, and have a good hunt the next day. Himmelwright liked that idea, and they hurried to get packed.

They took two tin cups, two spoons, and two tin plates stowed inside a camp kettle. They also took two double blankets, some rope, an ax, salt, coffee, sugar, condensed milk, bacon, bread, raw elk steaks, and some cold fried potatoes left over from the night before. They saddled a couple of horses and at two o'clock they were ready to start. They could expect it to be raining, as it was on their first visit to the upper licks, but Carlin pointed out that this time they would make a comfortable shelter for themselves and their gear. And he said he was still pretty sure that the elk were now coming down to their winter range near the river. Expect to come back with an elk, he told Himmelwright, slapping him across the shoulder.

When they reached the ford, they found the river higher than before, and the horses had some difficulty crossing against a strong current. The Lochsa here was a hundred yards wide. On the other side, the trail followed a large creek that flowed into the river from the east, across a brushy, thinly wooded flat. Carlin and Himmelwright rode up the creek and found a likely camping place a mile and a half from the river and half a mile from the springs. There was fir and cedar here and plenty of dry fuel lying around under the trees. They unsaddled the horses, and while Himmelwright picketed them in some bunchgrass near the creek, Carlin got to work on a shelter of poles and fir boughs. He propped up a pole five feet above the ground and parallel to a log lying five feet away. He placed shorter poles between the main pole and the log, and on these he laid saplings crosswise, forming a framework. He then piled enough fir boughs on this sloping roof to keep the interior fairly dry even in a hard rain.

He and Himmelwright placed the blankets and provisions in the shelter, and started walking toward the springs. Towers of steam rose above the hot springs in the cold, damp air. They passed several small springs, then descended through a thicket of fir and pine saplings to an opening in the woods about an acre in size where the main springs bubbled up from their sources under boulders and pebbles coated with white saline deposits. These were the salts that lured the animals to this steamy place.

A grove of pines, firs, and cedars separated this group of springs from another farther up the creek. It was now four o'clock. Carlin suggested that he should stay here and that Himmelwright should take his stand at the upper springs. Himmelwright did so, posting himself in the deep shade of the grove behind two fir trees. He cocked his gun and waited.

He saw no movement in his area of sight, and heard no sound except the roaring of the creek. It soon began to get dark, and before long the gloom among the trees became so intense that Himmelwright could no longer see the sights on his gun. He was thinking of going back down to Carlin and then returning to the shelter when he heard a twig snap sharply behind him.

He faced around, thinking it might be Carlin coming to get him, but he could see nothing moving in the darkness.

He turned his attention again to the pools, and shortly heard a low growl. He whirled and saw a grizzly bear coming toward him through the trees. His gun was pointed toward the bear, and he was about to shoot, when he saw that she had two cubs with her. Knowing better than to molest a bear with cubs, Himmelwright did nothing, and the three bears walked around him and into the lick. When the sow crossed the lick some twenty yards away from him, Himmelwright—believing it was safer to shoot now that the bear was well past him—aimed roughly along the barrel of his gun and fired two shots. Both missed.

He ran into the open where there was more light and fired again. The bear reared up, turned back toward Himmelwright, and began pawing the air. Seeing his chance, Himmelwright aimed along the top of the barrel and pulled the trigger. It simply snapped; there had been only three cartridges in the magazine.

As he reloaded, the bear and the cubs disappeared into the woods on the other side of the lick.

Carlin arrived just then, breathing hard, and wanted to know what was going on. Himmelwright said he was disgusted. He had just bungled the chance to shoot a grizzly and two cubs. And he said the cubs probably would have weighed a hundred pounds apiece.

Where did they go? Carlin asked, and Himmelwright pointed across the lick. After examining the spot where the old bear had torn up the ground, Carlin said Abe must have wounded the sow, and suggested they go after her.

That would not be a good idea, Himmelwright said. It was too dark and therefore too dangerous. They should wait until morning. They walked back to their bivouac in the rain, both deploring Himmelwright's rotten luck.

Their gloom didn't last long. Carlin's rough shelter was shedding the rain quite well, and that meant they would spend a comfortable night. Besides, there was supper of elk steaks, fried potatoes, and coffee to look forward to; it was a good life, after all.

While Carlin got a kettle full of water from the creek, Himmelwright found a piece of pitch pine and built a good fire. Then he rustled up enough dry wood to last them through the evening. After they had eaten supper and washed their dishes, they drank coffee, smoked their pipes, and contemplated a splendid day of hunting tomorrow. If they were really lucky, Himmelwright said, it might even stop raining.

The next morning at daylight they were back at the licks, still in the rain, waiting patiently for some game to show up. None did, and at eight o'clock Carlin came to Himmelwright's stand and suggested they go looking for the bears. They found the place where the old bear had taken Himmelwright's third shot, but the night's rain had washed away all the tracks on the trail leading out of the lick. There was no point going in that direction. They decided instead to walk up the creek, fifty yards apart, with Carlin in the lead. They could scout a lot of ground that way, Carlin said, and it seemed to him that a wounded bear would be too thirsty to get far from the creek.

They had walked about a hundred yards, out of sight of each other, when Himmelwright heard two shots fired in quick succession. He ran immediately to where Carlin was reloading his gun and pointing up the creek. Shoot! Shoot! he shouted to Himmelwright before he got off two more shots.

Carlin had wounded an elk, which was now staggering around some fifty yards up the creek from them. Himmelwright raised his gun and shot the bull in the shoulder. His second shot hit him in the neck and he dropped.

Himmelwright was disappointed. He had thought that Carlin might have found the bear. They already had an elk; what Himmelwright craved was a grizzly. But this *was* a fine big bull, he told Carlin, nudging it with his boot.

The bull had been badly shot to pieces by six bullets, and cleaning it was a disagreeable task. Once done, they rolled the carcass over a log and propped it upright, then resumed their search for the bears. They saw no trace of them, and returned to the lick and from there to the shelter. While Himmelwright went for the horses, Carlin collected their gear and they were back in camp by early afternoon.

Carlin wanted to go back right away and bring in the elk, but Spencer said it was too late in the day for that. They should wait until morning, and he would go along to help. A great idea, Carlin said. They could take the bear dogs in case the grizzlies were still hanging around up there.

As it turned out, Carlin stayed in camp the next day and Spencer and Himmelwright went after the elk, taking the bear dogs with them.

They found the elk, but the bears were nowhere to be seen, and the dogs proved to be quite a burden. On each ford of the swollen Lochsa, Himmelwright had to cross holding two dogs with one hand and the reins with the other.

When Himmelwright told Carlin about this later, Will laughed and said he wished he had been there with his camera. Abe was not amused.

On October 3, Spencer saddled his white mare, stuffed his pockets with biscuits, and told the other four he'd be back by early afternoon. It was raining as usual, and Spencer wanted to see how far up the bluff he would have to ride before this rain became snow. There had been eight inches of snow on the Lolo Trail when they came over it near the end of September, and it had rained in the river bottom most of the time since then. To Spencer, it seemed likely that the moisture falling as rain in the valley might well be making snow on the heights. If so, he and his party were in some danger of being snowed in. It was part of his job to make sure that didn't happen.

The two hunters from Missoula, before they returned home, had noted that the snow level was falling on the slopes above the river. And Jerry Johnson had said that if he weren't spending the winter here, he'd be getting out. None of the others in Spencer's group seemed much concerned about the weather—except for the rain, which by now was close to driving them all crazy.

Carlin had dismissed Johnson's warning, telling the others that the crabby old man wanted them to leave so he could have the hunting to himself. But Spencer was getting nervous. As he rode toward the switchbacks that had brought them down here, he found himself wishing he'd been able to get that note to the Missoula hunters before they left for home. He would feel easier if someone on the outside knew where he and his party were.

Because of the seemingly permanent cloud layer along the river, it had been impossible for days to see the terrain above. Spencer would have to ride through the clouds.

He was enjoying himself. It felt good to be away from the camp and on the move and he was glad he had decided to make this exploration. He was in no hurry. Once on the switchbacks, he let Molly go at her own pace, and he let his thoughts roam as they would. Only a light rain fell, no great discomfort to either horse or rider. After riding for some time up the face of the bluff he noticed that he could no longer hear the river. Only the squeak of leather harness, the breathing of the horse, and the gentle drumming of the rain on his hat disturbed this welcome silence. To amuse himself, he catalogued the scents of the forest: Wet fir and cedar and dirt, wet wool, wet horse. He took a biscuit from his coat pocket and sniffed its floury essence before biting into it. He told himself, for the millionth time, that he was a lucky fellow. Ten years ago, stricken by asthma, he had been almost an invalid, unable to do the things young men ought to do, and almost had a right to do. On doctor's orders he moved west, to higher country. And for the last eight years he had worked as a wilderness guide, knocking about in the woods for a living and getting paid for something he would have done for nothing, if the truth were known.

The trail, the rocks, and the bushes retreated into a gray haze as Spencer penetrated the cloud layer. He still had encountered no snow. So far so good, he told himself. A half hour later, he noticed he could no longer hear the rain on his hat. He was still in fog, but the rain had turned to a barely perceptible mist. Within another twenty minutes the gray mist was breaking into vague and isolated streamers, and he was squinting into the sun.

Now, he could see snow. There were pockets of it among the rocks and in shady spots near the trail, and he could see that not far above him the ground was solid white. And there was nothing but white across the canyon, which was in shadow much of the day.

He continued up the trail until nearly noon, estimating snow depths along the way. He reckoned that there might be twelve to sixteen inches on the Lolo Trail—a nuisance, but not a serious problem.

As he started back down, Spencer thought it would be unwise to spend many more days on the Lochsa. One heavy snowfall and they could be in real trouble, especially if Colegate's health should get any worse. His advice would be to get out while the getting was good.

That advice was not well received in camp. Both Carlin and Himmelwright complained that this was the first week of October, that the early snowfall meant nothing, and that they had not yet had any real hunting. And Carlin repeated his contention that Jerry Johnson's dire warnings should be ignored because he was a sour old man who just wanted them out of there.

Pierce said he was willing to go along with whatever the others wanted to do but that he respected Spencer's judgment.

Colegate took no part in the discussion. He had gone to bed, saying he was tired and needed some rest. It seemed to Pierce that the cook couldn't possibly be enjoying this endeavor, and it occurred to him that if he voted with Spencer, and if Colegate did the same, there would be three against two in favor of heading out. Then he reminded himself that Spencer and Colegate were only hired hands after all and probably not entitled to vote. So he said nothing.

Himmelwright said that if fortune smiled, and gave them just a few days of dry weather, he would be willing to forgo the rest of the hunt. Carlin said he felt the same way. He respected Spencer's opinion, he said, but he thought he was being overly cautious.

Spencer let the matter drop and left to take care of his horse. Himmelwright took Daisy and went hunting for grouse, and Carlin thought he had better look in on the cook.

Carlin stepped into Colegate's tent and asked him if there was anything he needed.

Yes, Colegate said, there was something he needed to say.

Then, lying on his back, his eyes closed, Colegate told Carlin that he had not been quite honest with him before. He was suffering from a condition that made it hard for him to urinate. In fact, he said, it had become almost impossible, and he was probably going to die.

Carlin asked him if his condition had anything to do with the prostate gland, and Colegate said that it did. According to his doctor, the gland was enlarged and pinching the tube that carried away his urine.

Carlin told him he would be right back, and he went in search of Pierce, who knew something about medicine. He found his brother-in-law in the other tent and asked Pierce to return with him to Colegate. When they got there, Carlin asked Colegate to repeat for Pierce what he had just told him.

Colegate did.

Pierce, expressing some alarm, asked Colegate if he had been using a catheter. Colegate said he had been—for almost twenty years.

When had he used one last? Pierce asked.

A day or so before leaving Post Falls, Colegate said.

Why did he stop using it?

He couldn't use it here in the mountains.

Why?

Because he hadn't brought any catheters with him.

He had left them at home?

Yes.

For God's sake, why?

He thought he could get along without them. He had before, for as long as a week or two.

But he was planning to be away from home for five weeks, Pierce said.

He understood that, Colegate said. But he thought he would be all right. And he hated to use them. His insides were sore from using them, he said, and it hurt every time.

Colegate heaved a great sigh. He was silent for a moment, then he said in a whisper that he was sorry.

Was there anything they could do for him? Carlin asked.

Not that he knew of, Colegate said. And he added that he probably wasn't going to die; he just needed some rest now, and then he would feel better.

Carlin said he should try to get some sleep, and he and Pierce stood up and went outside, leaving the tent flap open.

Carlin asked his brother-in-law what he thought of Colegate's immediate future.

Bleak, Pierce replied. Prostate problems were not unusual in middle-aged men, he said, and Colegate's condition was often the result. As long as he could not urinate properly, the poisons would continue to build up and eventually the kidneys would fail. Then he would die.

Carlin reminded Pierce that Colegate had some good days and some not so good. So he must be getting some relief the natural way.

Probably, Pierce said.

Meaning, Carlin said, that they should keep an eye on the cook's condition in case it became necessary to take him back to Kendrick for medical treatment.

The comment struck Pierce as odd, but he said nothing.

⁕

When Himmelwright and Spencer returned to camp, Carlin told them what Colegate's problem really was. Now, he said, they had to decide what they should do about it. Pierce spoke up, emboldened by his alarm at Colegate's awful truth. They should take Colegate back to Kendrick now, he said.

Spencer said he agreed with Pierce. He said also that he would advise going back soon in any case because they were in danger of getting snowed in.

Himmelwright thought it would be wise to take Colegate out, but he questioned the advisability of doing so in this cold and rain. The journey would be hard enough on the sick man, he said, even in the sunshine. Putting him through it in this miserable weather would be downright cruel.

Himmelwright had a point, Carlin said. It had been raining steadily for so long that there had to be a break soon; it wouldn't hurt to wait a few days and hope for better weather.

They decided that's what they would do. It didn't make sense to Spencer, who fretted about the worsening conditions on the Lolo Trail, and he decided he would talk privately with Colegate at the first opportunity.

He got the chance two days later when the hunters had all gone to the lower salt licks and he and Colegate had the camp to themselves. Spencer, sitting across the fire from the cook, told Colegate he was aware of his problem. He said he knew a little about this illness, which he called uremia, because it had killed one of his uncles. Colegate was going to die, Spencer said, unless he got medical help quickly.

Colegate said he would be all right, and that he was feeling better than before, but Spencer had no doubt he was lying.

Spencer thought he knew why Colegate was putting on this act: He didn't want the party to end on his account. So he offered Colegate a compromise.

He and the cook would leave tomorrow or the next day for Kendrick, and the hunters could remain here until they were ready to come out. They knew the way back; they didn't need the guide. Carlin and Himmelwright were both experienced woodsmen, perfectly able to do their own cooking. The only question was Colegate. Would he be willing to go?

Spencer put the question to him, fearing he might not have another chance to talk with Colegate privately. What did he think of Spencer's idea?

The cook didn't answer immediately. The question seemed to puzzle and confuse him. He looked down at his feet, then at the river, then into the trees, avoiding Spencer's eyes, and finally said, well, he didn't think so.

He was feeling better, Colegate said, and would soon be able to carry out his duties as he had promised. Then he startled Spencer by adding that if the guide wanted to leave, he should go ahead without him.

Spencer felt he was not getting through to Colegate. He tried again.

He said he knew what Colegate needed, and that he could be quickly taken care of in Kendrick. Then Spencer would bring him back so he could finish the job he'd hired out for, if that was what he wanted.

Colegate raised an arm and waved it in front of him as if brushing away a fly, and told Spencer again he would be all right. He was not going out, he said, until everybody went out.

He reached for a piece of firewood, effectively ending the conversation, and Spencer walked away in disgust.

It began to snow on the seventh of October, and on the eighth, the hunters decided that they would leave the next day, rain or shine. On the ninth, however, the camp got six inches of snow and the morning was almost gone before they found the horses and brought them in, so they put the departure off for another day.

They would be on the trail tomorrow for sure, Carlin said, and Spencer, addressing no one in particular, said it was about time.

8 Himmelwright awoke in the dark, knowing immediately that it was snowing again; there were sounds to be heard on a clear night that were muted by falling snow, and what he couldn't hear depressed him. What he *could* hear was Carlin's broken snoring across the tent and then someone's footsteps crunching in the snow outside. That would be Spencer, Himmelwright thought, taking care of the horses. It meant he had better get up.

He resisted the temptation to remain a while longer in his warm cocoon and sat up in the blankets, wondering what time it was. He reached for his boots and struggled into them. They were cold and clammy and stiff. By the time he had them on and laced, his fingers were numb. Tonight, he promised himself, he would wrap them in something and keep them in bed with him. He wondered, as he got to his feet, where he might be sleeping next. It would depend on the weather they found today on the Lolo Trail, and since it was impossible to know what that might be, there was no use thinking about it. He knelt again on the blankets, feeling around for his woolen coat, his hat, and finally, his gloves. He probably should wake Carlin, he thought, standing in the center of the tent, but he decided not to. First he would go see what Spencer was up to, and whether Colegate was still alive.

He untied the tent flap, kept it open only until he was out, and tied it closed again. Someone—Spencer, no doubt—had set a candle lantern on the kitchen box, and in its mellow gleam Himmelwright could see falling snow. The flakes came straight down; there was no wind. It was a light snow, Himmelwright noted with relief, and he judged from the level on the marker tree that it was no more than eight inches deep—about two inches more than yesterday. There was a light in Spencer's tent, giving the canvas a warm glow, and Himmelwright decided to look in on Colegate.

Spencer's bed was empty but the cook was still in his blankets, alive and groaning. Himmelwright closed the flap quickly and knelt down beside the older man. Colegate was rank with sweat. It seemed to Himmelwright that he could smell the poison collecting in Colegate's swollen body, pushing against his gleaming taut skin, and he remembered what they would do on the farm when a cow came down with the bloat, its belly near bursting with gas: They would push a clean ice pick into the ballooning gut and let the gas out. A terrible smell, but most of the time it worked. The cook's problem certainly was not gas, and there was no help for him in these woods.

Himmelwright didn't have to ask how Colegate felt, and he didn't. Instead, he said it hadn't snowed much in the night and they should have an easy ride up to the ridge. Himmelwright was immediately sorry he'd said it. For a man in Colegate's condition there were no easy rides.

Colegate, between groans, said he wasn't going. He got up on one elbow, stared hard at Himmelwright, and said there was nothing in the world he would rather do than thoroughly wet this bed. He lay back down and closed his eyes and declared he would willingly drown in his own piss if he could just get rid of it.

Himmelwright did not tell Colegate that of course he would have to go with them, no matter how painful the ride, for they could not leave him here. But it was true. Neither Jerry Johnson nor Ben Keeley would tolerate a sick man on his hands through the winter. Himmelwright, preparing to leave, started to give Colegate a sympathetic pat on the shoulder, but instead withdrew from him and stood up. He said he should be helping Spencer with the horses and left, again quickly closing the tent flap behind him.

He pulled in several deep breaths of the cold, clean air, ashamed of the relief he felt at escaping the odor of sickness in Colegate's tent. He thought he now understood why Spencer, the cook's tentmate, was up so early, and he marveled that the guide got any sleep at all, in there with all those gasps and groans.

In the distance suddenly he could see a light, turning off and on like a maritime code as Spencer carried his lantern through the trees and among the horses. Himmelwright took the lantern on the kitchen box and started walking toward Spencer's light. He found the guide arranging a wooden freight saddle on the back of one of the pack horses, talking softly to himself and the animal as he worked. Himmelwright offered to help, and Spencer, without speaking, reached under a nearby tarpaulin, pulled out another pack saddle, and handed it to Himmelwright. Both men worked silently. Spencer was beginning to load his horse when Carlin appeared, and then Pierce. Carlin expressed some surprise that Spencer and Himmelwright were getting packed so early.

Why not some breakfast first? he asked Spencer.

They would eat on the way, Spencer said. It would be near daylight by the time they got started, and that would be none too early since they had no idea what they would be getting into on the slopes above.

Carlin insisted, with Himmelwright's support, that they have some breakfast before getting packed. They would cook, he said, while the others worked with the horses, and they could enjoy a hot meal before heading out. Spencer said fine, if that was the way he wanted it. While Himmelwright made hotcakes and oatmeal, Carlin and Pierce went to get the tents, which would have to be emptied and properly folded for packing, and Spencer began saddling the horses. Himmelwright suggested they do Colegate's tent last since there was no point in getting him up until they were ready to leave. The night was fading now; the men could make out the shapes of trees, and getting about was easier.

After breakfast, Carlin decided to walk up to Jerry Johnson's place to say good-bye and ask whether he or Keeley would like to send a message to someone in the outside world. When he returned the camp was packed, the horses fed, and they were ready to move. It had stopped snowing and that pleased all but Colegate. The weather had ceased to be of interest to him. After the others struck his tent, he managed to walk painfully to the kitchen box. He sat there huddled in his heavy coat, watching in helpless misery as the others prepared for departure. He had the look of a man watching a team of doctors preparing to amputate his legs.

Finally, the others had to pack the box he was sitting on, leaving him leaning against a tree. Then they helped him to his horse, Himmelwright on one side and Carlin on the other. It took both of them plus Pierce to get the stricken cook into the saddle. He sat there in silence until the horse made a sidling move, and then he let out a groan that brought Spencer running through the snow to see what had gone wrong.

Well they couldn't leave him here, Himmelwright said to Spencer, who was staring at the cook with a tortured look on his face. Spencer said nothing, but returned to his own horse and mounted. The other three did the same, and the ten horses started slowly and quietly up the trail under a dark and threatening sky.

Spencer had planned to be out of camp by daylight, but one delay after another had made that impossible. It was now already ten o'clock.

The guide rode in front, followed by Carlin, Colegate, Himmelwright, and Pierce. The pack horses followed behind, loosely tethered to each other and to Pierce's saddle. This was an old and well-traveled Indian trail and easy to follow, even under eight inches of snow. It twisted through thick groves of fir and cedar and across occasional meadows before emerging upon the mostly bare and windy switchbacks.

The wind was not long in coming, nor the snow. The Carlin party began tasting the first small flakes in less than half an hour. For the next hour the snow fell lightly and fitfully, causing no great alarm. The trail remained clearly discernible and the day was brightening. But at midmorning the sky darkened and the breeze began whipping the brush and whistling through the dead trees.

The snow by now was falling hard and blowing erratically in the wind. Spencer, who knew the country well, began feeling disoriented. He began seeing here and there a lane through the burn that could be the trail, and after a while he began to fear that one of them might have been. At one point the party rounded a headland and he could make out through the blowing snow a familiar hogback in the distance, a sign that he was on the trail after all.

He gave no hint to the others that he was at all concerned, but Carlin, riding behind him, noticed that the snow was deeper here in the heights above the river and getting deeper by the moment.

Carlin began to worry. He could barely see Spencer's horse through the whirling snow. Turning in his saddle, he could make out Colegate's dark form but not the rider behind him. Colegate himself hardly noticed what was happening. The pain in his legs surged angrily with the horse's every step, and he tried to hold his thighs off the horse by placing his hands on the saddle, front and back, then stiffening his arms and lifting. It didn't help much.

Himmelwright, the next in line, rode as close behind Colegate as he could because he feared the cook in his misery might fall to the ground. Himmelwright could see the effort Colegate made to ease the weight on his legs, but there was nothing he could do to help. Himmelwright, like Carlin, had some experience in wilderness travel and like Carlin, he began to worry. He had no idea where the trail was. He trusted Spencer to know that, unaware that Spencer himself was no longer certain.

Behind Himmelwright, Pierce chewed on a piece of cold venison and wondered how long they could continue in this worsening storm. He tried to maintain his orientation by fastening his gaze on Himmelwright, who was barely visible, and by occasionally turning to check on the pack horses plodding behind him through the snow. He was staring at Himmelwright's back when he noticed with surprise that the figure ahead of him was getting suddenly closer. The other riders had all stopped, on Spencer's orders, and Spencer was walking through the drifts to the back of the string.

He passed Pierce without speaking and began pulling some picket ropes from a bag on the lead pack horse. Spencer handed

Pierce one of the ropes and told him they must now tie all the horses together; the visibility was so bad, and the drifting snow so deep, they could easily be separated.

Pierce dismounted and tied one end of the rope to the face harness of his horse. Himmelwright dismounted also and tied the other end of the rope to a hook on the back of his saddle. Himmelwright then took another rope from Spencer and attached it to the harness on his horse, leaving Spencer with the other end. Himmelwright could see Colegate trying to dismount and went forward to help him, and with Spencer's aid he managed to get the sick man lowered into the snow. Colegate stood leaning against his horse with one arm around the stirrup and the other in front of his face. He said nothing, and Spencer struggled forward through the snow, tethering the rest of the horses.

Spencer then returned and began knocking snow off the pack horses' loads while Himmelwright went to get Colegate into his saddle again. Colegate had slid down the side of his horse and was sitting in the snow, which was now so deep that only his head and shoulders could be seen. He refused to move, muttering only no, no, no, as Himmelwright tried to lift him to his feet. When Carlin arrived to help, Colegate told them both to go away. Spencer and Pierce emerged out of the blizzard and the four of them, two on either side, tugged and heaved until they got Colegate upright. As Carlin attempted to lift Colegate's left foot into the stirrup, the cook began to cry. The sound of his sobbing, though muffled by the blowing snow, cut Himmelwright like a dagger. He had known the man was seriously ill, but he had been as angry as the rest of them over the stupidity, or absent-mindedness, or simple unconcern that had caused the hunting party all this trouble. Now, fully aware for the first time of Colegate's terrible pain, he put an arm across the cook's back and squeezed a shoulder in sympathy. The other three men looked on in silent embarrassment until finally Spencer said he felt as sorry for Colegate as anybody, but they were going to get him onto that horse no matter how much it hurt, and they were going to do it right now.

They did it, forcing one foot into the stirrup, pushing Colegate upward and pulling his other leg across the horse's back and down into the stirrup on the other side. As the leg went over Colegate shrieked in pain. The horse, startled, shied suddenly and Colegate almost came off again. But at least he was mounted now, and they could continue on.

Spencer realized, after about fifteen minutes of bucking three-foot drifts, that this was no good. He did not know where he was going. While crossing a tilted meadow, unable to see the trail or make out the terrain around him, he called another halt and announced that they had to talk. Pass the word, he told Carlin, and Carlin shouted into the wind to Himmelwright, who shouted to Pierce. The riders nudged their horses into as tight a group as they could manage, and Spencer said they had a decision to make.

How close were they now to the Lolo Trail? Carlin wanted to know. Spencer said he wasn't sure. In fact, he said, he could be sure only of one thing: Their situation was desperate and it was time everybody realized that. The snow on the Lolo Trail would be at least four feet deep, he said. If the horses could move through those drifts at all, it would be slowly, and after three days without food they would play out. From then on, the men would have to find their way to Musselshell Creek on foot, over fallen trees, around boulders, through heavy brush, carrying all their gear on their backs. It might take as much as two weeks, and there was food for only eight more days.

However, Spencer said, it could be done.

But if the Indians were keeping the Lolo Trail open, Pierce said, they should have easier going.

There was no way they could keep it open in this weather, Spencer said, and he wasn't so damn sure they ever kept it open. It was the Lolo Trail that had brought them here, he reminded the others, and it was not easy traveling even then. Didn't they remember the horses' bloody legs? Spencer was losing patience with these New York men. He reminded them that they had twice been warned to get out of these mountains while they could, and had ignored both warnings. Then he apologized to Pierce, remembering that he, at least, had counseled prudence when the others had insisted on continuing the hunt. They might be able to make it back to Kendrick still, Spencer said, but only if they kept moving.

But what about Colegate, Carlin asked. He glanced toward the cook to make sure he wasn't listening, but he needn't have worried; Colegate was leaning over the pommel of his saddle, lost in reveries of his own.

What would become of him once they had lost the horses? He couldn't walk. Would they have to abandon him?

Probably, Himmelwright said, if they took Spencer's advice and tried to go out the way they had come. They could fashion crude showshoes, but even on snowshoes it would be impossible to carry Colegate along with their gear and provisions.

Pierce said it looked to him as though they could either try the Lolo Trail without Colegate, or find another way out.

And the only other way out, Carlin added, was the river.

That river, Spencer said, was too dangerous. He knew something about this stretch of the Lochsa. There was no footing for horses. There was a nasty canyon a short distance downstream that could not be penetrated on foot. They would have to use rafts, and as far as he knew, nobody had ever navigated that stream by raft or canoe even in summer, let alone in winter.

Was Spencer suggesting they abandon Colegate to die in the snow? Carlin asked.

The question angered the guide. He was telling these men only what they needed to know about the terrain they were trying to cope with, and he resented the insinuation. He said as much to Carlin, who quickly apologized.

Although he accepted the apology, Spencer said, he wanted it understood that Colegate was not his responsibility. He was only a hired hand in this enterprise, paid to know the country and to give the others the benefit of his best judgment. He was trying to do that. What they did about Colegate was for Carlin to decide since he was Colegate's boss and the leader of the expedition.

Neither Pierce nor Himmelwright had anything to add. Spencer had said his piece and could say more, but didn't.

For a long moment, no one said anything. Colegate was moaning softly and rhythmically—almost musically, Pierce thought as he chewed on his venison. The wind cried through the burned trees and the horses' whoofing breath made clouds in the air.

Carlin broke the quiet. All right, he said. They would go back down to the river and get to work on the rafts.

Then they'd better get moving, Spencer said, and turned his horse.

The others, still tied together, moved aside and fell into line, and the party began to retrace the steps so painfully taken. The going was not bad at first, because they had already broken trail through these drifts. But the snow was quickly covering the path they had made earlier, and Spencer knew they had to hurry. At least they would have daylight for a while and as they descended, the drifts would become less deep and the wind less fierce.

Himmelwright, riding behind Colegate, found himself wondering what the cook might be thinking about all this. Probably nothing, he decided. He was too sick to care. The prospect of freezing to death could hardly disturb a man whose every living moment was full of pain. Himmelwright couldn't decide whether he had more sympathy for Colegate or more anger. Luckily, he thought, he didn't have to.

Gradually, as he stared ahead, he could see Colegate's figure more clearly. He could now make out his cap, his horse's tail, even the place where the picket rope was attached to Colegate's saddle. The snow was falling loosely and fitfully now. The trail was twisting downward away from the wind, and things around them were resuming their natural shapes. They were going to be all right, Himmelwright told himself, at least all right for now.

A few more turns of the trail and they were in fir and cedar groves again, then riding past steaming hot springs, and finally the Carlin party was back where it had started that morning. There was the fire pit, filled with snow, there were the poles that had served as frames for their tents, and there was the crude corral they had thrown together for the horses.

Carlin took a shovel off the lead pack horse and began cleaning out the fire pit while Spencer unloaded the tents and the kitchen box. Himmelwright and Pierce together tugged Colegate from his horse and set him down on the box, then joined Spencer and Carlin in getting the tents up and the horses unloaded. Once that was done they would have to make supper, for it would soon be dark. The tent that housed Colegate and Spencer went up first and then Himmelwright and Carlin made the cook's bed and helped him into it.

They could tell that it had been a dreadful day for him, but there was nothing anybody could say or do that would help. So Himmelwright said only that he would bring some supper after a while, aware that Colegate would probably not be able to eat it.

As the two left the tent, they could hear Colegate moaning quietly in his blankets, but both pretended not to notice.

9 Spencer and Pierce were putting up the other tent when Ben Keeley walked into camp to inquire about the conditions above. He shouldn't have to ask, Pierce told him, because if conditions there were anything but awful they wouldn't be back here. They would be on their way home.

Keeley took his mittens off long enough to relight his pipe and then asked how Colegate had handled the ride up and back. Not well, Himmelwright said. Keeley said he guessed that Colegate's riding days were about over. Which was just as well, he added, because horses would be of no use now. That snow up there was not going away, he said, at least until spring. Unless they had enough grub to last them through the winter, which of course they didn't, they would have to find another way out of this canyon.

The best bet, Keeley said, would be snowshoes. The walking wouldn't be too bad on snowshoes, especially if there should be a crust on the snow. They had brought snowshoes with them, he assumed. No, Carlin said, he hadn't expected snow this early. Besides, he said, they had already decided to go down the river. A bad idea, Keeley said. And if they didn't have snowshoes, he added, they could make them. They had plenty of deer and elk hides that they could cut into strips and if they didn't know how to make the frames, he could show them. Carlin also knew how to make snowshoes, and he agreed they could pack out that way if it weren't for Colegate. The old man was far too sick to hike up that mountain and he was too heavy to carry.

Keeley suggested they build a sled and pull him. It was a thought, Carlin said, but he quickly dismissed the idea. It occurred to Carlin that this whole discussion was pointless. He turned to Himmelwright. They already had decided on the river, he said. Why were they talking about sleds and snowshoes? What they had to do was build a couple of rafts and float down the river. It was that simple.

As Carlin spoke, Himmelwright could hear the river rustling in the distance. It was a benign and pleasant sound. Yes, he said, that was the only practical option.

But Keeley pressed on, insisting they would be better off on snowshoes, going out as they had come in, on the Lolo Trail. He knew the river well; it had nearly killed him more than once, and he wouldn't consider trying to run those rapids and dodge those boulders in the winter time. What did Spencer think?

Spencer, who now was busy at the fire, cooking supper, said Ben was right; the river was a bad idea. And Pierce? The question surprised Pierce, who had assumed he would not be consulted. He was the tenderfoot in this group and he had no firm opinion either way. But he agreed with Carlin that the question already had been answered during that discussion on the mountain. Although he did not mention it now, Pierce felt that if it came down to it he would rather take his chances on the trail than in the river. Keeley's argument seemed powerful to him. Even Carlin, who had thought the discussion closed, found himself listening with interest to Keeley. What they needed, Keeley said, was a toboggan-type sled because runners would break through the crust and make pulling next to impossible.

But what did they have to make a toboggan from? Carlin asked. Keeley said the cabin he was helping to build for Jerry Johnson had a table in it, and a bunk, both made from milled boards. Maybe Johnson would sell them the boards, but then again, maybe he wouldn't. No, Keeley reconsidered, he was sure Johnson wouldn't. Johnson didn't like Colegate, and in fact he did not care for anybody in Carlin's outfit very much.

This was not fresh news to Carlin. He didn't want Johnson's boards anyhow because he couldn't imagine making a toboggan out of flat wood. And he didn't know why he was now letting himself be swayed, even temporarily, by Keeley's argument. The idea of climbing out of this canyon on snowshoes, under heavy packs and pulling a helpless man on a sled, repelled him. The more Carlin thought about the river the more appealing it seemed.

They would need two rafts, and on one of them they could build a seat for Colegate. There would be plenty of room for their gear and the trophies of their hunt. Of all the ways he could think of to get Colegate out of this place, the river route still seemed best.

There was, of course, the possibility that they could leave him here, and Carlin tried this out on Keeley. Did he think Johnson would be willing to take care of Colegate over the winter, even though they weren't the best of friends? Or would Keeley, for that matter?

Keeley knocked his pipe against a tree to dump the ashes and laughed. No chance, he told Carlin. Johnson not only did not like

Colegate, he didn't have enough grub to last two men through the winter. If Colegate didn't die, Johnson could be in trouble and if he did die, Johnson would have an unwelcome corpse on his hands. As for himself, he had nothing against Colegate but he had barely enough provisions to get by on alone.

Carlin hadn't really expected any other answer. He and Himmelwright both favored the river and Keeley's opinion didn't count because he wasn't one of them. It was up to him as leader of the party to make the decision, and he had made it. They would go out on the river, Carlin said. They would get busy tomorrow on those rafts.

Late that night, Spencer awoke from a deep sleep, alerted by some sounds other than Colegate's rough breathing; he was used to that. It was the horses he heard. Something had disturbed them and they were whinnying and apparently moving about. He should get up and check, he thought, but then decided there was no point in it. The horses probably had been spooked by a bear, and they would settle down again. Spencer went back to sleep.

Once again the next morning he was the first one up, and when he went to check, there was no bear, and no sign of the horses. The party's mounts and pack animals had broken out of the corral, which was only a few poles lashed to some trees, and they had all disappeared. They would probably wander back when they got hungry, Spencer told the others later, but even if they didn't—so what? They couldn't take the horses out with them on the rafts, nor could they ride them down the canyon; there was no footing for horses. And they had learned the hard way that the horses were no good in deep snow. So let them go, Spencer said.

Pierce had grown quite fond of his own mount, a roan mare named Joanna, and he said he hated to think of the horses starving. If they wandered back, would Johnson and Keeley feed them? Hardly, Himmelwright said. Johnson and Keeley had no hay and probably oats enough only for their own horses. Carlin told Pierce not to worry. They would leave the rest of their supply of feed here for the horses in case they should come back. If they didn't, well, maybe some Indians would find them and take care of them. That seemed to satisfy Pierce, but Carlin's assurances weren't needed, as it turned out. The horses all wandered back to camp in the afternoon.

On this day, the eleventh of October, the snow had turned to a light rain in the river canyon although the precipitation continued to fall as snow in the heights on either side of the Lochsa. At Snowy Summit, the depth had reached five feet. Carlin could not have known this but even so he was satisfied that his decision had been right. He felt comfortable with it, and he felt even better when the rain stopped and the clouds parted. In the afternoon that day sunshine flooded the canyon, raising everyone's spirits. It affected even Colegate, who said he felt better and asked to be moved away from the trees and into the sunlight where he could savor the warmth.

The weather had turned so fine so suddenly that no one had a thought any longer of building rafts—no one but Spencer, who kept insisting that time was short and this weather would not last. He got nowhere with Carlin and Himmelwright. As Himmelwright pointed out, they were snowed in already, so why the rush? He and Carlin wanted to do what they had come for and get in a few days of good hunting. The river would still be there when they were ready to leave. Even Pierce, who usually agreed with Spencer on such matters, caught the fever and in the late afternoon he and Himmelwright decided to take their rifles and walk down the river a bit before dark.

Carlin excused himself, saying he wanted to have a talk with Ben Keeley. He planned to offer the trapper a deal, and he set out for the camp where Keeley and Jerry Johnson were at work on Johnson's cabin.

When he got there he found Keeley and Johnson inside the cabin, seated at Johnson's table eating supper. Carlin said he had a proposition for Ben, if he didn't mind talking business during dinner. Ben said he didn't mind at all, and told Carlin to pull up that box in the corner to sit on. As Carlin did so, he eyed Johnson's table, trying to see it as a toboggan-style sled, but couldn't. Johnson offered him coffee. Carlin said no, but thanks. He hadn't brought a cup and he felt that Johnson, unaccustomed to guests, probably wouldn't have an extra.

Carlin then got to the point of the visit. He told Keeley he would pay him two hundred and fifty dollars in return for his grub supply and his assistance in getting down the river. Keeley told Carlin he was crazy. He knew that river too well to launch himself off on it at this time of year, on a raft he hadn't seen, that might come apart within minutes.

That was why he wanted Keeley along, Carlin said. He knew the river better than any of them, and obviously respected it. He could help build the rafts if he didn't trust them to do it right. And surely he could find some use for two hundred and fifty dollars.

To Ben Keeley, who had spent his whole life just scraping by, that was indeed a lot of money. It would make him, for at least a little while, a man of means. On the other hand, he had no taste for going down the Lochsa on a raft. He told Carlin he would think about it and let him know.

Carlin, saying he had things to do, got up and put the box back in the corner. He was out the door and fifty yards down the trail when Keeley caught up to him. He had thought it over, Keeley said, and he would accept the deal. For two hundred and fifty dollars, he would sell the party his provisions and his assistance in getting down the river. He did not like the deal, he said, because he was deathly afraid of the Lochsa, but he had realized he was not looking forward to spending the winter here with Johnson, who was becoming crotchety and hard to get along with. And he needed the money.

Carlin, who already had spent a small fortune on this expedition, was sure this was the wisest expenditure of them all. He and Keeley shook hands, and Carlin told the trapper he would get his money when they reached Kendrick.

Well, Keeley said, he'd been thinking he would get it now, when he turned over his store of food.

That would not be proper, Carlin said, because Keeley would not have earned the money until he had helped get the party back to civilization. People generally have to earn their pay before they get it, he pointed out.

This did not satisfy Keeley. What if Carlin drowned on their way down the river, he asked; who would pay him then?

They could all drown, Carlin said, in which case it wouldn't matter whether Keeley got paid now or later. Besides, he said, he couldn't pay Keeley now because he had left his money in the bank at Kendrick.

Keeley did not believe this for a moment. He had judged, correctly, that Carlin was not the kind of man to travel without funds even in the wilderness.

The deal is off, he said, and turned and started up the trail to Johnson's cabin.

Carlin, suddenly flustered and realizing that he needed Keeley more than Keeley needed him, called out to him to come back. He would pay him once the rafts were built, he said, and Keeley said in that case he would go along.

But Keeley said he would have to help Jerry finish the cabin before he did anything else. This did not sit well with Carlin, who was thinking that Keeley was now in *his* employ. He told Keeley he needed him to help get the work under way on the rafts.

No, Keeley said, not yet. He had promised Jerry that he would help him finish the cabin; anyway, there wasn't much left to do except the roof.

How long would that take? Carlin asked.

Keeley wasn't sure. Maybe a week.

Why so long? Carlin wanted to know.

Because there was just the two of them, and Johnson was an old man who was kind of slow and didn't like to climb. But Keeley added that if Carlin wanted to hurry it up, he and the others could help. If they all pitched in, he said, they could probably cut the time down to three or four days.

Carlin said he would ask the others what they wanted to do, and let Keeley know. He would talk to him again tomorrow, Carlin said, and Keeley returned to the cabin.

It was almost dark when Carlin reached his own camp. Himmelwright and Pierce had got there just ahead of him after a fruitless hunt, and Spencer was keeping the fire going for Colegate.

Carlin told the others that he had bought Keeley's grub and that the trapper would be going down the river with them. He had learned from Johnson that Keeley had floated saw logs on rivers in Michigan and Minnesota, and should be a big help in getting down the Lochsa. Keeley also was handy with an ax, he said, and would be useful in building the rafts.

Himmelwright thought this was good news, and so did Spencer, who said that maybe they could now get to work on those rafts.

Not quite, Carlin said. Keeley was obliged to help Johnson finish the cabin before he did anything else, and that might take another week.

Spencer, with some dismay, said that in his opinion time was running out. If they were going to get help with the rafts, they needed it now.

Carlin then repeated what Keeley had said: If he and Johnson had some help with the cabin they could cut the time down.

Well, Spencer said, why not do it? If he, Carlin, and Himmelwright joined the work force, leaving Pierce to care for Colegate, they could get the job done in a hurry, and then start in on the rafts.

Carlin had a better idea. They would need fresh meat while building the rafts, he said. He proposed that Spencer help Keeley and Johnson with the cabin, and that he and Himmelwright continue to hunt. Pierce would do some of the hunting and also take care of Colegate.

This did not entirely satisfy Spencer, but he said no more.

The hunters agreed that Spencer would offer his services to Keeley and Johnson tomorrow, and the three of them would get up early and try their luck at the lower salt lick.

⁂

Rain was drumming on the tent when Carlin and Himmelwright awoke before dawn, eager for the hunt. They were dressing by candlelight as Pierce continued to snore in his blankets. When Carlin tried to wake him, Pierce rolled over, mumbling fuzzily, and pulled a blanket over his head. Himmelwright reached down then and pulled the blanket loose, insisting that Pierce get to his feet. He reminded Pierce that they had to get to the lick before daylight, but Pierce muttered that Himmelwright should go and leave him alone.

Let him sleep, Carlin said. They would go without Pierce, and they'd better get started. He lifted the tent flap and peered out; it was still dark. Himmelwright tried once more. They were leaving without him, he told Pierce, but Pierce turned his face to the tent wall and said, good. Then go.

This worried Himmelwright, but Carlin said good enough. They were going. He picked up his rifle and went out through the tent flap, carrying the candle-powered hurricane lamp with him. Himmelwright got his own rifle and followed.

It was a light rain, falling straight down. Carlin said they would carry the lantern, to help them through the pre-dawn darkness;

later they would hang it on a tree and pick it up on the way back. The two men moved down the trail slowly, toward the salt lick about a half mile away. Every time they brushed against a fir branch they got a shower, but neither minded the brief discomfort. Both agreed it was a great day for a hunt. Today they would kill an elk, Carlin declared, giving his rifle a loving squeeze.

The prospect elated Himmelwright also, but he told Carlin he was concerned about Pierce. Was he all right?

Of course he was, Carlin said; he just didn't feel like getting up, and whether he did or not was his business. Himmelwright let it go at that. Pierce was Carlin's brother-in-law, not his.

The darkness began to fade as they neared the lick. Carlin suggested they halt and wait for more light before covering the last quarter mile; they might stumble in the dark and make alarming noises. It was still raining softly. The two conversed in whispers now, aware that other ears could be listening, and they agreed that Himmelwright would go first when they approached the lick.

The wan light of another day began to chase the night when the hunters heard a peculiar, faint sound—half whistle and half bellow, as Himmelwright would later describe it.

An elk! Carlin whispered, tugging on Himmelwright's elbow.

How could he be sure? Himmelwright wanted to know.

The same sound had come from the elk that Carlin shot earlier, he said. The very same!

Wonderful, Himmelwright whispered. They were in luck.

There was light enough now for moving. Carlin nudged Himmelwright, who started slowly down the trail toward the lick, placing each foot carefully and making as little noise as possible. Carlin followed closely behind.

That same whistling bellow came again through the damp woods, causing both men to pause momentarily, breathing hard.

They were moving again, about five feet apart, and in sight of the lick when Himmelwright turned and whispered to Carlin that something was there. A moment later a cow elk walked out of the brush and stood looking directly at Himmelwright. He froze.

There was no discernible breeze, and the elk, smelling no danger, lowered her head and began to lick the salt from the rocks bordering the warm spring. Himmelwright and Carlin quietly took positions behind nearby trees and waited. Within minutes a second cow and a calf entered the clearing, and behind them came still another cow.

A minute later the bull appeared. He passed slowly along one edge of the lick and into a patch of trees. The hunters could see only his rump, but in a little while he moved forward enough to put his head and shoulder in view.

Himmelwright shot once. Carlin followed immediately with two shots from his double barrels. The bull bounded away over a low hill and out of sight. The other elk, spooked by the firing, began moving away from the lick. Carlin took two shots at a young cow but failed to stop her and he began running in pursuit.

Himmelwright's bull, meanwhile, had bounded over a low hill and down the other side with great leaps, plowing furrows in the ground at every step. At the bottom he turned to the right and followed a game trail to the base of another hill. The elk was leaving great glops of blood on the ground, and Himmelwright could tell from the tracks that his prey was badly wounded. When he turned a bend of the trail he saw the bull, standing still and facing him, about seventy yards away. Himmelwright aimed carefully and fired again, but the rifle only clicked. Again. The rifle clicked once more. Himmelwright discovered that the empty shell, instead of ejecting, was being returned to the barrel. He hurriedly pulled the spent shell out and thrust in a new cartridge. Again he aimed, but before he could fire, he heard two shots from Carlin's gun and the bull bounded out of sight.

Himmelwright continued to follow the tracks and soon spotted the bull, standing in the river, facing the opposite shore and bleeding heavily. Himmelwright realized that if he shot now, the bull might find enough strength to leap into deep water where he could be washed downstream and away. While he tried to decide what to do, the bull lay down in the river, leaving only his head above water. Carlin's gun roared twice again. The bull got to his feet and took several steps downstream, then stopped and turned toward the shore. Himmelwright saw a chance to put a bullet in the heart and fired. He evidently missed the heart, for the bull turned and started for the opposite shore. He staggered to a halt, in water up to his belly, and Himmelwright, thinking a shot in the rump might spur him onward and away from deep water, fired again. After taking this shot, the bull flopped sideways into the water, struggled to his feet, fell again, and was washed downstream, lodging finally against a large rock.

Carlin appeared from over the hill, exhilarated by the hunt, and shouted to Himmelwright that this was the finest set of antlers he had ever seen. Magnificent, he said, but they must not let this trophy get away. He took off his pants and waded into the river.

Carlin grabbed the dead bull's antlers and pulled them around the boulder, then piled some rocks around the head and bent the neck to secure the animal. Then he waded back to the shore where Himmelwright waited.

Did Carlin get his elk? Himmelwright asked, remembering that Carlin had been chasing a wounded cow.

You bet, Carlin said, and he led Himmelwright to the dead cow, lying head downward on a steep hillside. She had led him on quite a chase, Carlin said. It had taken five shots to lay her down, but she would still make good meat for "the crowd."

Carlin and Himmelwright walked back to camp and returned to the scene of the hunt with pack horses, accompanied by Keeley and Spencer. In the lick they surprised a young cow elk, which Himmelwright shot, thinking it was a deer. They were now well supplied with meat, but Carlin and Himmelwright insisted that they had to retrieve the bull elk's head and antlers before the Lochsa carried the animal downstream.

Keeley and Spencer volunteered to ride their horses into the river to where the elk was lodged against the boulder, and put a rope around it. Keeley's horse balked at approaching the bull, but Spencer managed to get his horse close enough that he could jump onto the boulder with a rope and hatchet. He tied the rope to the antlers, then with the hatchet chopped off the head at the neck and waded back to his horse. He mounted and rode the horse to shore, pulling the bull elk's head and antlers.

The rest of the bull, unfettered, slid around the rock, then drifted down the river and out of sight.

Himmelwright and Carlin, loading two cows and a bull's head onto pack horses, agreed that it had been a great hunt. Too bad Pierce had to miss it, Himmelwright said.

Don't worry about John, Carlin said. He'd have his chance yet. There would be more good hunting before they had to work on those rafts.

10 Spencer and Keeley returned to Jerry Johnson's place, picking up along the way some cedar shakes that Keeley had split and cached near the warm springs.

He and Johnson were building a typical log cabin. Midway in each end wall was a king post, an upright that supported the ends of the ridgepole. The ridgepole was supported along its length by posts erected on timbers supported on *their* ends by the sidewalls. Between the sidewalls and the ridgepole, Johnson and Keeley had laid poles about two feet apart, and crosswise onto these they had lashed smaller poles that supported the shakes. Johnson handed the shakes up to Spencer and Keeley, who nailed them to the poles, overlapping them enough to keep everything dry below. Johnson and Keeley already had finished one side and started on the other, covering the uncompleted sections with tarps. At the end of three days, Keeley and Spencer had replaced all the tarps with poles and shakes, and the cabin was roofed.

Now, Spencer said on returning to his own camp, it was time to get started on the rafts.

Himmelwright agreed. He had been thinking about shapes and sizes and construction techniques, and he had in mind what they would need for those rafts. Dead cedar would be light and strong, he told the others, and that's what they should look for. But he would be of no help to them today, he said. He apparently had wrenched his neck while hunting a few days ago, because it was now so sore he could barely turn his head. Carlin said he had his own problem, a bad boil on his right ankle, and he would have to spend the day in camp. It wouldn't hurt to wait another day to go looking for timber, Carlin said, and spend this one resting and recovering.

Keeley said he was feeling fine. He would go with Spencer, and the two of them would try to find some cedar close by. They left Carlin and Himmelwright nursing their ailments, and Pierce tending to Colegate, and walked down the trail in the direction of the lower licks.

In mid-afternoon, feeling better, Himmelwright went down the river to see what Spencer and Keeley had found. When he reached them, near the warm springs, they already had felled several dead cedars and had begun peeling them. Himmelwright picked up a block of wood and weighed it with a small fish scales he had

A meal at the lower warm springs.

borrowed from Carlin. He needed to know the wood's specific grav-
ity, he said, in order to determine its buoyancy. And that, in turn,
would tell him how much cedar they would need to support the
men and dogs, together with their provisions and camp gear.

Spencer and Keeley were impressed by Himmelwright's engineering skills, but not by his proposed design. Back in camp that
afternoon, he suggested that each raft should be long and narrow,
in order to pass between boulders, and Carlin agreed with him.
Spencer and Keeley said the rafts should be shorter and wider or
the men could not handle them in swift water. After some debate,
Spencer and Keeley gave in, and the group adopted the
Himmelwright design. Each raft would be twenty-six feet long and
four and a half feet wide.

They also decided they would move most of the camp down to the timber so they wouldn't have to do so much walking back and forth. Carlin would remain in the upper camp for the time being, since his boil still bothered him, and so would Colegate and Pierce. Spencer, Keeley, and Himmelwright would move to the lower camp and begin working on the rafts immediately. The weather was fine—warm and sunny during the day but cold at night.

As the days passed, Colegate had become less and less involved in his illness, until it had assumed a life of its own. Colegate the person continued to fade away, replaced by the swollen shape that was by now only a presence in the camp, hardly more animated than the box it sat on. The others had ceased trying to converse with him, and ignored him unless he had to be moved, or fed (which was seldom). But they could not ignore the ailment that had turned their cook into this lump of putrefying flesh. The enlarged prostate, out of sight but never out of mind, was the enemy that had taken command of the expedition and ordered this desperate dash down the river.

And the enemy was going with them. They could not leave it behind without abandoning Colegate as well, and nobody was yet willing to suggest such a thing.

It *had* crossed everyone's mind. Spencer, afraid of the river, was sure he could lead the party back to the ridge on foot if Colegate weren't along. He was on the point of saying as much the day Keeley brought up the business of the sled. He didn't, because he realized he would be a guide no longer if it became known that he had even considered abandoning a sick companion.

Carlin, as head of the expedition in fact if not in title, was aware that the blame would fall on him if Colegate, still alive, were left behind. And his father, the general, would be humiliated. Himmelwright had gazed up more than once at the geese flying noisily south and envied them their freedom from the ethical chains that bound him. It was not a feeling he wished to express to the others.

It was Jerry Johnson who said exactly what he was thinking. He wanted the New Yorkers to take Colegate out with them because he had no desire to spend this winter with a corpse. Keeley had felt the same way Johnson did until deciding that he would be going down the river too. Now he would rather leave Colegate behind but knew it would be useless to say so. And although he didn't realize it, his silence now would later serve him well.

Himmelwright could still hear the chatter of geese as he snapped himself out of his reverie and raised his ax. They were about to launch themselves on a dubious enterprise, but he could not help feeling proud of his work. The first raft, the *Clearwater,* was coming along well and the weather had been a big help. It remained mild and mostly sunny in the canyon, but the workers on the river bank could look up toward the ridges and see the snow still there, deep and forbidding.

They had cut notches in the logs and inserted the fir cross pieces into them loosely. When they drove cedar wedges in between logs and cross pieces, the structure would be tight. Other wedges would go in at the ends of the cross pieces to hold the logs together. To further secure the logs, Himmelwright cut mortises into adjoining logs and inserted into them strips of wood four inches square which would be pinned down securely.

Each raft would be steered by a long sweep, or rudder, attached to the stern, a standard means of maneuvering in swift-running rivers. Spencer and Keeley would man the first raft, and so they would decide what they wanted in the way of deck furnishings. When their raft was ready for launching they added a kind of box about six inches high in the middle to hold the provisions and gear. They also built posts to which they could lash themselves in rough water.

Spencer, in the meantime, had made another reconnoitering trip out of the canyon on horseback to check the snow depths above, still hoping they could avoid the dreaded plunge down the Lochsa. The date was October 18. He saw that the sun had melted much of the snow on the south-facing slopes but that in other places it remained as deep as ever. He also reported on his return that some horses had revisited the spot where the party had turned around on October 10 in the failed effort to reach the Lolo Trail. The horses had trampled the area and then wandered back down to the river. It was still not possible to get out by that route, he told the others.

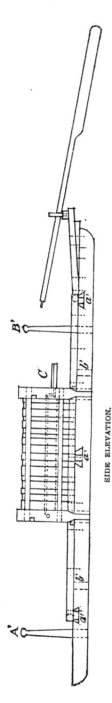

SIDE ELEVATION.

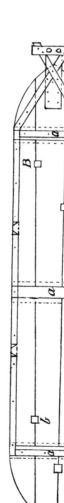

PLAN OF DECK.

END ELEVATION.

The *Carlin*, one of the party's two rafts. Dimensions were 26 feet by 4 feet, 2 inches. Posts *A* and *B* were to hold onto in rough water. The seat *C* was for Colegate to sit on; *a,a,a,* and *a',a,a'* are cross-pieces dovetailed and wedged into the logs; *b,b* and *b',b'* are vertical keys.

With the first raft completed, Carlin suggested their upper camp be abandoned because the whole crew would be working full time now on the second raft. This meant moving Colegate one more time, but it couldn't be avoided. It also meant they had to make decisions as to what they were going to take down the river and what they would leave behind.

Carlin, Spencer, and Himmelwright went to the upper camp to bring down the horses and found Pierce in the throes of a medical emergency. One of Colegate's swollen legs had lacerated, the flesh splitting open because it could not stretch any further. Colegate was in great pain, stuff was oozing out of the limb, and the smell was incredible. Pierce had put wet rags on the wound to ease the pain and had given Colegate a dose of morphine, but the cook was obviously in misery.

How could they move him now in this condition? Pierce asked Carlin, and Carlin replied, how could they not? They could not maintain two camps and still put all hands to work on the rafts. If Colegate was going to be in such pain as this, he said, it wouldn't matter to him whether he did his suffering in this camp or the other one. In that case, Spencer said, he probably should be moved at once because he wasn't going to get any better.

The other two agreed. Spencer brought up a horse and he and Carlin prepared to load Colegate onto it, but the sick man recoiled and cried out that he would not go. He raised his arms in a feeble attempt to fend them off, but Carlin insisted that there was no helping it; he had to go, and *would* go. Spencer put himself between them and told Carlin they should wait a minute. There might be a better way to do this, he said, and he proposed that they move the camp but leave Colegate here and take turns staying with him. This would mean keeping him fed, helping him to the latrine when necessary, and gathering firewood to keep him warm. It would be an unwelcome chore, since Colegate was not good company. He spoke hardly at all, and he smelled bad.

After some hesitation, Carlin asked Himmelwright what he thought. Abe said he could see no harm in doing it that way for a few days. If he were in Colegate's condition he wouldn't want to get on that horse either. Pierce agreed, and Spencer volunteered to take the first Colegate watch, as they called it.

Spencer saw the men off to the new camp, then busied himself gathering wood for the fire. He had padded Colegate's box with one of the cook's blankets, and Colegate sat there with another blanket around his shoulders, staring glumly at the fire. He could no longer get his boots on, because of the swelling in his legs and ankles, and several days earlier Pierce had cut a couple of pieces off one of his own blankets and tied them around the sick man's feet. Spencer wondered now if they ought to be changed or adjusted, but he could think of no reason to do so and left them as they were.

Once all the camp chores were taken care of, Spencer sat for a few minutes, then decided he needed something to do with his hands. He picked up a broken pack saddle from the heap under the tarp, thinking to fix it. When he remembered they weren't going to need that pack saddle, he threw it down on the ground and sat on it. He sat silently across the fire from Colegate, wondering what was going through the man's mind.

What did he see in that fire? Although Spencer had not been well as a youth, because of his asthma, he had never before been in such close quarters with a dreadful illness. His own helplessness in the face of it dismayed him. He wondered if the smell from Colegate was the smell of death. What should he do? he asked himself. Just sit here?

Pierce came up the next morning to relieve Spencer, and the guide walked down to the new camp. He had changed his mind. He had spent the night worrying about it, and he was now convinced that Carlin had been right; they had to move Colegate now. They had waited too long to start building the rafts, and now the job needed all hands. Leaving Colegate at the upper camp was no favor to the cook, since he would have to be moved later anyhow, and he planned to tell Carlin that. But when he arrived at the lower camp, Keeley was the only one there. The other two had gone hunting, Keeley said, and he was glad to have Spencer's help since Pierce was not much of an axman.

Spencer picked up an ax and got to work, and a couple of hours later Carlin and Himmelwright returned empty-handed to camp.

Spencer told Carlin they should bring Colegate down, and they should do it today. He half expected a jibe from Carlin, who had wanted to do it yesterday, but Carlin said only that he agreed and that they should go and get Colegate now. The four of them left Keeley with the rafts and led two horses back to the upper camp. Spencer caught and saddled Colegate's horse, and he and Carlin hoisted the cook up and onto it. As he had on the fruitless attempt to reach the Lolo Trail, Colegate cried out in pain when they lifted his leg over. He appeared unable to hold himself erect, but Carlin and Pierce thought they could keep him on the horse by riding close beside him on either hand. It took some doing, because parts of the trail were not wide enough for three horses side by side, and in these places either Carlin or Pierce would drop back while the other held tightly onto Colegate's arm. The two camps were only about a half mile apart, but the transfer of Colegate took a good half hour.

Once there, they lifted Colegate down to the ground and arranged some cedar boughs for him to sit on. Pierce asked the cook if he thought the wet rags had done any good, but Colegate could say only that he didn't know; maybe they had, and maybe Pierce should put on some more. Both Pierce and Carlin worried about infection, but Himmelwright said that any easing of the pain was worth the risk. Keeley said under his breath to Spencer that the sick man was a goner, any way you looked at it. Spencer simply nodded, and went back to the upper camp to bring down the rest of the horses.

The second raft, which came to be called the *Carlin,* had the same dimensions as the first, but its flotation logs were hewn on top and bottom so that they had a flattened shape. Himmelwright thought this would make the raft lighter, and therefore more buoyant, without sacrificing size. Besides that, it would make the deck easier to walk on.

The second raft also had a square, boxy structure in the center to hold provisions and gear, but this one had a bottom raised some six to eight inches above the deck, to keep the contents dry. Attached to the back of this structure was a chair for Colegate. It was simply a shelf on which Colegate could sit, and a pair of posts he could hang onto.

There was no more hunting for several days and the party was running out of meat. On October 30, therefore, Himmelwright took his rifle at dawn and walked up the river looking for elk.

A bit later on that same day Spencer made a final inspection trip by horseback in the direction of the Lolo Trail. The men, while building the raft, had noticed the snow levels rising on the hillsides above the river, and Spencer was determined that if there was any escape route short of the Lochsa he would find it. What he found was that the snow had melted considerably in the low areas but that on the approaches to the Lolo it was deeper than before. Spencer, now satisfied that it was useless even to think of getting out by this route, reported the same when he got back to camp.

Spencer's news was discouraging, but Himmelwright's was not. He returned to camp shortly after Spencer's arrival with the heart and sirloin of a cow elk he had shot some four miles up the river. The next day he and Spencer took a couple of horses and packed out the rest of the meat.

Then Himmelwright and Carlin, along with Keeley, went up the trail to Jerry Johnson's cabin where Keeley had stored his provisions. They took what they thought the party would need and left the rest for Johnson, who was glad to have it.

Spencer had told Carlin the trip down the river would take about a week. Johnson, hoping to hold on to as much of Keeley's grub as possible, declared that it would take only four days. Carlin considered Spencer's estimate optimistic, and told Johnson so; he figured they should take enough food for fifteen days, just in case. That was ridiculous, Johnson said, but Carlin would not budge. He and Himmelwright picked out provisions for fifteen days, and then discovered that they had no sugar. Keeley had been sharing with them, and Carlin realized now that they had eaten all his sugar and had none of their own. Would Johnson sell them some of his? No, Johnson said, he would not; he had barely enough for himself. Himmelwright told Johnson he would trade him his entire fishing outfit, which he said was worth twenty-two dollars, for two pounds of sugar. That was eleven dollars a pound, he pointed out, but still Johnson refused to deal.

Carlin stepped in at this point and raised the stakes. He said Johnson could have his 45-90-300 single-shot Winchester rifle, plus ammunition, fishing hooks and tackle, in return for three pounds of sugar. This was not one of the rifles Carlin had brought with him from New York; he had bought this one from Keeley. Johnson was familiar with the rifle, and for that plus the ammunition and fishing tackle, he would part with three pounds of his precious store of sugar.

Keeley and Himmelwright loaded the food on one pack animal and Carlin told Johnson they were leaving the horses with him and hoped he would not let them starve. Johnson said he would not be responsible for the horses, but Carlin said they were leaving them anyhow, and Johnson could do with them as he liked. Himmelwright wished Johnson good luck through the winter, and the three men left for the warm springs.

Carlin by now was in a fine mood. As they led the horse down the trail he joked with Keeley, saying he'd bet Ben would have been willing to go with them for nothing, just so he wouldn't have to spend the winter with old Jerry.

Maybe, Keeley replied with a laugh, but Carlin would never know for sure. And meanwhile he had Carlin's two hundred and fifty dollars.

The second raft was finished now, and in the nick of time, Carlin thought, because the weather had worsened. Heavy, dark clouds had moved in, spitting rain and occasional snow.

The temperature had dropped so drastically that Pierce and Spencer were making jackets and mittens out of spare blankets. Colegate, whose condition had worsened along with the weather, suffered terribly from the cold. The splitting of the skin on his upper leg had released enough fluid to reduce the swelling and ease the pain in his limbs. But his lungs were filling with liquid, and he could no longer lie down without choking. Spencer built a sort of chair for him out of a block of cedar and Colegate sat on that throughout the long days and longer nights while the others piled blankets on him to keep him warm and took turns feeding the fire.

At one point Colegate surprised everyone by saying, in a barely audible voice, that he would rather die on this chair than spend the winter with Jerry Johnson. It was the first time in weeks that he had offered an opinion on anything, out of the blue. The others knew that Colegate did not like Johnson, and that the feeling was mutual; but Colegate startled them by going on to say in the same breathy monotone that he was afraid of Johnson. Afeered, as he put it. Pierce asked him what Johnson had done to make him afraid, but Colegate dropped his chin on his chest, clutched his blanket more closely around him, and fell silent.

11 On November 2, Carlin walked down the river for several miles to see how difficult the first day's rafting might be. He saw two large rapids, one of which he thought quite dangerous, but he told the others later that there was a channel on the left that probably would take them around it. While he was gone, Himmelwright filed a saw for Jerry Johnson, as he had earlier promised to do, and Pierce sewed a canvas cover over two bags of flour to keep them dry. The men dragged and prodded the rafts into the shallow water near the shore and prepared the poles that would go on board. The weather was bad and getting worse. That afternoon, all agreed that they would load and launch the rafts as early as possible the next day.

Himmelwright and Keeley walked up to Johnson's place to deliver the saw and to tell Old Jerry that they were leaving in the morning. Jerry told them again that anyone foolish enough to try to float down the Lochsa on those long, narrow rafts, deserved whatever happened to him. But good luck anyhow, he said, and Keeley and Himmelwright returned to camp.

On the morning of the 3rd, as the men prepared to leave, Johnson arrived, saying he wanted to see whether those rafts would float or sink. As Johnson looked on glumly, the rafters loaded everything they had including the tents and the three dogs. Johnson didn't care much about the tents or the dogs, but he wondered why Carlin insisted on carrying so much armament, which would probably be lost the first time those ungainly craft hit rough water. He suggested to Carlin that he leave his three-barrel paradox with him for safe keeping through the winter, but Carlin said he would need it if they ran out of meat. Then Johnson said, as he had before, that if this river were navigable, the Indians wouldn't avoid it the way they did, and Lewis and Clark wouldn't have damn near starved to death on the Lolo Trail. No one bothered to respond to this comment, but it made Spencer wish he were up there on the Lolo with a couple of snowshoes under him.

The rafts were loaded, and it was time to go. A hard, cold rain was falling. Spencer and Keeley would go in the first raft, followed directly by Carlin, Himmelwright, and Pierce in the second. Himmelwright and Pierce helped Colegate down the bank and through the shallow water and placed him on his chair. Carlin had suggested roping Colegate to the chair, but Spencer had pointed out that in case of an accident there might not be time to loosen those ropes. So Colegate would have to hang on as best he could, and either Carlin or Pierce would ride the back of the raft with him.

None of the men had thought it would be so hard to move the loaded rafts out of the shallows, over the rocks, and into the current. Keeley and Spencer, using pike poles, nudged their heavy craft over and around the rocks until it was fairly free and then jumped aboard, Keeley at the tiller and Spencer up front where he could use his pole to keep the craft away from boulders. After a nudge or two from Carlin and Himmelwright, the raft was free of the shore.

It moved sluggishly downstream and lodged briefly against a large boulder, but Spencer, using his pole, pushed it clear. Suddenly the current caught it and moved it faster. Keeley clung to the long-handled sweep, peering ahead over the top of the gear enclosure. Spencer stood with legs spread wide and one hand on the framework. The *Clearwater* and its crew were on their way.

Meanwhile, the other three pushed and shoved their raft out of the shallows and continued poling after all were aboard. Himmelwright took the sweep, Carlin rode the rear with him, holding onto one of the posts beside Colegate's chair, and Pierce went forward, bracing himself against the framework of the gear enclosure.

Colegate seemed hardly to know what was happening, or to care. He sat on his seat, stiff as a statue, expressionless, staring fixedly up the river at something in the far distance—or perhaps at nothing at all.

Carlin looked back at the shore, waved once to Johnson, and was astonished at how rapidly the shore passed by. They were really moving! Carlin felt a sharp thrill surging through him. His anxieties forgotten, he did a little dance on the deck and thought to himself what a grand adventure this was going to be. He turned and shouted something like that to Himmelwright, but Abe was staring steadily ahead, grim-faced, feet planted firmly, leaning into the tiller.

Jerry Johnson stood on the shore watching until the last raft was out of sight around a bend of the river. Then he spat once on the ground and started walking back to his cabin.

The second raft was about a hundred yards behind the first, traveling well through easy water. After half a mile, Himmelwright turned it to the shore and while Carlin tied it to a tree, Pierce walked down around the bend to see whether Keeley and Spencer had made it safely through the first rapids. They had, and then had landed on the opposite bank. Pierce returned to his raft to report that all was well, so far, with the *Clearwater*. He and the others cast off in the second raft, went around the bend, and into the rapids. Keeley waved to them to pull over to the bank where he was, but Himmelwright, having trouble maneuvering, decided to sail on by and into another rapids not far below.

A third of the way into the whitewater, Himmelwright lost control. The raft struck a pair of nearly submerged boulders. It hung there for a moment as Himmelwright fought desperately with the sweep, but he could not hold it, and it turned sideways to the current. The force of the roaring water pushed the upstream side of the raft down and under and Colegate was suddenly out of his seat and sliding into the river. He was sucked under the raft and about to be swept away when Himmelwright grabbed him by the collar of his coat and hauled him back aboard. One of the terriers, the one called Montana, went overboard and would have drowned had Pierce not caught him by a foreleg and pulled him back.

Spencer and Keeley, meanwhile, had launched the *Clearwater* again and spotted Carlin's crew ahead of them feverishly trying to avert disaster. They ran their own raft ashore and hurried down to help. They waded out into the river as far as they could, getting to within twenty feet of the others before the steady, hard current threatened to sweep them away. They could faintly hear Carlin and Himmelwright yelling to them but, over the river's roar, couldn't make out the words. Finally, Spencer took the other end of the pole Keeley was using to balance himself, told Keeley to hold on tight, and waded out another eight feet, as far as the pole would reach. Spencer was up to his chest in the river, but he could now hear

The place where Carlin's raft hung up on a rock and Colegate almost went overboard.

Himmelwright well enough to understand most of what he was trying to tell them. He wanted Spencer and Keeley to tie their raft to a tree with a long rope and let it float down and alongside Carlin's raft so they could transfer Carlin's load from his raft to the other.

Spencer and Keeley waded back to their own raft and pulled it slowly between the rocks toward the *Clearwater*'s foundering sister ship. They secured it with a long line to a fir tree, then poled it out broadside to the other raft and lashed the two together. They transferred Colegate, the dogs, and some provisions from raft to raft, and thence to shore. While Spencer built a fire for Colegate, Himmelwright returned with Keeley to Carlin's raft to transfer more of its load. They were poling the *Clearwater* back to shore when Himmelwright heard a shout from the raft where Carlin was now alone. Looking back, he saw that Carlin's raft, lightened of its load, had righted itself and was slipping into the current. He ran the length of the raft he was on, leaped aboard the other one with Carlin, and the two of them—Himmelwright with the pole and Carlin at the sweep—rode that raft down through the rapids and ran it aground on a rocky bar. They waded to shore with a rope, tied the raft to a tree root, and walked up the river to the new camp.

Spencer had a good fire going, Keeley had put up a tent, and Pierce was trying to dry out Colegate's clothes and blankets, one piece at a time. The sleet continued relentlessly. To Himmelwright, who a few days ago had thought the gurgle of the river pleasant and benign, the Lochsa now spoke with a mocking snarl. He could feel hostility in the very air, and he could hear no laughter in the camp.

Carlin wrote in his diary that night: "All in all, we've had a rough sort of day."

12 Throughout that Friday night, November 3, Spencer, Keeley and the hunters kept the fire blazing and by morning had managed to get everything dried and stowed in one of the two tents. Colegate, whose seat was protected by the fly, was dry by now but feeling worse; Carlin suggested that yesterday's wetting had done him no good, and the others agreed. He was coughing and complaining of chills, although Pierce, after feeling the cook's forehead, reported that he was feverish. Colegate refused to eat any of the breakfast Spencer had cooked but did accept a cup of sugared coffee, which he cradled in his mittened hands and slowly sipped while the others dined on biscuits and the warmed-over roast.

Himmelwright, comforted by his coffee, decided that the river didn't sound as hostile this morning. The rain drew a sort of curtain between the human travelers on the north bank and the firs and boulders that lined the Lochsa on the other side, blurring the details and reducing everything to shades of gray.

Spencer set his tin plate on the ground and said they needed to make a decision. They were carrying too much stuff, he said, and they needed to lighten the rafts. Carlin asked him what he would leave behind. To start with, Spencer suggested, how about the trophies of the hunt? The antlers would be of no use in getting down the river, and they probably were carrying more firearms than they needed. Some of the camp equipment, although nice to have, was a nuisance without horses to carry it.

Carlin objected. One of the reasons for this hunt, he said, was to have trophies to show for it. He told Spencer he would hate to leave those behind. It was just a suggestion, Spencer said, and he looked to Himmelwright and Pierce for support. Pierce said the trophies could be abandoned as far as he was concerned, but Himmelwright complained that this was easy for Pierce to say; he hadn't done much of the hunting.

Keeley was inclined to side with Pierce, he said. He didn't give a damn about the trophies and would like to clear the rafts of everything they didn't absolutely need.

Spencer told Carlin he could do as he liked, but that Spencer had an obligation as the guide to offer advice on matters like this. Carlin then agreed that Spencer probably was right. But he said he would rather save the trophies and abandon some of the camp paraphernalia.

Spencer suggested that anything they didn't want to take they could leave with Jerry Johnson, including the antlers and scalps. That seemed to satisfy both Carlin and Himmelwright, but Carlin insisted that Spencer be the one to broach the matter to Johnson. Spencer agreed to walk up to Johnson's place and ask the old man to accept temporary custody of the trophies and camp equipment. If Johnson agreed, Spencer and he would come down with horses and pack the stuff back.

Spencer lingered in camp only long enough to wash his breakfast dishes, then set out on foot for Jerry Johnson's cabin.

Pierce stayed in camp to keep the fire going and Carlin, Keeley and Himmelwright went down to the river to pull Carlin's raft off the bar. It was lodged securely among the rocks, held tightly there by the current, and it took the three men a good two hours of hard work to pull it loose. Once free, they pulled it into deeper water and tied it to a stump. Keeley and Himmelwright started gathering wood for Colegate's fire, and Carlin walked down the bank to check the river below.

He saw signs of elk and bear, and near a gravel bar that formed an island in the river, he saw an Indian sweat lodge. He wondered if that meant the Nez Perces had been using this island in summer.

The river would be lower then, and the gravel bar would be no island at all. In fact, he decided, the right-hand channel even now would probably be too shallow for the rafts.

He walked back through the rain and joined the others, all now thoroughly soaked, who had gathered around the fire with Colegate and Pierce. The men fell into a routine that the rain had imposed upon them: drying their clothes. Pierce had put together a crude rack of sticks and tree branches that he had braced in an upright position with poles. Keeley, Himmelwright, and Carlin took off their shirts first, hanging them on the rack close above the fire. Then the tops of their two-piece long johns. They dried themselves from the waist up with towels, and then put on underclothes and shirts already dried. With their uppers warm and dry, they doffed their pants and underpants and hung them up in turn, and repeated the toweling and dressing. Why were they bothering with all this, Himmelwright thought as he held one bare foot a little closer to the fire; they would not stay dry very long. Then he began hearing little grunts of pleasure from the other two and realized that he also was enjoying this hard-earned comfort and the feel of warm wool against his skin. The rain continued drumming on the canvas fly above their heads, and the river still grumbled a few yards away like a spoiled child, but here beside the fire it now seemed downright cheery.

Pierce, looking out hopefully for a break in the clouds, was the first to see Spencer approaching from the east on his way back from Jerry Johnson's place. He was alone and on foot, Pierce told the others in some alarm. Did this mean Johnson had refused to accept the trophies and equipment for safekeeping? It seemed like he would have a couple of horses with him if they were going to move the stuff to Jerry's, Keeley said. The old guy had probably told Martin to go to hell.

Colegate emerged briefly from his half-stupor and muttered that he could have told them they would get no place with Johnson.

But when Spencer reached the camp he told the others that Jerry Johnson would be there in the morning with the horses, and that everything would be as they had planned.

All but Colegate spent the next couple of hours gathering firewood to keep the sick man warm and fuel the drying of the clothes, then set about choosing and separating the things they would leave with Johnson.

They would have no use for Colegate's harmonica, Himmelwright said, and he put it in a corner of the tent beside some other odds and ends to be left behind. Pierce made a mild objection, saying that decision should be left to Colegate. Well then, Himmelwright replied, why didn't Pierce go and ask Colegate whether he wished to keep the harmonica with him? So Pierce did. Colegate said nothing, but nodded and held out his hand. Pierce went into the tent, got the harmonica, and put the instrument in Colegate's open palm. Colegate thanked Pierce in a single, whispered word, and sat holding the harmonica, putting it neither to his lips nor in his pocket.

Keeley cooked supper that evening, complaining that the New York hunters had wasted more meat than they saved. There was no excuse for running out of meat in this country, he said, and yet it looked to him as if they might.

Himmelwright was about to snap back at Keeley for impugning his outdoorsmanship when he remembered that gut-shot bull elk. At the time of the hunt he had gloried in the picture of the noble beast standing wounded in the river, its magnificent head and antlers etched against the mighty firs and cedars rising up behind. Now, stung by Keeley's complaint, all he could remember of that hunt was the sight of a thousand pounds of bone, gristle, and meat drifting headless down the dark river. Himmelwright said nothing, and fetched a stick of wood for Keeley's fire.

Carlin was not so willing to let the remark go unchallenged. He observed from his seat on the kitchen box that Keeley had no right to complain about the way the game was handled because he had not done any of the hunting. If Keeley was worried about the meat running low, why didn't he go shoot a few grouse? Carlin asked. He could have the use of the best grouse dog in Idaho, he added, nodding to where Daisy was lying, as close to Colegate's chair as she could stand to get.

Carlin's response got no reply from Keeley. Pierce said nothing because he had a feeling that Keeley was right. Spencer remained silent because he also had done none of the hunting and because the matter was none of the guide's business anyway.

The men ate their supper of venison and biscuits in silence, sharing the meat with the dogs, then washed their utensils in the river and went out again for firewood. The rain continued to fall, but only lightly now. This was such a welcome turn of events that no one dared make note of it for fear of changing good luck to bad.

Himmelwright's mother had arrived in Chicago on October 20, the day she was supposed to meet her son there, and was wondering by now whether she had got the date wrong. Abe wasn't there, and she had heard no word from him. She wrote a letter to General Carlin at Vancouver Barracks, asking whether he had any knowledge of Abe's whereabouts. The general replied that he had heard nothing of or from the hunting party, but added that he had not expected to hear; the boys were a long way from the nearest telegraph office, he wrote. He presumed that Mrs. Himmelwright was correct; there had been a mix-up in the dates, and she had nothing to worry about. But the general said he understood her concern, and would be in touch.

The general realized now that he was not the only person who wondered where the Carlin party might be; it had been five weeks since the hunters left Kendrick, and they had planned to be out of the woods by now. If Himmelwright had told his mother he would meet her in Chicago on October 20, he was way overdue, and she was right to be worried. Maybe he should be more worried than he was.

The next morning the general wired Captain Louis Merriam at Fort Spokane, asking him to take the train to Kendrick to seek word of his son and his son's companions. Keep track of the expenses, the general said; he would pay them out of his own pocket.

Merriam took the Northern Pacific to Moscow, Idaho, and from there to the end of the line at Kendrick. It was the last week of October. The talk around the stove in the lobby of the St. Elmo Hotel was mostly about the weather. Nobody could remember a year when there had been so much snow so early in the country between the Coeur d'Alenes and the Bitterroots. One old-timer told Merriam that they could assume the New York men had made their way out to the Montana side. Otherwise they were in there for the winter, since there was no way to get out now in this direction.

Of course you couldn't get out with animals, someone else said. But men on snowshoes shouldn't have much trouble unless they were encumbered. The talk turned to other bad winters and other hunting trips, and Merriam realized he now had as much information as he was going to get. He would let the general know tomorrow by wire that these hunters were probably not coming out of the Bitterroots the way they went in—at least not according to the gossip in Kendrick.

13 On Sunday, November 5, it rained all day. Himmelwright was the first up, at daylight, and he went immediately to check on Colegate. He was awake and complained to Himmelwright that he couldn't get warm. Spencer joined Himmelwright, and while Himmelwright went looking for dry wood, Spencer built a fire of the material brought in the day before. Spencer's ability to bring flames to life under the worst conditions never failed to impress Carlin, who wrote in his diary during this period that "Spencer has a great knack for making a good fire out of almost anything." Within moments all five were up and busy about the camp, caring for Colegate, fetching wood, and cooking breakfast.

They had Spencer's assurance that Jerry Johnson would be here today to pick up the trophies and equipment they were leaving behind. As soon as breakfast was over they started packing the things they were taking with them, and loading them on Spencer's raft. They struck and folded both tents but left the canvas fly, which was Colegate's shelter, until the last. When that was on board, Carlin, Keeley, and Pierce pushed the raft out of the shallows and into a relatively light shore-side current. Then, maneuvering the craft from the shore with long ropes, Keeley and Carlin guided it carefully downstream to the place where the other raft had landed so ungloriously two days earlier. Keeley and Carlin secured Spencer's raft to a couple of fir trees, and with Pierce's help moved half the stuff on Spencer's raft to the other one. It was now about 10 o'clock. The rain had turned to sleet.

Jerry Johnson, on foot and leading two horses, came into camp declaring that he'd rather see snow than any more of this damned rain. Amen to that, said Keeley. All except Colegate helped pack the horses, and for a second time they bade Johnson good-bye.

The old trapper led his two horses back up the trail, thinking that these men probably would never see their trophies and their camp gear again. He was pretty sure they would drown, starve, or die of exposure somewhere in the canyon of the Lochsa. It would not be his fault; he had warned them more than once that they were digging their graves by launching those rafts on this river. Their plight didn't trouble him because he didn't care for any of them with the possible exception of Spencer. He respected the guide as both savvy and prudent, and it saddened him somewhat that the foolishness of others would probably cost Spencer his life.

As for Ben Keeley, Johnson said aloud to the horses, to hell with him. Johnson had looked forward to having company through the winter for a change, but he had wintered alone many a time and could do it again. Anyhow, he thought, he and Keeley would have been on each other's nerves before spring. It was probably better this way.

Ben Keeley, as he watched Johnson and his horses walk out of sight through the rain, was thinking much the same thing. This jaunt down the Lochsa was a chancy venture for sure. But spending the winter with old Jerry in a cabin under six feet of snow might have been just as daunting.

Keeley had spent such a winter once, on the Selway with an old miner named Jesse who could hardly stand the sound of human speech. Keeley had got trapped by an early winter much like this one, and Jesse had taken him in. Old Jess seldom uttered a word himself, speaking only when necessary, and Keeley had quickly learned that a vow of silence was all that stood between him and the cold, wet snow. That was the worst winter of his career, and he had escaped as soon as the snow melted enough for traveling. He had thought to thank Jesse for saving his life, but decided that the old man wouldn't appreciate so much needless chatter.

Keeley heard Carlin shouting that it was time to go, and saw that Pierce and Himmelwright were helping Colegate down to the rafts, one on each side of him. It was a journey of only about fifty yards, but it took a long time to get Colegate there and then to get him aboard the raft that carried his chair.

The raft carrying Spencer, Keeley, and the dogs would go first, and it moved away into the current at about 11 o'clock, followed by raft number two. They were not long getting into the rapids. In the first half hour they plowed through several, and then came to a gravel bar and some pine trees that formed an island in the river. The channel on the right hand side seemed to offer the best route past the island, but Carlin had warned Keeley that it was too shallow even for rafts. The left hand channel was deep enough, but there were some dangerous rocks dotting the water at the far end.

Since they had no choice, Spencer and Keeley chose the left channel and poled into it. They struck the rocks and hung up on a couple of them, but managed to work the raft loose. Himmelwright, steering the second raft, saw Keeley's error and missed the rocks by keeping to the left of the channel. Both rafts made a landing below the island on the right bank and everybody waded ashore but Colegate, who remained aboard on his chair.

Why were they stopping now? Pierce wondered as he stepped into the shallow water. They had got past the island, missing the rocks, so why not keep going? He didn't seek the answer from anyone because no one else was raising the question. And since he was the greenhorn in this group, he didn't think it would be proper for him to raise it himself.

Himmelwright sort of answered the question anyhow. He volunteered to walk down the river far enough to scout the next few rapids and locate another landing spot. Carlin, who had previously done the same thing on the stretch just covered, now remarked that he had seen signs of elk and bear on the flat adjacent to the river at this place. And he pointed out the sweat lodge he had seen the day before.

Why hadn't Pierce known that Carlin had scouted the stream on foot? he asked himself. Probably because he was so busy fetching wood for Colegate's fire that he hadn't noticed. Well then, the stop-and-go made sense. They didn't want to set themselves adrift in these currents until they had some idea where they were going to land. Pierce felt anew his separateness from the others. He also was finding it more prudent than ever to keep his notions to himself.

When Himmelwright returned he said he had found a landing site farther down the river, but he added that there was some pretty rough water between here and there. Spencer suggested that since Himmelwright knew better than the rest what lay ahead, perhaps he and his raft should take the lead this time. Carlin didn't think that was a good idea. Since they had a sick man on their raft, they should let Spencer and Keeley go ahead and show the way. Himmelwright could tell them exactly where the landing site was and what they could expect in getting there. The others agreed and the men returned to the rafts, taking the landing ropes aboard with them.

Spencer and Keeley bent to their poles and shoved off, followed closely by Carlin, Pierce, and Himmelwright. They had been on the river or between runs for two and a half hours. Now they were making up time. The two rafts sped down the Lochsa through the cold rain, around a bend, then around another bend and toward the rough water, gathering speed. Himmelwright, guiding the raft with the long sweep, heard an ominous roar ahead. He glanced at the banks running past them and felt his mouth go dry. He had told Spencer and Keeley that when they reached this spot they should stay close to the right bank because there were a couple of huge boulders in the center. Through the slanting rain he could barely see the raft ahead of him, yet it was clear that it was keeping to the right bank. But as he watched he saw it bounce against rocks, break loose, then bounce again, and stick.

Spencer and Keeley were hung up in swift water, and both were waving frantically to Himmelwright and motioning him toward the center. Carlin shouted something but Himmelwright couldn't understand him and didn't care; he was devoting all his attention to the awful scene rushing toward him.

One of the two boulders in the center was huge—it rose about six feet above the water—and the other was only slightly smaller. They were barely farther apart than the width of the raft. Himmelwright knew that only by a miracle could he steer between them. And it quickly became clear that it would take another miracle to survive the plunge beyond. The water that squeezed swiftly between the boulders then fell several feet straight down on the other side. There was no way around. He would have to go through. Himmelwright shouted to Colegate to hold on, but the roar of the water snatched the words away from him.

As the raft flew toward the rocks, Himmelwright experienced for the first time the sense of suspension that some others have described: The feeling that time has suddenly slowed almost to a stop. The big boulder on the right moved past so close that

Himmelwright could almost have touched it, and then the smaller one on the left passed slowly by. It seemed to Himmelwright that the raft was now suspended in midair at the lip of the fall, hanging, hanging, and then was going deliberately down and down, into a swirling blackness. The front end disappeared into the eddy and then, unbelievably, bobbed up again.

They had made it through. What luck, Himmelwright thought. What incredible luck. Carlin and Pierce were looking grim and holding on, one on each side of Colegate, and Colegate was clutching his chair, his head rigid, his eyes staring aft toward Himmelwright.

The raft turned slowly around and around in the eddy, then drifted into the current, and Himmelwright steered it to the landing place he had earlier picked out.

He and Carlin tied the raft to a tree, and all three of them ran to help Spencer and Keeley. But they met the other two men walking toward them, roping their raft down to the landing place. After finding they could not get the raft off the rocks in any other way, they had jumped into the river up to their waists and pried it free.

Keeley and Spencer had watched the other raft scoot between the boulders and Keeley told Carlin now that he had figured the four on that raft were goners for sure, when they went over the jump. How had Himmelwright managed it? Himmelwright, still not sure, said he didn't want to think about it.

Spencer said Himmelwright deserved a rest, and suggested he and Carlin make this examination of the river downstream. They scrambled over rocks and fallen trees looking for troublesome water and found a nasty rapids at a spot where a narrow gorge pinched the river. Submerged rocks roiled the speeding water into four-foot waves that looked frightful, but Carlin and Spencer agreed that with the river this high there should be enough water to keep the rafts above the rocks. They located a likely landing spot and returned to confer with the others. They agreed to make one more run today and then camp. Everybody was tired and wet, and Colegate sorely needed a warm fire.

Keeley said he thought maybe Carlin's raft should go first this time, and Carlin agreed that it was his turn. He and Himmelwright and Pierce returned to their raft, where Colegate waited silently on his chair. Carlin warned the cook that he should be prepared for more bad water ahead. Spencer and Keeley, still on shore, untied Carlin's ropes and tossed them aboard. Carlin took the steering sweep and Pierce and Himmelwright poled the raft into deeper water. Behind them, Spencer and Keeley called the dogs; the animals had been exploring the game-rich flat in a frenzy of sniffing and running. Carlin, remembering his own recent survey of the place, felt a fleeting regret that they all couldn't stay a while and do a little hunting.

The drifting was easy, and if it hadn't been for the rain, it might even have been pleasant. Himmelwright gripped the gear enclosure and Pierce braced himself against a stern post within reach of Colegate's chair, as the raft gained speed through the water. Pierce, looking back, could see Spencer and Keeley coming along behind them with Daisy, Idaho, and Montana.

This easy ride didn't last long. Carlin could hear the roar of the gorge before he could see it, and he realized that he and Spencer could have been wrong about the depth of the water ahead. The rocky walls of the canyon closed in upon them, and the wild water under them began tossing and rolling the raft "like an ocean steamer," as Carlin wrote that night in his diary. Himmelwright, in the bow, got the full force of the waves coming over the raft and would have been swept off if he had lost his grip on the post he was clinging to. Pierce managed to keep Colegate on his chair, and the raft somehow remained upright.

Once out of the rapids, Carlin steered to shore and he and the others were waiting there for Spencer and Keeley to join them when the other raft came rolling through the gorge and sped on by. Himmelwright and Pierce poled their raft back into deep water and followed, and Pierce found himself wondering again why they, too, hadn't just kept going.

The drifting was easy again now, and after about three quarters of a mile Carlin spotted the other raft on the bank and saw Spencer and Keeley motioning him to shore. He tried to get to the bank but the raft was heading instead toward some rocks, and the sweep had no effect. Carlin dropped the sweep and grabbed a pole and all three men, poling desperately, managed to get clear of the rocks. As they drifted past the other raft, Himmelwright threw a rope, which fell short. Pierce threw another, and Spencer caught it. But the raft kept moving and Spencer hung on as he was pulled into the water. Still he hung on, dancing over rocks and driftwood, until he was able to snub the rope around a stump.

They had arrived at another flat, dissected by a fast-running creek and almost treeless. There would be little dry fuel here, but it was now almost four o'clock. It would soon be dark, and everyone was weary and wet. They would camp here tonight, Carlin said, and make another river survey in the morning. While the three dogs explored the flat, the men brought Colegate ashore, put up a tent and the fly, and went looking for firewood.

They worked until after dark gathering enough wood to maintain a fire through the night. After supper they found some dry cedar and used it to make a floor under the fly to lay the provisions on. Then they began drying blankets and clothes and got to bed at 2 a.m.

Pierce took the first watch, keeping the fire going for Colegate. He would be relieved in two hours by Spencer, who would later make the breakfast. Through the whole day and far into the night, the rain had not stopped.

14 It was still raining hard at daylight when Spencer announced to the camp that breakfast was ready. After a meal of fresh bread and venison washed down by coffee, Carlin and Himmelwright cleaned their utensils at the water's edge and set off on foot down the river. Keeley helped Spencer clear away the cooking equipment and then the two of them began making a bow oar for their raft. Poles were fine in shallow water, but in some places the water ran too deep for poles; they needed some way to steer the craft from the bow as well as from the stern.

Carlin and Himmelwright, meanwhile, found the downriver hike strenuous. The bank, rocky and brushy, made walking hard—much harder than the rafting, in Carlin's opinion. They passed two islands and counted several minor rapids plus one big one. They also saw much evidence of other travelers here—old campfire sites and choppings that Himmelwright said had been left by railroad survey crews. Himmelwright, at one time a railroad surveyor himself, recognized the signs. He told Carlin that the Northern Pacific had once considered running rails down this canyon. My God, was all Carlin could say to that as he stared at the hostile landscape around them.

After traveling about three miles down the river, the two returned to camp, arriving at noon. Keeley showed them the bow oar he and Spencer had made, and Carlin said he had been thinking also of adding a bow oar to his raft; that plus the stern sweep would give the steersmen more control, he thought. Spencer said he might want to wait until they had a chance to see how this one worked.

Pierce had been busy all morning with the fire and with Colegate, who was draped with blankets but shivering just the same. Pierce said he didn't know what to do; he simply could not get Colegate warm. None of the others knew what to do either beyond what they had been doing. So they struck the tent, took down the fly, and moved Colegate, with much stumbling, through the rain to the raft. The dogs, aware that the camp was moving, ended their exploration of the flat and hurried down to the river.

Spencer and Keeley shoved off first with Keeley at the sweep and Spencer standing by with a pole in one hand and one arm wrapped around a post. Once in deep water, Spencer dropped the pole and grabbed the new oar to help with the steering. He was surprised at how well it worked.

Both rafts managed to miss a number of big boulders dotting the river. They both passed by the first island without incident, but Keeley decided to land on the second one and then motioned for Himmelwright to do the same.

They were in a fix now, Keeley said, because neither the left nor the right channel was passable. A quick examination proved him right. On the left, the current drove directly into a ledge of sharp rocks. On the right, there was a big boulder in the center of the channel and a string of smaller ones extending from the boulder to the shore. The current flowed toward the boulder and in swift water it would be impossible to drive a raft between that boulder and the island. When Carlin and Himmelwright studied the island from the shore, it had looked passable to them because they couldn't see across the island to the rocks in the left channel.

Well, Spencer said, there was a way to get the rafts to the other end of the island: Rope them through the right channel. With every healthy man on a rope, they should be able to hold the first raft off the big boulder, land it at the bottom, and then go back for the second. The Spencer-Keeley raft would go first because they needed to be sure they could hold it before sending the second one through with Colegate aboard.

The maneuver worked. Both rafts made it safely to the bottom of the island, but there was still a long, fierce rapid visible in the distance below.

Spencer and Keeley shoved off first and the others climbed a pile of driftwood and watched them go. They saw them enter the rapids, then suddenly shoot off to the right and reappear moments later as tiny specks far down the river.

Himmelwright, Carlin, and Pierce then climbed down from their driftwood perch, boarded their own raft, and set out for the rapids with Himmelwright at the sweep. He entered the rapids at the center and quickly realized that this was the roughest water he had yet encountered. For two hundred yards it tossed the raft so roughly that Himmelwright was once again almost washed overboard, and Carlin was certain the raft would overturn and throw them all into the water. Then, as suddenly as it had begun, the bouncing ended. Below the rapids they drifted through a deep pool for half a mile before reaching an island where Spencer and Keeley awaited them.

The men agreed they couldn't have stumbled upon a better campsite. The island was thick with trees and relatively dry, with abundant fuel close at hand. After some discussion they decided they would spend two nights here. They were all wet and cold and tired, and they needed some rest. They might be able to shoot some grouse or larger game, Carlin said, and they would also have time to do some fishing.

Himmelwright and Pierce brought Colegate ashore, and while Spencer built a fire, Carlin and Keeley put up the fly and both tents. The dogs, as usual, went exploring with all three noses close to the ground.

Carlin said to the others, as they stood around the fire, that in his opinion they had earned a bit of brandy. They were all so cold and wet on the outside, he said, that they needed something to make them warm on the inside. Spencer got out the tin cups while Himmelwright fetched the jug. He poured a shot for Colegate first and paused to see how the cook would take it. Colegate lifted the cup to his lips with both hands, took a small swallow, then closed his eyes and lowered the cup to his lap. He was smiling—for the first time in many days—when Himmelwright passed the jug to Carlin.

All but Keeley seemed to find some comfort in their tin cups. Keeley began to fret that this journey was taking too long. They had been on the river for four days, he complained, and they had covered only ten miles. He had no objection to spending two nights here, he said, but after they resumed traveling, why not keep going?

Pierce, who had been breathing in the rich brandy smell from his cup, suddenly raised his head and shot a startled look at Keeley. That was the question *he* at one time had wanted to ask.

They could have made twice the distance, Keeley said, if they had not wasted so much time landing every few minutes and constantly exploring the river ahead on foot. He wanted to turn the rafts loose, he said, and trust to luck in running the river.

No one agreed with him.

Carlin said this river was too dangerous for that. He wanted to know what lay ahead before turning *his* raft loose.

Keeley said it didn't make any difference what lay ahead. They had committed themselves to going out by raft because there was now no other way. So they might as well just go, he declared, and take their chances.

Keeley's demand had taken his raft mate by surprise, and Spencer didn't like the notion at all. He said that if they were to survive, they would need to use caution, and that meant learning as much about the river as they could before launching themselves into it. Time spent that way, he said, was not time wasted.

Himmelwright said that Keeley was wrong in assuming they would go out by raft or not at all.

Then what other way out was there? Keeley asked.

Shank's mare, Himmelwright said; also known as on foot.

Keeley tossed a meaningful glance in Colegate's direction. Really? he asked.

Carlin said there was no point in arguing about the matter because it had already been settled. They would continue to explore the river ahead in advance of every start as long as that was possible.

Himmelwright and Pierce volunteered to start collecting firewood. They would dry their clothes when they got that done, they said. Before he dried *his* clothes, Carlin said, he thought he would go fishing. He cut a pole and took some fishing line and his book of flies out to the end of a small gravel bar, thinking the rain might improve his chances. It didn't. Carlin made several casts into the river, and decided the water was too high and too fast.

He returned to camp and helped Spencer pull off Colegate's shirt and pants and hang them up by the fire to dry. Carlin stooped to unwrap the blanket pieces tied around Colegate's feet and almost fainted from the smell. Gangrene was eating away at the cook's swollen legs, as they had all known for some time. But this was Carlin's first good whiff of the stench that poured from the rotting flesh. Everyone had noticed that even Daisy, Colegate's own dog, would not lie close to him. Fortunately for the rest of the party, Colegate had to spend the nights sitting up by the fire in the open air; his presence in one of the tents on a rainy night would be almost unbearable, Carlin realized. It made him feel a bit guilty to think of this as a blessing, since he did feel sorry for the sick man, but there was no denying that it was.

Holding his breath, Carlin quickly untied the blanket pieces on Colegate's feet and placed them near the fire. Spencer had managed with difficulty to pull the cook's wet undershirt off and get a dry blanket around him, but both men understood that his wool underpants were on to stay. Like his outer pants, they had been ripped apart enough to accommodate his enlarged legs. Carlin poured the cook another shot of brandy and placed it in his hands, a little embarrassed by his own sudden burst of compassion.

Keeley had been busy moving gear and provisions off the rafts and piling them under the trees where they would stay fairly dry. When he returned to the fire he told Carlin that his new bow oar worked so well that he thought Carlin's raft should have one too. It would give the crew a little more control of the raft than they had with just the poles and the stern sweep. Spencer then said that if Carlin wanted one, he would be glad to make it tomorrow. Carlin accepted the offer, and Spencer went looking for a lodgepole pine to make it from.

The party spent the rest of that day drying things out and preparing supper. By late afternoon the rain, which had been coming down hard, faded to a light drizzle, and by nightfall had stopped entirely. The men went to bed early, hardly believing their good luck, after arranging for Keeley and Carlin to keep the fire going for Colegate.

Keeley, who had the first watch, sat under the fly on a kitchen box expecting at any moment to hear again the sound of rain on canvas. But there was only the wind in the trees and Colegate's occasional rough snoring. Just before Carlin arrived to take his watch, Keeley walked out into the open to relieve himself and caught a brief sight of the half moon sailing through scudding clouds.

Was this a sign their luck was changing? he asked Carlin. He certainly hoped so, Carlin said, and Keeley went into his tent.

Carlin put some wood on the fire and sat on the kitchen box, wondering what he had just said. He realized he was afraid to hope their luck was changing, because when he thought of all they had been through on this river, their luck so far had been pretty good.

Above him, between the trees overhead and the ridge across the river, he could now see not only the moon but some stars. He picked up his diary, intending to record the day's events, and instead began composing a poem. He called it "A Night on the Kooskooskee River, Idaho: A Reverie." It included these lines, clearly influenced by the English nature poets popular in America at the time:

A hundred mountains round me rear
Their hoary heads on high,
And join in admiration of
A clear and brilliant sky.

A thousand stars from farthest space
Their silver-white rays send,
Which with the moon's more mellow light
Harmoniously blend.

Ten thousand rippling waves have caught—
Despite the river's roar—
The stars above, and, trembling,
A hundred thousand more....

O Nature kind! Thy proffered cup
With rarest grace o'erflows;
It soothes the mind and heals the soul,
And priceless gifts bestows....

After completing nine stanzas celebrating the river and the night, Carlin began the humdrum business of noting the day's activities, and was still at it when Spencer came to relieve him.

Abe Himmelwright's mother had by now been in Chicago since the 20th of October. A week later after her first letter to General Carlin, Mrs. Himmelwright again wired the general and the general replied it was too early to become concerned. But he would make inquiries at Kendrick and get back to her. He already had heard from Captain Merriam that the old-timers in Kendrick didn't expect the Carlin party to get out until spring, at least in that direction.

The general sent a wire immediately to the St. Elmo Hotel at Kendrick, asking whether anything had been heard from the hunters. He was startled to get his reply from Charles Colegate. Charles said that someone in the hunting party should have come out long before this because he had reason to believe his father was very sick. But he said nobody here had heard anything and the old-timers were saying that the Carlin party was probably snowed in.

Charles had come to Kendrick because Dr. Webb thought someone in the family should be there when they brought George out. The doctor had assumed that George would become seriously ill within the first two weeks, and that someone would do whatever it took to get him back to Kendrick. It would be Charles's job to put him on the next train and accompany him to Spokane.

General Carlin was unsure how he should deal with Himmelwright's mother. He didn't want to alarm her unnecessarily, but he had promised to keep her informed. He sent her a wire saying the illness of the camp cook may have caused a change in the hunting party's plans. He also said that bad weather may have delayed the party's return to Kendrick; he would stay in touch.

Charles kept his mother informed. Fannie Colegate grew more perplexed by the day. If George was sick, as she knew he must be, why hadn't they brought him out? If he was dead, why hadn't they brought him out? If they were all snowed in, as the old-timers were telling Charles, why wasn't someone going in after them? She didn't know—because Charles hadn't told her—that there was now some six feet of snow on the Lolo Trail, the primary access to the hunting grounds of the Bitterroots. Charles wasn't quite sure why he hadn't mentioned this to his mother. Probably because he didn't want to kill any hope she might still have of seeing her husband again.

Charles himself kept hoping that any day now, in spite of the deep snow, the hunters would come out of the mountains and deliver his dad to him, either dead or alive.

15 Until recently General Carlin's chief distraction had been his impending retirement from active service and the ceremonies that would attend it. Now, as the cold rains of autumn fell on Vancouver Barracks, a friend and former partner of Martin Spencer suddenly thrust the general's retirement into the background.

In Missoula, Montana, William Wright had been watching the weather reports with mounting alarm. Wright, a veteran guide and mountaineer, had kept in touch with Spencer and knew he had taken a hunting party into the Bitterroots. He also knew that the party had spent a night at the Hotel Spokane, and he wrote to the only person he knew there, one John L. Randle.

After taking note of the weather, and expressing concern for his partner, Wright added:

> If Spencer has not got out of the mountains before now, he will not get out before spring—not that way [to the west] as the snow is from four to six feet deep in the mountains and it is impossible to get out any horses unless it is this way [toward Missoula, to the east]. Even then one could not do so unless they went in from this way and took a pack train of oats. It has snowed for over a month on the range. I came out with a party in about two feet of snow. Two men going out about a week ago started with six horses and got out with two, and would not have got out then only for some Indians who had helped them. Do you know of anyone who knows where [the Carlin party] were going and how much grub they took? How many horses did they take? General Carlin had better send out a relief party to hunt them up. If you see him, tell him I really think so, for if they have not got out they will not, unless they come on snowshoes.

Randle turned the letter over to the one person *he* knew who would know what to do with it, Captain Louis Merriam at Fort Spokane, a part of General Carlin's command as chief officer of the Department of the Columbia. Merriam telegraphed Wright for the latest weather conditions on the upper Lochsa, and Wright replied with what essentially he had said in his letter to Randle: There was six feet of snow in parts of the Bitterroot range and that no one had heard anything from or about the Carlin party. Captain Merriam then telegraphed General Carlin, saying the hunters had run afoul of bad weather, had not been heard from, and could be trapped in the mountains by snow. Within hours he had the general's reply:

> Thanks for information. If possible, go to Missoula and ask Colonel Burt, commandant at Fort Missoula, for a party of men, pack animals and subsistence and guide, and go in relief of Will and party. I will pay the expenses.

Merriam left for Missoula the next day aboard the Northern Pacific, but got only as far as Cataldo, Idaho, where heavy rains had washed out the rails. The railroad returned its passengers and crew to Spokane, and Merriam reported to the general that he would stand by at Fort Spokane for further orders.

General Carlin by this time had heard directly from Wright that his son and companions were probably trapped in the mountains by snow.

The general had Randle's assurance that Wright knew the country well and could be trusted on such matters. The general had met Spencer at Spokane in September and was satisfied that the guide was competent, hardy, and knowledgeable. If the situation was as serious as Wright seemed to believe, why had Spencer not come out of the mountains before now? Was it because he could not?

The general ordered Merriam by telegraph to take a party and try to get into the mountains by way of the Lolo Trail. And he told his aide-de-camp, Lieutenant C.H. Martin, to take the train immediately to Missoula, assuming the tracks had been repaired, and report there to the commanding officer, Colonel A.S. Burt.

By now everyone in the general's headquarters knew what was happening, and one of the officers, First Lieutenant Charles P. Elliott of the 4th Cavalry, volunteered to go in search of the general's son. The general, expressing his gratitude, told Elliott to take a few men and leave as soon as possible for Kendrick. The lieutenant had no trouble putting a detachment together. Sergeant Alexander Smart and Privates Hamilton F. Markland, Ethelbert Norlin, and David Ruhl, all of E Troop, 4th Cavalry, volunteered because they were tired of barracks life. Elliott and the four enlisted men left the next day by train for Spokane.

A couple of days later, Lieutenant Gordon Voorhies of the 24th Infantry at Fort Walla Walla, also a part of General Carlin's command, reminded the general that he and Will were good friends and that he would like to be involved in the search. In that case, the general said, Voorhies should take some troops to Kendrick and organize two more search parties.

Next he sent word to Himmelwright's mother, still in Chicago, that she might as well return to New York since nobody knew how soon her son and the others would be brought out. But he assured her that the party was well provisioned for a long stay and that she should not be concerned about the young men's safety.

⸎

The seventh of November was a clear day on the Lochsa, but cold. Keeley, having seen some ice on the rocks at the river's edge, declared he would take the temperature drop over more rain any day. It meant the men would not have to spend so much of their time and energy drying clothes and blankets. There was enough dry fuel in this campground to keep a good fire going, and spirits were on the rise. Himmelwright decided after breakfast that he would walk down the river to see what lay in store below. Carlin and Pierce went looking for game, and with Daisy's help Pierce shot four grouse. They saw signs of elk and bear, but brought back only the birds, which Pierce dressed out for supper. Keeley did some minor repair work on the rafts, which had been used badly by the river, and Spencer spent most of that day drying things and making an inventory of the provisions.

He noted that they were running low on flour. That caused Keeley to bring up again his complaint that they were wasting time with this stop-and-go running of the river. They would probably run out of food, Keeley said, before they ran out of rapids and rocks.

Carlin reminded Keeley that he might be eating more than his share, considering that Keeley was eating grub he had already sold to Carlin. Then Keeley reminded Carlin that he had been asked to come along because Carlin wanted his help in getting down the river. And if his help was so badly needed, why didn't they take his advice?

Spencer intervened at this point, declaring that Carlin and Keeley had reached a standoff, and they could now change the subject. Then Spencer went back to work on a bow oar for Carlin's raft.

Himmelwright returned near dark after a long walk down the river, weary and discouraged. He had walked eight miles down and eight miles back with nothing to eat since morning but a small piece of bread. He reported that the first five miles would be fairly easy but that the last three were one long rapid. He described the water as very swift and rough and probably impassable. They might have to rope the rafts all the way through those last three miles, he said.

Lining two rafts down three miles of swift water would be a full day's work, Carlin said. They might be wise to take only the first five miles tomorrow and start fresh on the bad part the day after.

Keeley had started to light his pipe with a piece of burning wood from the fire, but when he heard that he stopped and threw the stick on the ground.

Spencer, who knew what was coming, put a hand on Keeley's arm and told him not to get excited. Will was only thinking out loud, he said; no decision would be made until they got a good look at those rapids. If Abe was right, he said, it might pay them to be satisfied with five miles tomorrow.

Keeley said nothing. Spencer picked up the stick, re-lit it, and handed it to Keeley, who threw it back into the fire.

Early the next morning, in clear, cold weather, the party broke camp and this time Pierce rode with Spencer and Keeley. The two rafts covered the first five miles quickly, as Himmelwright had predicted, and landed at two large eddies. From here they admired a beautiful creek that came down to the Lochsa on the left in a series of lovely falls, then blanched at the heart-stopping view down the river.

Pierce stayed with Colegate and the rafts, and the other four walked down the bank for a closer look. These rapids, they agreed, were the worst they had seen. The river dropped steeply here and for a mile the water flowed swiftly among countless boulders. Then it narrowed, with a huge boulder in the center leaving a channel on either side, each full of smaller rocks. Farther down, it was even worse—more boulders and rougher water.

They could not run these rapids. If they tried, they would surely upset; and if they were not upset and failed to make a landing, they would be carried into a row of boulders that would smash both rafts and probably drown them all. And they could not line the rafts down the right side, where they had landed, because it had a perpendicular wall with no bank to stand on.

The four returned to the rafts, where Pierce had a fire going, and made camp. They would cross the river in the morning and inspect the left-hand side. Colegate was so cold he could not move. Spencer and Keeley had to carry him to shore and set him by the fire.

In his diary that evening, Carlin wrote: "Some of us think we are in the canyon, but Spencer thinks not."

Spencer was right. The fearsome Black Canyon of the Lochsa was some fifteen miles farther down the river. They were roughly halfway there, and they had already covered the easy part.

The next morning, November 9, it was raining again and still cold. They would have to cross the river today and that would take some planning. They had camped at the foot of an eddy some two hundred yards upstream from a waterfall of several feet. Should either raft get caught by the current while crossing, it would be swept down over the falls and smashed. To avoid that, they pulled the rafts to the head of the eddy and started across there, with Keeley and Spencer in the lead. They had spotted a gravel bar at the head of the rapids and planned to land there and then work the rafts through the left-hand channel with ropes.

They got across safely and roped the first raft through the channel and down to the gravel bar. The other raft, carrying Carlin, Himmelwright, and Pierce, as well as Colegate, made the crossing also, but Himmelwright's pole lodged in the rocks and the current swung the craft sideways at the head of the channel. Carlin leaped into the water with a rope and tried to hold the stern upstream but was swept off his feet. He managed to regain his footing as Himmelwright jumped in with his rope and the two of them were able to land the raft on the gravel bar a few yards downstream from Spencer and Keeley. Carlin, Himmelwright and Pierce got off their raft, leaving Colegate aboard because he would be unable to walk down the rocky bank.

Keeley boarded Carlin's raft and prepared to pole it around the rocks as the others slowly let it down the channel on ropes. All went well until they came to a spot where the water rushed swiftly around a large rock in the center. The men on the bank decided they had better take Colegate off before maneuvering through this hazard. They moved Colegate to a small level spot near the river and left Pierce with him. Then Carlin and Spencer tied a long rope to the raft and carried the other end of it down the river and stood by to snub the line around a tree when the raft came abreast of the large rock. Keeley and Himmelwright, also on shore with ropes, let the raft drift with the swift water for some thirty feet, but were unable to control its speed. Carlin and Spencer tried desperately to get it snubbed, but the current carried it past them and dragged all four through the water and over the rocks for several more yards.

They got it under control finally and landed it, then walked back up the river to bring down Colegate. They all but carried him over and around the rocks that lined the bank since Colegate could barely walk even on level ground. It took all four men, working in relays with Pierce's help, to move the invalid to where they had tied the rafts. They thought the worst was over, and they put Colegate back on his seat. But what they had been through proved only a foretaste of what was to come. For the next mile, while Pierce rode the raft with Colegate, the other four lined it down through the roaring turbulence, shouting and cursing as they went.

They had picked out a camping spot near a small eddy, and when they came to within fifty yards of it, the raft got away from them and ran aground on a gravel bar. It was raining harder by now, and Pierce said they must build a fire quickly because Colegate was suffering from the cold. Pierce himself was weak from the fright of this terrible ride and had to be helped to shore. Spencer made the fire while Carlin scrabbled about for firewood and Keeley set up the fly.

They still had Keeley's raft to bring down, but Keeley said he didn't want to go through this again. He would run it down, he said, and show them how it was done. Spencer and Himmelwright thought that was a bad idea, but Keeley persisted, and Carlin said that as far as he was concerned, it was Keeley's raft and he could do with it as he pleased.

Spencer told Keeley that if he wanted to run these rapids he would run them alone, because nobody else was that foolish. This did not seem to deter Keeley, and Spencer finally agreed to go with him. It made him feel like a fool to do it, Spencer said, but if Keeley tried to do it alone he would either drown or break his neck.

Keeley and Spencer walked back up the river. Himmelwright went along because he said somebody should be on shore to throw a rope to if things went bad. He would stand at a place where the current reached into the bank. If Keeley and Spencer wished to land there, to avoid worse water downstream, they could throw him a rope.

With Himmelwright posted at a fair landing spot, Keeley and Spencer continued up the river to the raft and started to bring her down. The first hundred yards or so weren't bad. Then the raft began to move at tremendous speed, and Spencer, manning the stern sweep, shouted that they had better try to land. At that point Keeley's bow oar struck a rock and flew out of his hands. He quickly grabbed the bow rope, and as the raft sped toward Himmelwright, he threw it. But Himmelwright could not hold it and the raft flew past him, crashed into a large rock, and upset.

Himmelwright ran down the bank, scrambling over rocks and driftwood, and when he came opposite the raft Keeley threw him the rope. He snubbed it around a rock, but he needn't have bothered. The raft was half under water on its side, with the current holding it there securely. Keeley had managed to throw himself onto the rock, but Spencer was swept into the water and saved himself by clutching a dangling rope, then pulling himself back aboard.

Himmelwright shouted to them to stay where they were while he went for help. He hurried back down the bank to where the others had made camp, arriving just before dark. It was still raining, and nobody had eaten since breakfast. Colegate was stiff with cold. The daylight was fading fast, but they were in real trouble now and had to get back up the river bank without delay. Carlin, cursing himself for letting Keeley have his way, reminded the others that half their provisions were on Keeley's raft.

Leaving Pierce with Colegate, Himmelwright and Carlin quickly gathered some extra ropes and hustled up to the accident site. All four men, working hard, could not budge the raft. Keeley and Spencer tried to push it off the rock, but because of their positions they had a hard time getting a purchase on it. Carlin and Himmelwright pulled from the shore with the ropes while the other two pried and pushed. Finally, they gave up. They secured the raft with ropes from bow and stern, and then helped Keeley and Spencer use the ropes to get ashore. The four made their way back down the river in the dark and put up the only tent they now had. Pierce had started supper, and after they had eaten, Spencer got a big fire going. It had stopped raining but everything was wet and all but Colegate spent the evening trying to get their clothes and their few remaining blankets dry.

Himmelwright said he could think of nothing he wanted more right now than a shot of brandy—and then remembered that the brandy was on the other raft.

It was an unpleasant night. There were too few blankets to keep them all warm in this cold, and the ones they had were clammy

A cold morning on the river. Carlin, standing at right, is wearing the shirt he made from a blanket.

with damp. Himmelwright realized shortly after going to bed that he didn't want that brandy nearly as much as he wanted another blanket. Pierce stayed up late to keep Colegate's fire going. Spencer, who was glad to get out of his cold, soggy bed, relieved Pierce at midnight.

Colegate was beyond complaining. People draped blankets over him, giving him the driest ones, as he sat stiffly on his seat, breathing heavily and now and then mumbling to himself. He didn't seem to recognize anyone. He didn't seem to listen when anyone spoke, even when speaking to him. Pierce, who spent more time with him than anyone else, often wondered what was going on inside Colegate's head. Keeley said he didn't want to know, and anyway didn't care. For some time now they had been treating the sick man as though he weren't there; they didn't hesitate to talk about him in his presence, confident that it could make no difference to him what they said. Carlin had referred to Colegate more than once as "a goner." Keeley said once that if Colegate had had the good timing to crap out back at the hot springs, they wouldn't now be struggling down this river in the rain. Spencer snapped at Keeley, telling him that kind of talk was no help at all. And Carlin pointed out that if Colegate had died then, Keeley would be spending the winter with grumpy old Jerry instead of gliding down this beautiful stream with jolly companions.

Nobody laughed.

16 Thomas Beall, a rancher and sometimes miner who now lived near the mouth of the Clearwater River just east of Lewiston, Idaho—a man who had spent some thirty years in the Clearwater country—got word at about this time that the U.S. Army needed his services. General Carlin wanted Beall to help guide Lieutenant Clough Overton's rescue party into the Bitterroots in search of a group of lost hunters.

Before leaving for Kendrick, Beall told the *Lewiston Tribune* that the party would include a detail of troopers, several packers, six horses, and six mules. He said they would head for the Lolo Pass on the Idaho-Montana border, establish a camp there, and radiate on snowshoes in all directions in search of some trace of the missing men.

Beall did not hold out much hope of success. He pointed out that the winter begins early in October in those mountains in normal years, and that this winter promised to be an unusually bad one. With several feet of snow on the ground, he said, travel would be impossible on horses and precarious even on snowshoes.

Beall told the *Tribune* that as he was coming out of the Bitterroots six weeks earlier he met a couple of men who had been lost in the mountains for two months, subsisting on berries and bulbs. Their strength finally had given out and they had collapsed after getting stuck in a ravine and were accidentally discovered there. People starved in that country even in decent weather; Beall wouldn't bet a nickel on the survival of anyone marooned there in winter.

As if to support this bleak assessment, a rumor began circulating in Kendrick that the Carlin party had lost its horses and was facing starvation. But Captain Merriam told the *Spokane Review* that he didn't think young Carlin was in serious trouble.

"Willie has roughed it a great deal," Merriam said. "He is a husky young fellow and I think he has the executive ability to keep the party together." Then he added that "I sincerely hope they lost their horses early," because then the hunters would realize that they had no choice but to set up a good camp and prepare to spend the winter.

There was reason to believe that Will and the others were indeed spending the winter on the Lochsa. That was the assumption, anyhow, of the two men who had been visiting with Jerry Johnson and Ben Keeley when the Carlin party first arrived at the warm springs.

One of these was K.A. Larson, a farmer in the Lo Lo area west of Missoula who knew the country well, and the other was a man named Houghton. They had helped Johnson and Keeley pack in a winter's supply of food and had been visiting at the cabin for two days when the Carlin party arrived on September 26. On the 27th, as Larson and Houghton prepared to leave, they told Carlin that it would not be wise to linger; all signs pointed to an early winter. It was raining as they left, with several pack horses, en route back to Montana. Shortly after leaving the river bottom they ran into a bad snow storm that continued without letup until the snow on the trail was so deep they floundered in it. At one point the horses had such difficulty coping with the drifts that the two men considered abandoning them. They continued on, however, and after four days of struggle they arrived, worn out, at Lolo Hot Springs. When Larson arrived home, he told his family that he had met some hunters who were camped on the Lochsa with Johnson and Keeley. His daughters happened to be in Missoula later, when the Carlin party was in the news, and they told the *Missoulian* roughly what their father had told them—that Carlin and his friends had been staying with a trapper named Keeley in a shack on the Lochsa, and would probably spend the winter there.

Lieutenant Voorhies reached Lewiston with a detachment of twenty-one men from Fort Walla Walla and pitched camp near the Clearwater River east of town. The party's three wagons, each drawn by six heavy mules, were loaded with rations for three months. Voorhies had orders to proceed as far as possible with the wagons in the direction of the Lolo Pass and establish a camp to supply Lieutenant Overton's party.

William Wright, aware of the difficulties Larson and Houghton had met in fighting their way out of the river bottom, still remained convinced that the best route to Jerry Johnson's place was from Missoula, to the east. General Carlin was not so sure. He was beginning to think it more likely that if Willie and the others were to be rescued, it would be from the west; he suspected that they were avoiding the deep snows to the east and working their way down the Lochsa in a westerly direction. If so, they had a long trek ahead of them and they should be running out of food. They had taken provisions for five weeks, he recalled, and already they had been in the mountains for almost eight. The general also was aware of Larson's and Houghton's surmise, but he was not willing to assume that the hunters were spending the winter with Jerry Johnson.

There would be others going in from the Missoula end and from Weippe, he told Elliott during one exchange of telegrams; the lieutenant should consider going in from the west, up the Middle Fork of the Clearwater and into the Lochsa. But the general said he would let Elliott make that decision, based on what he might learn at Kendrick.

The hunters were up early on November 10, after a miserable night. The weather was clear and cold, so cold that there was thick ice on Carlin's raft. They ate a quick breakfast, and all but Pierce walked up to the other raft to see if they could get it off the rock where it had lodged the day before. The river appeared to be a little lower this morning, and that gave Carlin some hope that they would achieve the goal that had escaped them yesterday. But the raft was as solidly stuck as before. They aimed now to rescue the provisions. They assembled a small raft of three logs held together with ropes, and Keeley rode this across to the large raft. The others then pulled the small one back with a rope and Spencer rode it over. He and Keeley pulled the canvas cover off the big raft's baggage, loosened the ropes that secured it, and by taking a little at a time got all the provisions moved to shore. They then discovered that with the load removed, they could work the big raft free of the rock, and they landed it safely on the bank.

Keeley and Spencer were so cold by now that their fingers and feet were numb, so Himmelwright and Carlin built a warming fire before doing anything else. Spencer said he had so much pain and energy invested in that cargo now that he wanted to take no more chances with it. He said he and Keeley would pack it down on their backs if Carlin and Himmelwright would rope the raft down. They did, arriving at the lower camp in mid-afternoon.

Pierce had been keeping a fire going for Colegate, and he helped Carlin collect enough firewood to last through the night. Himmelwright decided to use the remaining daylight to scout the river below, while Spencer and Keeley went back up the river to carry down the rest of the equipment on their raft. Himmelwright got down the river only a quarter of a mile, because of the fading light, but he saw enough to lower his spirits even further.

The river was filled with rocks and rapids, and the men would be able to line the rafts through only with great difficulty; to try to run those waters would be suicidal, Himmelwright said. They decided they would take a longer walk down the river tomorrow in good light and see if the going looked better farther on.

Carlin felt especially low that evening. Among other things, he was worried about the ropes. They were badly frayed from constant rubbing against the rocks and he wasn't sure there was enough strength left in them to hold the two rafts in that current even if the men had the strength to line them down. And there was still the Black Canyon ahead of them. Carlin continued to hope that they had already reached it—since the terrain on both sides of the river seemed steep enough to him—but Spencer insisted that it was still some miles away.

And Spencer, who had been doing most of the cooking, reported that they were down to forty pounds of flour, about a week's worth. They were also out of fresh meat. Carlin had tried for days to catch fish, but in this fast, deep water they would not rise. Even the grouse that had been fairly plentiful before seemed to have disappeared.

They agreed that for the time being they would eat no more flour, and live on cornmeal and beans as long as they lasted. Keeley gazed pointedly for a moment at the three dogs lying near the fire and then raised an eyebrow in Carlin's direction. No, Carlin told him a bit sharply, they were not that desperate yet.

17 On the morning of November 11, Spencer prepared a breakfast of beans and cornmeal while the others gathered firewood. After a quick meal all but Pierce walked down the river to see what hazards lay below. Their worst fears were confirmed. For a good three miles, the Lochsa below camp was a jumble of large boulders and small, so close together that it would be impossible to float a single log between them. No one was willing at first to say what all four now realized: The rafts would be of no further use.

They had rounded a bend in the river and paused on a gravel bar covered with driftwood and split by a stream that would later be known as Lost Creek. Ahead of them the river stretched straightaway to the southwest for three quarters of a mile before disappearing between near-vertical rock buttresses. As far as they could see it was the same—boulders of all sizes, fallen logs and rapids, and the howl of the water cascading through it all.

Himmelwright sat on a log and laid his head in his hands; he had nothing to say. Carlin, after a long silence, bent over, picked up a pebble, and threw it with a curse onto the ground. Keeley and Spencer stood staring down the river for a few moments and then turned and started walking back toward camp.

Carlin slapped Himmelwright across the shoulders. Better start back, he said. They all had some talking to do, and he wanted Pierce to be a part of it. The four men picked their way wearily back up the river bank in a light, cold drizzle.

Pierce had kept the beans and cornbread warm, and after lunch Carlin suggested they all move away from the fire a bit. He was fairly sure that Colegate would pay no heed to anything said in his presence, but he would feel better, he told the others, if they were out of earshot.

It was time to take stock of their situation, Carlin said, and come to an agreement on their next move. They were now absolutely stuck. The useless rafts would have to be abandoned. By Spencer's reckoning they were at least fifty miles from the nearest help. That would be the Wilson ranch, some twenty miles below the forks of the Lochsa and the Selway. The only way to get there was on foot over some of the roughest terrain on this part of the continent. Their boots, almost destroyed by the rocks, would not last much longer. They were all weak from exposure and bruised by whipping branches and sharp rocks. In their condition, they would be lucky to make four or five miles a day, and they had food for only a week.

Spencer said they might consider returning back up the river to the hot springs, on the chance a rescue party might find them there.

But what if that didn't happen? Keeley asked. They would starve, that's what. Jerry Johnson had only enough food to feed himself through the winter, and he would guard it with his life.

Spencer withdrew the suggestion; he realized on second thought that there would be no rescue party breaking through those deep snows, at least not until spring. Spencer knew something about the upper Lochsa in winter, having tramped through the region on snowshoes with his former partner, Wright—and remembering Wright gave Spencer a momentary lift. Wright knew that Spencer was in the Bitterroots with the Carlin party, and Wright would surely start making inquiries if the party didn't come out. It was a cheering thought, but only for a moment. Even if people started looking for them, how far would they get in this weather? Horses were useless and snowshoes were too slow. Carlin was right; they were absolutely stuck.

Well, Carlin said, they couldn't sit here and starve. They would have to walk out. Did anyone believe there was any way out but down the river? No one did. So that was decided. They would start in the morning, climbing the side hills as high as they had to in order to avoid the nearly impassable Black Canyon of the Lochsa.

And now, what to do about Colegate?

It was the question no one wished to address, although everyone knew what the answer must be. The sick man obviously could not walk out of this wilderness. He could barely sit up, he was so far gone. Both of his legs, from the knees down, were so consumed by gangrene that the odor was unbearable. His presence of mind had become a fragmentary thing, and even now as the others considered his fate, he sat by the fire with his chin on his chest, engulfed in his blankets, showing no sign of awareness.

Pierce, who spent more time with Colegate than anyone else, had tried to keep track of his glimmers of humanity, mainly because

Pierce was afraid he might otherwise come to think of the cook as simply a thing to keep warm. Pierce wondered out loud whether someone should stay with Colegate now to keep him warm in his last days.

Nobody liked that idea. As Keeley said, Colegate could linger on while someone sat there uselessly waiting to bury him. Besides, as Himmelwright pointed out, that would mean leaving a share of the remaining food behind. Carlin wondered if anyone would like to volunteer to stay here with Colegate until he died and then try to walk out alone. He got no takers.

Well, Carlin said, glancing over his shoulder at the immobile Colegate, it made no sense to stay here with him until he died, for that would mean self-sacrifice beyond all reason. And they had their families to think about.

For God's sake get to the point, Keeley cried out. They all knew what they had to do, he said; there was no point in going on and on about it while sitting here in the rain. He stood up in frustration and strode to the tent and back, then sat down again on his log.

All right, all right, Carlin said. They would start walking in the morning, and Colegate could come along with them as far as he could. After all, he added, they didn't know whether any of them would make it all the way out.

This still didn't satisfy Keeley, who demanded that Carlin face the facts. One fact, he said, was that Colegate could not walk. He could not walk from his chair to the river. He could not walk far enough to feed his own fire. He was a helpless invalid on the edge of death. Another fact was that no one was strong enough to carry him. Therefore fact three, which was that the rest of them, in order to save themselves if possible, were going to abandon him here on the river bank because they had no other choice.

And let's not forget, Keeley said, that the son of a bitch brought this on himself.

This little speech seemed to end the discussion. Nobody spoke for or against Keeley's assessment of the facts, although there were some things that might have been said had everyone not been so tired and frightened.

Himmelwright was thinking that it was true about Colegate: He had brought his fate down upon himself by lying at the outset about his health and later refusing to admit that he was sick. But Himmelwright also could recall the night on Bald Mountain, now so long ago, when he had prayed that Colegate was not sick although he feared that he was. He did not want to hear such bad news then, and was much relieved when he didn't.

Carlin wondered how different things might have been if he had only remembered to get in touch with Dr. Webb before leaving Kendrick. Webb would have told him what he was getting into. But he had trusted Colegate and taken him at his word. He could feel uneasy about that, he thought now, but he didn't need to feel guilty.

Spencer, as angry at Colegate as the others, couldn't focus the anger as sharply. His advice had been to get out of this canyon in the first week of October, before the heavy snows descended. His advice went unheeded, but he couldn't blame Colegate for that.

Keeley's torrent of "facts" bothered Pierce the most, but he knew better than to show it. He agreed that Colegate's death, when it came, would be his own doing, but he remembered Spencer's unwelcome advice to abandon the hunt and his own failure to more vigorously support it. They were in this fix partly because of Colegate's empty assurances, but partly also because the hunters were having too much fun to take their problem seriously. Pierce knew as well as Spencer that they should get out while they could, but since he was only along for the ride, so to speak, and the tenderfoot of the bunch, he didn't press his views on the rest. So he had to figure, Pierce thought, that some of the blame was his.

Carlin had tried to soften the edges of the decision that had to be made by carefully pointing out options and consequences. But Keeley had struck at the heart of the matter, and more: He had put the blame squarely on Colegate, and forced the others into unwelcome reflections on their own roles in the tragedy. It occurred to Pierce that Keeley, for all his rough behavior and sometimes rash decisions, was the one innocent man in the party. He may have been too quick to lay blame, Pierce thought, but no one had more right.

That evening Carlin wrote in his diary: "Everyone feels very much dispirited at having to leave Colegate. There is hardly a word spoken by anyone tonight."

18 William Wright by now was convinced that his partner, Martin Spencer, and Spencer's clients were in deep trouble. He was afraid others might not share his awareness of their danger,

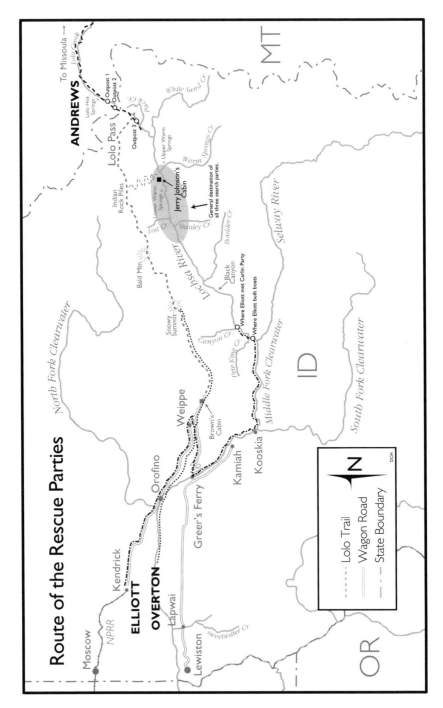

Route of the Rescue Parties

and he sent a wire to Kendrick, urging that it be passed along to anyone who might be in touch with the general. It said the hunters could be starving by now and that their horses, if they still had them, would be of no use.

The word got back to General Carlin, who reached Elliott by telegraph at Spokane. He told Elliott that instead of going to Kendrick he should take his detachment to Fort Missoula by way of Fort Sherman at Coeur d'Alene, Idaho. At Fort Sherman he was to pick up several more men and some mules. He told Elliott that Wright seemed to think there was a better chance to get through from the east than from the west.

Before leaving Spokane, Elliott and the enlisted men bought heavy winter clothing, out of their own pockets, and Elliott bought or borrowed snowshoes and an arctic sleeping bag, as well as several toboggans. He looked up a friend, an experienced guide named J.P.M. Richards, who drew him a map of the eastern end of the Lolo Trail showing camping spots and details of the terrain.

Elliott told a reporter from the *Spokane Review* that he would pick up horses, mules, and a few more men, at Fort Sherman and then go to Missoula. Using the animals to break trail through the snow, he would attempt to cross the divide into the headwaters of the Lochsa and begin the search for the snowbound Carlin party. Elliott's troops would take the animals as far as they could, he said, and then resort to snowshoes and toboggans. It could be an all-winter campaign, Elliott told the reporter, but he was prepared for that.

Elliott and his men boarded the train again the next morning and left Spokane for the brief trip to Fort Sherman, an Army post at the northern end of Lake Coeur d'Alene. The fort, on the outskirts of the town of Coeur d'Alene, was one of many that had been scattered across the region as a means of keeping the tribes under control. By 1893 the fort had long outlived its mission and was nearing the end of its life. General Carlin knew the place well because he had been posted there, as a colonel, before taking command of the Department of the Columbia at Vancouver Barracks. He was still remembered well at Fort Sherman and in the town, and one of the lake's important bays was later named for him. Instead of protecting the settlers from the Indians, Fort Sherman's men most recently had been trying to maintain labor peace in the hardrock mining districts east of Coeur d'Alene. In the previous year, while he was in command there, General Carlin had been ordered to take troops to the Kellogg-Wallace area and help put down an uprising of the miners against the mine owners and managers.

Elliott was disappointed on reaching Fort Sherman to find that the detachment that was to join him was not ready to go. That meant he was in danger of missing the paddle-wheel steamboat that was about to leave for Harrison near the southern end of Lake Coeur d'Alene, connecting there with the O.R.&N. line to Missoula. Should the boat leave without him, he would have to take his troops and his horses and mules back to Spokane by train, and thence by the Northern Pacific to Missoula. It would cost him a day that he didn't want to lose. Elliott rode down to the dock and explained to the boat's skipper, one Captain Sanborn, why he had to get to Harrison that day. Sanborn was sympathetic. He had known General Carlin and had met the general's son, Will. He would be glad to hold the boat, he said, and Elliott rode back to the fort.

There he discovered that the packer who was to join the party, a man named Hager, couldn't leave now because his brother had dropped dead. They would find a packer later, Elliott decided, and he ordered the preparations to proceed. While Captain Sanborn waited with steam up, Elliott and his men prepared to load eight horses and ten mules, plus equipment and provisions. When the detachment finally steamed away from the dock at Coeur d'Alene, it included, besides the men from E Troop, Dr. Nathan Purviance, Sergeant Guy Norton, and Corporal William Harris, the latter two of the 4th Cavalry. Norton had volunteered for this duty because Himmelwright was an old shooting chum of his; he confided to the others that Abe had always called him "Fatty Norton." Elliott now had eight men and eighteen animals.

Captain Sanborn had barely left the dock when a small boat came alongside with a telegram for Lieutenant Elliott. It was from General Carlin, ordering him not to go to Missoula as now planned, but to go instead to Kendrick, the original destination. Captain Merriam had notified the general by wire that there had been a bad washout on the Northern Pacific Railroad between Spokane and Missoula.

Elliott decided to continue up the lake and catch the O.R.&N. at Harrison, but a subsequent telegram ordered him to proceed to Kendrick by way of Spokane. He returned back down the lake to

Coeur d'Alene and caught the Northern Pacific, reaching Spokane late on the night of November 11.

The rest of the detachment left Spokane the next morning at 7, but Elliott stayed behind long enough to buy two toboggans and three pairs of snowshoes. Dr. Purviance had remained at Fort Sherman, but the packer, Hager, apparently having settled the affairs of his dead brother, rejoined the party at Spokane. Elliott left Spokane by passenger train at 9 a.m. on the 12th and met the rest of his detachment later that morning at Oakesdale, Washington.

If the lieutenant had any doubts about the reliability of his new packer, they vanished as the train neared Moscow, Idaho, some ninety miles south of Coeur d'Alene. The car containing the horses and mules jumped the track, and Hager, riding in the boxcar just ahead of it, leaped off at the risk of his life and signaled the conductor. The train came to a stop with the horse car still attached and no great damage was done.

"Hager was badly bruised," Elliott reported later, "but continued on with [the] detachment and did his duty like a man while he was with me."

The train reached Kendrick at 6 p.m. There Elliott hired a guide, Henry Ables, who claimed to know the Bitterroot country well, and another packer and snowshoe expert, a man from the North Fork of the Clearwater named Norbert LaMothe. LaMothe presumably replaced the injured Hager.

❦

Meanwhile, the Northern Pacific had repaired the washout east of Cataldo and Lieutenant C.H. Martin of the 14th Infantry, General Carlin's aide-de-camp, was riding the train from Vancouver Barracks to Missoula. Merriam had been ordered back to Kendrick, and Martin was to help lead a rescue party into the Bitterroots from the east. When Martin reached Fort Missoula he found that Colonel A.S. Burt was away and that Major Chambers McKibbin was the acting commandant. McKibbin assigned Martin to a search party to be led by Captain George Andrews, 25th Infantry, with Martin Spencer's partner, William Wright, as the guide.

Wright was fairly sure that he knew where Spencer was, and he thought there was a good chance he could get there, on snowshoes if necessary.

On November 10, the day Lieutenant Elliott was in Spokane for the second time, Captain Andrews led his party out of Fort Missoula enroute to Lolo Hot Springs, on the Montana side of the pass. In his command were fifty-three men of Company F of the black 25th Infantry, three escort wagons pulled by four mules each, three teamsters, a supply of grain, and fifteen days' rations for the men.

Ahead of them lay forty miles of primitive road, deep in mud, and much of it under the swollen waters of Lolo Creek. The troops, armed with axes, picks, and shovels, had to make frequent road repairs so the wagons could get through. At one point, in order to lighten the loads, Andrews halted the company at a vacant cabin and left some of his rations there along with a small detachment to guard them.

On the night of the 12th the company was overtaken by its pack train, which had started with one wagon that had to be abandoned because it held up progress. First Lieutenant Carroll A. Devol, 25th Infantry, in charge of the train, was accompanied by the guide Wright, Lieutenant Martin, and two packers, Sergeant J. Buck of B Troop, 10th Cavalry, and Corporal J.W. Green, Company H, 25th Infantry. The train itself consisted of five pack mules.

Andrews managed to get all of his three wagons, now lightened, to Lolo Hot Springs at noon on the 13th after three days of hard, slow travel. The wagons had forded the creek forty-eight times. To avoid having to march his men through the water, Andrews had led them on foot trails along the sides of mountains as often as he could. These trails, like most of the journey, he described later as "very difficult."

Captain Andrews's assignment was to support Lieutenant Devol's small group by supplying rations, breaking trail, and providing other support until the animals could go no farther, after which Devol, Wright, and a few others would continue on snowshoes. If all went well, Wright would be able to lead this small contingent to Jerry Johnson's cabin near the warm springs and bring the Carlin party out.

On the day Andrews reached Lolo Hot Springs, Lieutenant Elliott and his four enlisted men were riding on the wagon road to Weippe, having left Kendrick at 5 o'clock that morning. Somewhere behind them, the packer LaMothe and Elliott's new guide, Ables, were bringing the pack train, lightly loaded because Elliott intended to drive the mules hard. The pack train camped that night at the ferry station on the North Fork of the Clearwater River, some twenty-five miles east of Kendrick. Elliott, making better time, overtook Lieutenant Overton four miles beyond the ferry, and proceeded on to Reed's ranch, forty-two miles from Kendrick. He spent the night there and reached John Gaffney's farm at Weippe at 9 the next morning.

Gaffney was well known throughout the region for his intimate knowledge of the area and for his willingness to help anyone passing through. Gaffney's advice, as it turned out, proved crucial to Elliott. The two men spent much of that day poring over maps, some of them crudely hand-drawn. During their conversation Elliott decided he would not go into the Bitterroots on the Lolo Trail after all. Gaffney had convinced him that he would be better able to penetrate that region by way of the Lochsa River, which Gaffney knew as the North Fork of the Middle Fork of the Clearwater. He would leave the Lolo Trail to Overton and his party, who were not far behind him.

When Overton reached Weippe, with his horses, mules, packers, and his guide Tom Beall, Elliott turned over to him two toboggans, three pairs of snowshoes, and the arctic sleeping bag. Overton would need them on the Lolo far more than Elliott would need them on the Lochsa. The next morning at 7, Elliott left Weippe for Kamiah, a tiny settlement on what is now known as the Middle Fork of the Clearwater—again in advance of his pack train. And Overton proceeded on toward Brown's Cabin and the Lolo Trail.

From Weippe, Elliott's route took him down the mountain north of the Clearwater to Greer's Ferry, and then up the south bank of the river to Kamiah, an ancient wintering place of the Nez Perce Indians. There Elliott bought some more supplies, figuring that the mules were broken in enough now to carry heavier loads. He left the goods there to be picked up by the pack train when it arrived, and rode up the river another six miles before calling it a day.

On the Lochsa, some seventy miles upstream from Kamiah, the one-time pleasure hunters were spending part of this Sunday morning, November 12, getting packed. It was not a good day for beginning a journey. A disheartening cold drizzle had befronted them at dawn, getting everything wet. Pierce and Spencer had managed to keep a fire going through the night, but a cold wind had been blowing down the river, making it impossible to get warm.

They had decided they were on the wrong side of the Lochsa. There was no good side, as Carlin put it, but the south side was worse because it got almost no sun. The north side would be better, but to get there would be difficult. It would mean poling the raft across a fierce current that could easily whirl them downstream into a death-dealing collision with a rock ledge that jutted into the river below.

The goal was a point of rocks some fifty yards down on the opposite bank. Keeley said that if they put their minds and muscles to it, he was sure they could make the crossing and cheat the current. Carlin and Himmelwright were not so sure. Carlin pointed out that the current curved in toward the side of the river they were on; they would not only have to cross it, but pole the heavy raft against it in order to reach the other side. He didn't think that was possible.

What did they have to lose? Keeley wanted to know. Their chances of seeing civilization again were not so hot no matter which side of the river they started out on. The advantage of being on the north side, he said, would offset the hazards of the crossing.

Spencer said that Keeley had made a good point. Walking out on the south side would be much more difficult because of deeper snow and steeper terrain. And when they reached the south fork, later to be known as the Selway, they would have to be on the north bank anyway. So they might as well cross here, while they still had the raft.

Himmelwright then proposed a solution that settled the matter. He pointed to a tall white pine near the bank not far from where they were standing in the shelter of a large cedar. He suggested that they chop the pine down so that it fell across the river. Then, he said, they could pole the raft downstream of the tree while tied to it, and the rope would hold them against the current.

After a skimpy breakfast of beans and cornbread, Keeley took the ax and walked over to the tall pine that rose some fifty feet into the sodden sky. He began to chop expertly, with rhythmical blows, while the others started to separate the things they would take from those they would leave behind.

They kept two flat stew pans, filled the smaller one with coffee, and fitted it inside the larger one. They kept two small frying pans. Himmelwright packed his camera, which was small and light, and Carlin took the film out of his and threw away the box. Except for a few small objects—a knife, spoons, a few coins, a small hatchet, fishing tackle, and their guns—they packed nothing else but their blankets, their dwindling store of food, and an ax. They still had a few pounds of flour, some cornmeal, the beans, and a chunk of bacon they had been using to grease the bread pan. Spencer estimated that if they found no game and caught no fish, this food would last them about five days.

His estimate made no allowance for feeding the three dogs.

The packing done, Himmelwright went down to where Keeley was whacking chips off the tree and took his turn with the ax. Carlin picked up his gun and went hunting, thinking without much hope that he might get some meat for the camp. He found no signs of game and saw only a single grouse, which eluded him. He got out his book of flies and tried fishing, again with no luck.

At noon it began to snow, and at 3 o'clock the pine still stood. By now it was clear that the long hike out would not begin today. Pierce and Spencer went looking for another night's firewood, and Carlin decided the time had come to break the bad news to Colegate.

He approached the sick man reluctantly, not sure how Colegate would respond. He began by saying the party had got something of a shock, and now had to change its plan for getting down the river. Colegate said nothing, but nodded, and turned his eyes away from Carlin to the river. Carlin then told him that it was no longer possible to proceed on rafts; the river below was too full of boulders and rapids. Therefore, it would be necessary for them to walk out, if they could. He said that from now on it would be every man for himself, and each should bear his own burden.

Colegate continued to stare at the river. He reached out from the blanket draped over his shoulders, and pulled it closer.

Did he understand? Carlin asked him.

Colegate gave Carlin a blank look, and nodded, and Carlin got the impression that the cook was nodding not because he understood what Carlin had told him, but that he just wanted him to go away. Carlin realized with some regret that Colegate was not used to being spoken to; communicating with him had become so difficult that the others had given up. Carlin's words had fallen not on deaf ears but on a confused and wandering mind on the verge of closing down.

Carlin walked back to where the other four were tending to camp chores and told them he had given the bad news to Colegate.

How did he take it? Himmelwright asked.

It was hard to say, Carlin said; it apparently had made no impression on him.

19 During the night the skies cleared, and Spencer awoke early enough to see a tapestry of stars winking down at him from above the canyon. As the stars faded, he lay in his blankets sorting out the various ways he felt about the day that was soon to begin. He hoped Abe's plan to cross the river with the pine tree's help would work, but he worried that it might not. He was glad the rafting was over because he was afraid of this river, but he knew he and the others were in for some hard hiking and climbing. They had a long way to go and the Black Canyon still lay ahead. Would they have enough food? What if they found no game? The river was full of fish, but they had not caught any lately. Spencer deliberately put Colegate out of his mind because, he told himself, Colegate was no longer a factor. He could drive himself crazy thinking about Colegate, and what would be the point of it?

The sick man himself dozed on the kitchen box beside the fire that Pierce had tended since midnight. It was about the last thing Pierce would be able to do for Colegate, and with each stick he added, he hoped to God that the cook would continue in his doldrum and not come alert on the last day. As long as Colegate remained in his stupor, it would not be so hard to walk away from him when the time came. Pierce could think of nothing worse than to hear Colegate calling out to them to stay or take him along.

Pierce took some of the burning embers from Colegate's fire and carried them in a tin plate to the small circle of rocks where he and Spencer would cook breakfast. Spencer was out of his blankets now, pulling on his boots. He couldn't believe it wasn't raining or snowing, Spencer said. A whole day of sunshine—what a gift that would be. Carlin and Keeley came to the fire as the darkness retreated, followed shortly by Himmelwright, who had another idea.

The big pine tree, he now noticed, was not going to fall correctly the way it was leaning. It was leaning over the river, he said, but too much in the downriver direction; if they felled it that way, it would be hardly any help at all in getting the raft across.

Then what should they do? Carlin asked.

Fall another tree against it, Himmelwright replied. And he pointed to a pine standing not far from the first. If they chopped the second tree just right, it would fall against the big one, causing the big one to drop into the river in just the right direction. Himmelwright said that was the only way he could think of to make the big pine fall where they needed it. Did anybody disagree? Nobody did, but there was some grumbling because there were now two trees to chop down instead of one.

Breakfast was over well before the first sunbeams fell on the river bank. Himmelwright took the ax down to the second tree and began to chop. The ax Himmelwright used was the only one in camp, but there was the hatchet, and Keeley took that down to the big pine and started working on it. Carlin and Spencer packed the cooking gear and blankets, and carried them to the bank beside the raft. They left the tent standing, along with the fly, because they didn't plan to carry them out. They left Colegate where he was on the kitchen box because the box also would be left behind.

As Keeley and Himmelwright laid into the trees, Carlin took his rifle and went looking for game. If he could shoot a deer or an elk, they could cut it into pieces easy to carry and have meat for several days. Carlin didn't have much hope of that happening, since signs had become scarce, and it didn't. After a couple of hours of fruitless hiking over gravel bars and through heavy brush, he returned empty-handed to camp.

By noon the woodchoppers, spelled by Spencer and Pierce, had laid the smaller pine against the big one, and by 1 o'clock both were ready to fall. Spencer motioned the others back, and with the ax he dealt three blows that wrung from the tree the tearing sound of live wood splitting. Spencer jumped away as the big pine began to fall. It arched over the rocks and plunged into the river with a thunderous boom that shook the ground and sent water flying. As it settled, the men on the bank watched it roll in the current, dip and bob, and then sink until the top third of the tree was out of sight.

They hadn't expected this. They had assumed the whole length of the tree would float, giving them something to rope onto almost all the way to the other shore.

Damn, Spencer said, still holding the ax. Himmelwright felt betrayed, since the idea had been his, and he said only that the pine tree shouldn't have done that. The others had nothing to say until Carlin declared that what they had left to work with was better than nothing. They could still rope onto the tree for most of the way, he said, and if they were careful they could make the opposite bank. They had picked out a landing spot some fifty yards downstream where a rocky point jutted into the water. If they missed it, there would be no second chance, and they probably would all drown in the rapids and eddies below. They therefore planned to make a first crossing with the raft unloaded, drop Himmelwright on the opposite shore, then return for Colegate and the packs. On the second crossing, if they were in danger of missing the landing they could throw a rope to Abe and trust him to help them to shore.

Keeley volunteered to tie the long rope to the downed tree. He took off his pants and boots, thanking the Lord for this sunny day, and waded out on the upstream side of the pine, clinging to the branches. When he got out too far for wading, he pulled himself forward from branch to branch until he reached the farthest part of the tree that was above water. He tied the end of the rope to a thick limb, because the trunk was too far under, and made his way back. Gasping and shivering, he took off his wet underwear, toweled himself with Pierce's shirt, and put on his dry pants and boots. It was the coldest water he had ever dipped himself into, he muttered as he slid into his suspenders.

Pierce remained on the bank with Colegate while Carlin crawled out on the prostrate pine, flipping the rope across the tree to the downstream side. He got as much of the rope over as he could, then crawled back. It would come the rest of the way, he said, when they put some pull on it. He gave the rope to Keeley and said he and Himmelwright would pole the raft while Keeley held the rope that anchored them to the tree. When they reached the other side, Abe would get off and they would haul and pole the raft back to the south bank.

The crossing went as planned. Himmelwright leaped off just upstream from the point of rocks, with a whoop and a feeling of elation. The others returned on the raft to the south bank, landing a few yards below the starting point, and walked up to where Pierce and Spencer waited. Carlin and Keeley gathered up the packs, and Pierce and Spencer lifted Colegate off the box and carried him by his armpits down to the raft. With the dogs aboard and Colegate braced on his seat, Keeley again took the rope while the other three picked up their poles. They had only one bad moment on that final crossing, when the current near the north bank threatened to grab the raft and run with it. Carlin tossed the short rope to Himmelwright and by poling and roping they made the landing. They carried Colegate off, and while Pierce gathered wood for a fire, Carlin said he would like to see what the current would have done to the raft had they not been able to land it. He untied the short rope that tethered it and tossed it onto the bank. Then he gave the raft a push with his pole and watched as the current caught it, whirled it around, and carried it spinning and bouncing for some two hundred yards into a jumble of large rocks left of the center of the river.

Pierce built a small fire near Colegate, who was sitting now on a piece of driftwood some twenty feet from the water's edge and facing downstream, in the direction they would go. They had only a couple of hours of good daylight left, Carlin said. They had better get going. Pierce asked Colegate if there was anything he needed. Colegate, who had not said a word all day, remained silent. Spencer picked up his bedroll, held it for a moment and put it down again. The walking would be hard enough, he said, without lugging blankets. He was leaving his behind. Good idea, Keeley said, and he left his blankets, which he had started to roll up, on the ground. Carlin and Himmelwright did the same, and so did Pierce, after some hesitation. There was now a pile of blankets on the ground beside Colegate. The sick man reached out, pulled one blanket off the top, and laid it across his knees. Pierce took it and rolled it, putting one of Colegate's shirts inside, and with two short pieces of rope he tied it onto Colegate's back. Pierce intended it to mean that they were expecting him to come along with them. He realized as he made the gesture that it was for his peace of mind, not Colegate's. But it was for Colegate that he scurried about for a little more firewood, which he laid down close to the cook's blanket-wrapped feet.

The others were waiting for him a bit impatiently as he pulled on his pack and picked up his rifle. Then they started to walk out—Spencer in the lead, followed by Carlin, Himmelwright, Keeley, and Pierce. The two bear dogs tagged along, rummaging in the underbrush as usual. They made their way between the rocks that formed the little headland, up a small rise, and around a bend. Pierce paused at the last moment and looked back. Colegate sat quietly, his head bent forward, the afternoon sun shining on his gray felt hat. He appeared to be gazing into the fire at his feet, and he gave no sign that he knew what was happening. But as Pierce watched, Colegate stood up, balanced unsteadily for a moment, and took a few steps in the direction the others had gone. He stopped, then took another halting step, and stopped again. He was still standing there with Daisy beside him when Pierce, in a turmoil of confusion and despair, turned away, and hurried around the bend toward the others.

◆━━━◆

People had been here, there was evidence of that. From the rocky point a steep trail of sorts wound up the bank and ended under a fallen log. Spencer found a compass in the grass that some earlier traveler had lost or discarded. The men had begun to traverse a steep slope almost immediately after leaving camp, finding their way through trees and heavy brush on game trails and the remnants of Indian paths. Much of the time there was nothing to guide their feet but their own instincts. At one point they came to the edge of a deep ravine that cut a gash in the slope from far above them all the way down to the river. They scrambled to the bottom of it, clinging to bushes and fir branches, and crossed a rushing creek, one by one, on a log. Then they struggled up the other side. Keeley was carrying the ax, Himmelwright, Carlin, and Pierce were

Baking bread in the pine bough lean-to.

carrying their guns, and all five were laboring under their packs. They stopped frequently to rest, and when they did, the remaining two dogs lay down, panting, and rested too. After the first hour, Carlin began to have second thoughts about the virtues of hiking out. Then he remembered the sight of the raft breaking apart on the rocks below their last camp. This was better, he decided, as they continued climbing.

Spencer said they should seek the high ground, so as to be above the cliffs that bordered the river in places such as the Black Canyon. But they should not get so high that they were wading through deep snow. They would not need the river, he said, because there were enough streams here to keep their canteens full. But Carlin reminded Spencer that they were running low on food. They shouldn't get so far from the river that they couldn't fish. Keeley then reminded Carlin that even down on the river he hadn't been able to catch any fish—at least not lately. Himmelwright, who could tell that Carlin was getting riled, pointed out that Carlin had been fishing with flies. He needed spoons. But they had no spoons, Keeley said. If they decided to fish, they'd make some, Himmelwright replied, and Keeley only grunted.

After two hours of hard traveling both up and down the canyon wall, they reached a broad flat not far above the river. Here the way became easier and the prospects seemed brighter. Near the flat's western edge, Spencer said they had walked far enough. It was nearly 4:30 and the sun had dropped below the ridge across the Lochsa. Spencer estimated the distance covered at about two and a half miles, which wasn't bad considering the rough terrain and the loads they were packing. He would cook the supper, he said, if the others would gather some pine boughs and build a lean-to they could all sleep under.

Spencer put some beans to soaking in a pan of water, and baked a skillet of bread in the folding reflector oven. The men would have the bread, with coffee, for supper, and boiled beans and more bread in the morning. There was nothing for the dogs. As the men munched on bread washed down with coffee, the two bear dogs, Idaho and Montana, lay nearby, intently watching. Pierce, watching the dogs watch him eat, was haunted by his last sight of Colegate and his dog. He had said nothing about this yet to the others, but he knew that he probably would, in time.

As one of two chief marshaling points for the Carlin search operation, Kendrick was enjoying perhaps the liveliest November in its history. The St. Elmo Hotel was almost always filled with soldiers, newspaper reporters, and provisioners. People who had never heard of the town were seeing the Kendrick place name in papers throughout the Northwest. Every train that arrived carried somebody involved in the search or reporting on it, and every day, new reports of horrendous weather reached Kendrick, causing the locals to advise the soldiers that they might as well go back to their barracks. Either the lost hunters were safely camped someplace or they were not; and if they were not, there was nothing the soldiers could do about it.

In normal years, the mountains were considered safe until October 15. But in this mid-October there had been five feet of snow on the Lolo Trail. On November 10, the snow depth in some places was eight feet. Animals could not move through that much snow, and men could move only on snowshoes. If the snow was soft, they could not move at all.

Charles Colegate, who had wondered at first why so few were interested in his father's fate, now wondered why so many were. It would only later occur to him that it wasn't his father they were interested in; the public didn't know or care about George Colegate's problem because the few Kendrick people who did know didn't talk much to reporters. The public's attention was focused on the general's son and his two companions—the New York men, as they came to be called. The dominant feeling in Kendrick was that these New York men had become the victims of their own eastern foolishness. The townspeople, who lived close enough to the wilderness to respect it, had all heard about the rancher who met the Carlin party at Brown's cabin and warned the hunters. And they had heard from the rancher himself that young Carlin then seemed pretty cocky for a tenderfoot.

Charles wanted desperately to go out on the search with one of the military parties. He begged Captain Merriam to take him, saying he knew how to handle himself in the woods. He talked to Lieutenant Voorhies, to Lieutenant Overton, and to Lieutenant Elliott, and they all said no. When Dr. Webb learned of this through Fannie Colegate, he immediately wired a note to Charles, telling him his post was in Kendrick and he was not to abandon it. The Army officers had taken a liking to the young man, and Merriam told Charles that the Army considered him a part of the rescue operation just as much as though he were out on the trail. To show his sincerity, Merriam got the general's permission to put Charles on the Army's tab at the St. Elmo Hotel.

George Colegate's catheters, wrapped in white tissue paper, still sat in their box behind the hotel's registration desk, and Charles considered it one of his duties to make certain the clerk checked the box every few days. Dr. Webb was pretty sure Colegate was dead by now, but he didn't tell Fannie or Charles that, and the box behind the desk gave the boy some sense of hope and usefulness.

Although Fannie Colegate had six other children, she wanted Charles home. He had been long enough in Kendrick, and for no good purpose, she told her friends. She was going to send for him. But first she wrote to Dr. Webb, asking him if he thought there was any chance of George coming out of the wilderness alive. Webb replied that it was impossible to rule that out, since the human body was a marvelous mechanism, but he thought the chances were ninety to ten that George was already dead. And he added that George might not be the only one. Webb had been following the news of the various search parties, and it seemed clear to him by now that even if the lost hunters did come out of the wilderness, it would not be to Kendrick; everyone was saying there was too much snow on the Lolo Trail. Even if they did come out to Kendrick, with George still alive, there were others in the town who could see to his care and his transportation to Spokane. Charles might as well come home, he said. He didn't tell Fannie that he was surprised the boy was still there. When he told Charles that his duty lay in Kendrick, it was only to dissuade him from joining one of the search parties.

Webb's letter arrived on a Wednesday. On Thursday Fannie wrote to Charles, enclosing some money, and told him to take the next train home.

Charles had developed a liking for Kendrick, and he had made friends there. One of them was Corporal Harris of the 4th Cavalry Regiment. Harris had been acting as a sort of courier between Kendrick and Weippe, and he had let Charles go with him on a couple of these horseback trips. Charles was convinced by now that he wanted to join the Army, the cavalry in particular. He admired all the cavalry men he met, especially Harris, who was a debonair, non-stressable, take-it-or-leave-it sort of fellow. When he told Harris he would like to be in the cavalry some day, Harris told him to forget it. Army life looked pretty good out here on detached service, Harris said, but it was not so good in camp. There was nothing in the world more boring, he said, than barracks life. Day after day of being shouted at, ordered around; of cleaning stables, standing inspection, and never any excitement—at least that had been his experience. None of this discouraged Charles. One day he asked Captain Merriam if the captain thought he would make a good soldier, and Merriam said he had no doubt of it, no doubt at all. Merriam also told Charles that if he wanted to learn good soldiering, he probably should spend less time with Corporal Harris. This surprised Charles, who had great respect for his friend, and he asked Captain Merriam to explain. Merriam said he could describe Corporal Harris in one word: sloppy. But he told Charles that Harris might still be a good man in a pinch.

Charles didn't quite understand all this, but he was pleased with the captain's assessment of him—so pleased that he didn't mind that he had to leave Kendrick on the next train for Post Falls.

20 On November 14, a Tuesday, Captain Andrews sent two wagons back to the vacant cabin where he had previously stored some of the provisions, with orders to bring the rations in. Then, with Lieutenant Devol and William Wright, he made a horseback reconnaissance of the area in the vicinity of Lolo Pass. The party found three to four feet of snow on the divide, well packed and passable for horses. The three followed the trail into the Bitterroots for some twelve miles, and agreed that the prospects of getting in by this route were good. Andrews decided he would keep his base camp at Lolo Hot Springs, on the Montana side, and establish three outposts on the trail leading west. The first would be nine miles from base on the meadows of the Little Clearwater. Outpost number two would be five miles farther on, at the top of the divide; and number three would be six miles from there near the headwaters of the Lochsa.

These posts would create a supply line some twenty miles long from base camp into the Bitterroots. From outpost number three, Wright would proceed some sixty miles by horseback and snowshoes to Jerry Johnson's cabin. There was no snow to speak of at this time in the Bitterroot Valley in Montana or on Lolo Creek, and Wright was confident that there also would be little or no snow in the valley of the Lochsa.

Lieutenant Devol had not felt well that morning, and by the time the three had returned to the hot springs he was worse. Captain Andrews told him to stay in camp for the time being; he would assume full responsibility for the operation.

Lieutenant Martin volunteered to take charge of outpost three, and Andrews placed Second Lieutenant V.A. Caldwell of his own company in charge of the pack train and the search party proper, as he later defined the assignment. Andrews himself would look after the base camp and outposts one and two.

The next morning, the ailing Devol left for Fort Missoula and Caldwell put together a pack train of seven mules supplied with eight days' grain and rations for seven men who were, or would be, manning the outposts. This train set out for the Lochsa and reached outpost three that evening. The party included Lieutenant Martin, the guide, Wright, and two enlisted men. At 8 p.m., after they had set up a camp, it started to rain. By midnight it was snowing.

The next day, November 16, Andrews sent detachments of six men each to outposts one and two, on foot with two days' rations. Andrews had no mules to send with them because the wagons he had sent back for the stored provisions had not returned. The non-commissioned officers in charge of the three outposts had orders that were much alike: Get breakfast at daylight, then send two men and a mule in each direction until each detachment meets one coming from the opposite direction. On meeting, these detachments were to exchange orders, information, and supplies, and return to their own posts. The men were to carry axes, blaze the trail thoroughly, and cut out the worst of the fallen timber. In this way, Andrews hoped to keep the trail open and supplies and information flowing from base camp to all three outposts and from the outposts back to base.

Things did not work out exactly as planned. Sergeant William J. Haynes was to establish outpost two, on the divide, when pack mules with tents and supplies arrived at outpost one. But Andrews had no mules to send to outpost one. Haynes and his party set out for the divide anyhow, and established outpost two in deep snow with almost no shelter.

The detachment at outpost one, under Corporal Jonah Parker, was without tents on the night of the 16th, but he built a "hunter's camp," according to instructions passed along from Andrews.

Caldwell and Wright found the Lochsa choked with ice and rising so rapidly that it was becoming impassable. One of the mules stumbled while crossing the stream and fell, and would have drowned had Wright not whipped out his knife and cut the pack loose. Wright himself lost his rifle during the struggle to save the mule. The men and mules returned to outpost three, and Caldwell sent word to Andrews that it would be impossible to go down that stream. He suggested using the Lolo Trail instead, setting up two additional outposts beyond outpost three, and he proceeded to do that. From the last of these, Wright would go alone on snowshoes to "old Jerry's" place.

On November 16, Caldwell sent word back to Martin, at outpost 3, that he was four miles from there. "The mules are playing out. Guide and packer say we can't get them through. One mule staked himself and can't go further.* Guide and I are going on with three mules and our horses; please keep the trail open and work grain down as far as possible. If we are not back in six days, something has happened."

The next day Martin sent the following message to Andrews:

> River trail found impracticable. Took over five hours to make less than two miles. Caldwell, guide and packer will attempt Lo Lo trail today. Sixty miles over, with thirty miles snow to buck. Will be necessary to establish two more outposts. Please send over immediately all oats and rations you can spare, also four more men. No more tents necessary, good cabin here. Several mules in bad condition.

Captain Andrews acquired a riding mule that day, and rode down Lolo Creek in search of the missing wagons. He found them, and the mules, at the cabin where the provisions had been left. Because of the cold nights, the ice had frozen on the edges of the creek, narrowing the channel and causing the water to rise. The creek was now too deep to ford. Andrews ordered the wagons left with the detachment, and pack saddles put on the mules. He and two civilian teamsters, Billy and Barney Wheeler, loaded as much grain and rations as six mules could carry, and Andrews returned to base camp. The wagons would be left where they were until spring.

As soon as he arrived at the hot springs, Andrews dispatched the teamsters and the loaded mules to outposts one and two. Two mules were to be left at outpost one, and four at outpost two; two of those four would later be taken to outpost three.

The next morning, Andrews sent Corporal D.D. Harrod and three men to relieve Sergeant Haynes at outpost two, with orders for Haynes and his men to proceed to outpost three. There they were to report to Lieutenant Caldwell for duty at outposts four and five. There would then be twelve men, including officers, enlisted men, two civilian teamsters and one citizen volunteer, distributed

---

*By "staked himself," Caldwell probably meant that the mule had tried to jump over a fallen tree, or some other obstacle, and accidentally had run a branch or sharp stick up into his belly. This kind of accident happened sometimes to horses, less often to mules, and rarely to cows.

among outposts three, four, and five. The citizen volunteer was E.S. Hathaway of Missoula, a friend of Captain Andrews. The six mules were to be distributed so that there would be two each at outposts three, four, and five.

Lieutenant Elliott, after buying provisions in Kamiah, spent the night of November 14 some six miles upstream near the present town of Kooskia, where the South Fork joins the main Clearwater River. The pack train following him stopped that evening at Kamiah to take on the goods Elliott had bought, and remained there that night. On the following day, Elliott rode another eight or ten miles up the Clearwater to Smith Creek, stopping at Wilson's ranch on the way to buy potatoes and red beans. At Smith Creek he ran into a man named Hinds, a prospector, probably, and Rory Burke, an expert swiftwater man who had worked with LaMothe. Also at Smith Creek was a trapper named J.T. Winn, who was about to go into the mountains. Elliott told Hinds, Burke, and Winn what he was doing, and they told him there was a miner nearby who might be useful to him. John Freeman, they said, knew about boat building. Elliott hired Burke and Winn on the spot and asked one of them to fetch Freeman for him. From Hinds he borrowed a saw, a drawing knife, a square, a chisel, and a plane. Then he continued on to Pete King Creek, where he spent the night of November 16.

At about noon the next day, at a place he called Pete King's Bar, or McLain's, Elliott found McLain himself and a man named Cunningham, sawing out lumber with a whipsaw. The two prospectors would use it, they said, to build a flume to carry water from a nearby creek into their sluice box—a device that passed water and gravel over a series of riffles in the hope of catching whatever gold might be carried with the gravel. This type of placer mining had been common in the region since the 1860s, and there was hardly a white man on the river who wasn't engaged in it. Elliott asked the two if they would cut for him enough half-inch cedar planks to make two boats. McLain and Cunningham said they would, if he would provide the cedar.

The pack train joined Elliott here, carrying the provisions he had bought in Kamiah and at Wilson's ranch. And this, it turned out, would be as far as the train went; "civilization" ended here, and any further progress would have to be made by boat and on foot. LaMothe felled a cedar tree that morning, and by noon the two sawyers were working on the log. They had dug a pit and built a framework over it sturdy enough to support a tree trunk. After they rolled Elliott's log onto it, one of the sawyers got into the pit and the other stood on the platform. The whipsaw, some seven feet long, had a handle at either end. Cunningham, standing on top, had one of the handles, and McLain, underneath him, had the other. They pushed and pulled the saw between them, up and down, up and down, through the length of the log. The two changed places frequently, because the man on the bottom had the worst of it; he got the sawdust.

And Elliott got his planks. They were crude as well as green, and the thicknesses were imprecise, but Elliott felt he was lucky to have them. He had thought there would be places on this stretch of the river, ranches or placer mines, where he could pick up lumber, but no one had lumber to sell. Until finding Cunningham and McLain, he had about decided he would have to build a raft. Instead, he could now start building two boats.

The boats he had in mind would be twenty feet long on the keel and twenty-six feet overall. They would be two feet wide on the bottom and four feet, six inches wide on the top. That was the plan, but the plan had to be modified to suit the lumber. Elliott would use the thickest planking for the bottoms and the thinner wood for the sides. He began the building that day in fair weather and in late afternoon John Freeman, whom Elliott described as "the only man besides myself who understood anything about tools," arrived in camp.

In mid-afternoon on Nov. 18, Lieutenant Martin and the guide, Wright, rode into base camp at the hot springs and told Captain Andrews what he already had learned from Caldwell: The original plan to go down the valley of the Lochsa had to be abandoned. They also told him the pack mules were too tired to buck the snow any further, but that Wright had three fresh cayuses at the mouth of Lolo Creek. If they could get these horses, they would try to get over the Lolo Trail and down to Johnson's camp. Andrews sent a soldier to bring in the cayuses, but he had little confidence in the

Lolo Trail route. He told Martin and Wright he wanted to know everything there was to know about the new plan and its prospects.

During a long and earnest conversation in Andrews's tent, the captain learned that even though the mules were now useless, Lieutenant Caldwell was unwilling to give up on the Lolo Trail. He still thought they could supply his proposed outposts four and five with horses, and would abandon the plan only if Andrews ordered him to. The captain pointed out that it would take at least three days to get the cayuses to outpost three, and that by the time they got them there they would be far from fresh. The wagons with grain and supplies were some five miles below base camp, cut off except by men on foot. Wright and Hathaway were the only snowshoers in his command, he added, and he had twenty men out on the trail along with animals, all of whom needed to be supplied. All that was worrisome enough, Andrews said. But his main concern was the weather. With the exception of one day, the 16th, the weather had been fair, and this couldn't last. He said it was sure to snow soon, and a heavy storm would be a serious matter for the whole command. Finally, he told Martin and Wright that the more he thought about it the more certain he was that the whole effort had to be abandoned.

By 9 o'clock that night, Andrews had sent couriers out with written orders to retreat to base camp. These men traveled in relays, on foot, from post to post and reached Lieutenant Caldwell at outpost three at 9:30 the next morning. Caldwell's orders from Andrews:

> Return as soon as possible with your entire outfit to this place. I trust this will reach you in time for you to make No. 1, at least, tomorrow (Sunday), if the weather continues fair and you need not rush your stock, but if it should threaten snow, limit your pace only by that of the slowest man or beast. Further effort on the part of this expedition is abandoned and I do not wish to risk any avoidable delay in getting you all out.
>
> Pick up Nos. 2 and 1 as you come in, or if the men are not there, pack in what they leave if you can. Use your own judgment in all things, except do not delay one moment longer than an orderly and well regulated retreat demands.
>
> Do not hesitate to leave grain if it impedes you or your animals are weak, but keep one day's in any case.
>
> Take command of all men and animals that you run across. All previous orders are revoked.

By 6 p.m. on the 19th, the searching party and men from all the outposts were in base camp. It began snowing hard that evening.

After a fairly comfortable night on their pine flat above the Lochsa, the hunters—who now thought of themselves not so much the hunters as the prey—ate a breakfast of beans, bread, and coffee, and by 8 o'clock were walking again. Colegate's dog, Daisy, who evidently had been following them, arrived during the night looking tired and bedraggled, and had to be coaxed into moving on. As long as they were crossing the flat it was easy. There were signs of elk and deer everywhere, and Carlin wanted to stop and do some hunting. The others said no, they had better push on, and they did. At one point they crossed a trail that ran back into the mountains and found fairly fresh Indian choppings and blazes. The going got harder as the day progressed. The packs became heavier, and their straps began to cut and burn. The terrain by mid-day was brushy and steep, and the footing was bad—so bad that the travelers had to do much of the climbing on their hands and knees, grabbing onto bushes and pulling themselves across downed timber.

Later that day they found an old line chopped out by a surveying crew—probably railroad surveyors, Himmelwright said. They kept an eye on the river, and by early afternoon had all the assurance they needed that further rafting would have been disastrous. They saw many places where it would have been impossible to get a raft through. At one point they passed a waterfall of some six feet, with dangerous boulders both above and below it. Yet Carlin, at least, found the river beautiful. "I had never seen such clear-looking water," he wrote in his diary that evening. Himmelwright shot a grouse that day and Carlin caught two fish weighing half a pound each. They stopped walking and climbing at about 3 o'clock, having covered some five miles of mostly hard terrain.

Spencer, who was now doing most of the cooking, fried the fish and made a broth of the grouse, giving the bones to the dogs. The weather was still fair, firewood was abundant, and the men had a good camp. They went to sleep that night feeling more optimistic than they had in days.

The weather continued fair, and on Wednesday morning the 15th the travelers had breakfast of coffee and bread and were on their way again at 8 o'clock. The route took them across numerous small flats and steep hillsides, most of the time in heavy brush. By mid-morning, last evening's good spirits had flown. Short rations and hard work were telling on both the men and the dogs; they were all tired and hungry. Of the three dogs, Colegate's black spaniel seemed to be suffering the most. Everyone had been cut and bruised by rocks and brush, and all were weakening. Carlin was having occasional dizzy spells, but he didn't mention it, and he wondered how many of the others were experiencing the same thing.

Among the five men there was only one timepiece now since Pierce had accidentally dropped his in the river weeks ago. Himmelwright still had his, and he was carrying it in his hip pocket when he stumbled and fell backwards against a large rock. He pulled the railroad watch out of his pocket and saw that the crystal had been pulverized. What the hell, he said; who gave a damn what time it was? And he threw it down the hill as far as he could.

Spencer said he was surprised Abe had carried it this long.

Sentimental reasons, Himmelwright said, without explaining.

During that day, with Daisy's help, they shot three grouse. Carlin wanted to do some more fishing, but darkness caught them on a desolate flat some distance from the river. There was hardly any firewood here, and no trees large enough to provide shelter, but Spencer managed to make enough fire to stew the grouse and bake bread.

After supper it began to rain. It was going to be a miserable night for everyone, including the dogs. Within a couple of hours the rain had turned to sleet, and Carlin, hunkered down in his coat, began to fear he would leave his bones in these mountains.

21 The next day, November 16, was no better. After a night without sleep, the men made a daybreak meal of coffee and bread, and began walking in mixed snow and rain. They traveled at first along the rocky north shore of the Lochsa, up and over the steep bluffs they were encountering near the river. Hunger was a serious problem now. All five stumbled frequently from weakness and dizziness, and they moved only short distances each day before giving in to fatigue.

Approaching Black Canyon.

At mid-morning on this day they came to the highest bluff they had yet seen, rising above a fast-running creek. Before trying to cross, Spencer said, they should rest. He found some fairly dry driftwood under a boulder and built a small fire. They warmed themselves and made a pot of coffee. With energy renewed, they started up the creek. There was no way to cross it without a log, but there was no log in sight. Finally, Keeley chopped a tree down, felling it across the creek to form a bridge. The snow and sleet had frozen on trunk and branches, and it was so slippery that Carlin feared one of them would surely fall off and drown. No one did, and they proceeded slowly up the side of the bluff for about a thousand feet, slipping and sliding in the wet snow. They followed the ridge for a quarter of a mile, then descended again to the river. They picked their way among rocks and downed timber and after rounding a bend they came upon the Black Canyon.

This time there was no doubt about it. The view of those perpendicular cliffs filled Pierce with despair and chilled Keeley to the bone. Spencer knew about the place, and feared it even though he had never seen it before. Gazing at it now, he understood its reputation. It was a terrifying sight. The river, flowing smoothly between high walls of stone, was deep, dark, and foreboding—almost black. It moved silently here, but from somewhere downstream came the rustle of rapids still out of sight, and the moaning of the wind.

The five men stood in the cold rain for a moment without speaking, then four of them turned to Spencer. He was their guide. He would know what to do. Spencer had assumed that when they reached this spot they would simply climb up and around the Black Canyon, but it did not look so simple now. They would be in snow up there, even if they had the strength to climb that high; they were having enough trouble putting one foot ahead of another down here on solid ground. But they couldn't go back, and they couldn't go ahead. They would either starve on the river rocks or start climbing.

Spencer knew what had to be done, but it didn't have to be done today. It had been a hard morning, and they were all too tired. He suggested they start their climb first thing tomorrow, and in the meantime get a little rest. He said Himmelwright, Pierce, and he would locate a suitable camp while Keeley and Carlin tried to catch some fish.

Carlin agreed they probably would never find better fishing. They were sitting on large rocks near a clear, deep pool teeming with fish. Dolly Vardens, Spencer called them, otherwise known as bull trout. They milled lazily around in the pool, and many of them were big—too big, as it turned out.

They had no large hooks or spoons, so Carlin and Keeley each took some line and tied several flies together. They put lead sinkers ahead of the flies and then cast out, slowly pulling the flies toward them across the pool. They hooked plenty of fish, but the fish were too large for their flimsy tackle and broke the hooks. Carlin was about to land one that he took to weigh five pounds, when it broke away. Keeley almost landed another that was even larger. In two hours of fishing they hooked and lost at least thirty fish and lost some twenty flies. They quit finally and walked to the new camp with one half-pounder that Keeley had caught. The others were so disappointed that the anglers returned to the pool and in another hour of casting and pulling they managed to catch two more trout weighing about a pound each. Himmelwright had shot a grouse, and the evening meal was almost festive. They stewed the fish and the grouse and drank the juice and bits of flesh out of their tin cups.

Carlin said that if they had a good trolling spoon they could catch fifty pounds of fish out of that pool, and the fish would keep them going even if they found nothing else to eat. After supper, feeling new hope, they searched around in their packs looking for something to make a spoon out of. Keeley made one from the bowl of a teaspoon, and Carlin made one by hammering out a fifty-cent piece. Spencer produced a piece of copper wire he had been using to clean his pipe. They now had two spoons, but they still had only small hooks, and an inventory showed they had just twenty-four left.

Their camp that night was cold and wet, but they found enough wood nearby to keep a good fire going.

They got under way again the next morning without trying the new spoons. That could wait, Spencer said; what they needed today was an early start. The route took them up a steep, brushy hillside on a game trail until they were some fifteen hundred feet above the river. Then the trail disappeared. Across the chasm on the south side of the Lochsa they could see the route they would have had to travel had they remained on that side. It appeared to be impassable—an almost perpendicular slope dotted with outcroppings of rock. Himmelwright thought he could see goats up there, and Spencer confirmed it. There were several, moving easily around on the rocky cliffs. Himmelwright gazed at them in awe. He remembered his disappointment, in Spokane, on learning that they would not be able to penetrate goat country. There would be other times, he had said, and yet here they were, watching mountain goats from just across the river. He could hardly believe it, and continued to stare at the cliffs beyond the Lochsa until he heard someone telling him to move it.

They had not seen this much snow before on the trek down the river, and they had to proceed with great care. Keeley led the way most of the time because he seemed to have a greater knack than the others for finding the best places to step and turn, for knowing when to go up and when to go down.

In the afternoon they made a difficult descent to the river in order to find a camp before dark that had both water and firewood.

They settled on a small point on the shore between vertical cliffs, knowing they would have to make another wearying climb the next morning. It had been a hard day, and at the end of it Carlin estimated that they had advanced only two and a half to three miles.

Carlin and Keeley took their new spoons to the tip of the point and fished for a while, but nothing rose to their lures. Spencer built a fire, and the others made a crude shelter of pine boughs to shield them from the cold wind whistling down the river. During these labors, Pierce found part of a copy of the *Spokane Review* from last summer, under a rock, and Spencer found a cleaning rod for a .45 caliber rifle. Someone had come up the river this far only a few months ago; it made the wilderness seem less wild and lonely.

As the gloom of dusk settled into the canyon, Colegate's black spaniel, Daisy, began to whimper. She crouched trembling on the ground near the fire, exhausted, hungry, and in pain. Pierce said there ought to be something they could do for her, and Carlin told him that there was one thing they could do. He borrowed Spencer's revolver and shot the dog in the head. She was past any other kind of help, he said, handing the gun back. He and Keeley hung the dog in a tree, then cleaned it out and skinned it. When the carcass had cooled, they cut off the best parts, got a pot of water boiling, added the meat and a tablespoon of flour, and made a strong broth. The soup was good, but the meat was tough and stringy. What the men didn't eat they gave to the remaining two dogs, but only one of them would touch it.

Near their camp was a huge, hollow cedar some six feet across at the base. Keeley thought it would be a good idea to build a big fire inside it; they could sit in their shelter in front of the opening and keep warm, he said. He took some burning wood from the cooking fire, placed it in the base of the tree, and fed some small pieces to it, one by one. Within minutes he had a tremendous fire going. The flames leaped up the chimney formed by the tree's hollow interior and shot out through an opening some twenty feet above. They had a regular furnace, Himmelwright said, and he planned to make good use of it. He got Pierce to help him round up some sticks of driftwood, and they made a rack to dry their clothes on. It had stopped raining by now, and with this warming blaze they could expect to get a good night's sleep. The other three joined in the labor, and soon all their wet clothes were steaming in the heat.

Keeley hadn't counted on this much heat, however. It got so hot the men had to leave the shelter and move back and then move back again, taking the drying racks with them. They ended up lying in the firelight some distance from the source, stretched out on the rocks and feeling better.

The next morning, November 18, the weather was fair but the prospect gloomy, for the route lay straight up the side of the canyon.

Spencer asked Keeley if he really wanted to carry that ax up that mountainside. Keeley said someone had better, because they were apt to need it. Then who? Spencer wanted to know. Carlin, Pierce, and Himmelwright were carrying guns. Spencer had the cooking gear plus his own pack. Keeley said that if they had to build a shelter of some kind they would need the ax. He would carry it as far as he could. When he felt he couldn't pack it any farther, they would talk about it again.

This may have been one reason why Carlin, in his diary that night, wrote that Keeley "has been a splendid fellow all through, doing all he could and not grumbling at all."

Did they really need three guns? Spencer then asked the others. Carlin said he wasn't ready to abandon his beloved three-barrel paradox, and Pierce and Himmelwright both said they wanted to keep theirs. They'd better get started then, Spencer said, and the five began the long, slow climb toward the skyline, followed by the two dogs, Idaho and Montana.

As they climbed, they encountered high, perpendicular faces of rock they had to walk around. Then they found themselves in moose brush, clinging, slapping stuff difficult to move through. After the moose brush they ran into a thicket that slowed them still more, and at length they emerged on a ridge that ran parallel with the river far below. They trudged silently along this ridge until Pierce, the last in line, asked for a brief halt. He wanted to confirm something, he said. Was that Bald Mountain? He pointed up to the northeast. Indeed it was, Spencer said; he reckoned it to be about fifteen miles away. Carlin had thought they were below Bald Mountain a couple of days earlier. If he was right then, he said now, it meant they must have traveled farther than he thought. For at that time, the mountain was—or seemed to be—directly above them, and now it was well off to their right.

They had camped on that mountain September 24, a little less than two months ago. And now, after all they had gone through, on horseback, by raft, and on foot, it was still only fifteen miles away. It seemed to Pierce that the snow-clad peak might as well have been the moon, for all that distance meant.

As Himmelwright gazed at Bald Mountain he remembered the afternoon they had walked to the top and surveyed the wild country spread out all around them. Carlin remembered the anger he had felt toward Colegate that day for putting the expedition's future in doubt. And Spencer remembered the crashing and thrashing in the dark as his big white mare, Molly, bolted down the mountain, dragging a stump behind her. As for Keeley, he wondered why they were all standing here instead of moving on down the ridge.

They found what appeared to be a trail and followed it until it disappeared, but by mid-afternoon they were too tired to go on. Spencer tried to get down to the river but found it impossible from where they were. So they descended some fifty yards and made camp in a rocky flat above a small creek. The terrain around them was so difficult and steep that it took Carlin almost an hour to get down to the creek and back with a bucket of water. It was a poor camp, with little firewood and few boughs for making shelter or bedding. For supper they had some bread and a thin broth made from a grouse that Himmelwright had shot. They had eaten the last of the beans by now and the only food left was coffee, tea, some flour, and a tiny bit of sugar.

In this whole day, they had covered a mile and a half.

⸎

Lieutenant Overton found the trail north of the river so deep in snow that the mules could not push through it, and he sent them back. He and the rest of his men went forward on snowshoes, pulling their subsistence on toboggans. As they proceeded eastward they cached provisions under blazed trees to sustain them on their return, and on the 18th of November they reached a place called Beaver Dam, not far from Snowy Summit. They were still some fifty miles from the warm springs where they believed the Carlin party to be camped. Nevertheless, Overton and his four troopers pushed on.

On the other side of the divide, Captain Andrews was ordering his extended detachments back to base camp, and on the 19th all of his outposts had been abandoned. The next day, he tried to move his wagons out by way of the Lolo Creek road but had to abandon that effort as well; the creek ran so high his men had to leave the wagons and the unhitched mules, now packed with food and equipment, were forced to swim part of the time. Rather than try to continue on the creek road, Andrews gambled on the Lolo Trail, which continued across the divide into Montana.

The trail was steep and snow-covered. Several of the mules fell, tumbling and sliding down the mountain side, and one was killed. After two days of hard travel on foot, Andrews' company reached the Schmitz Brothers ranch and stopped to rest. Lieutenant Devol, apparently feeling better, arrived at the ranch with two wagon loads of hay, two days' supply of grain, and two days' rations for the men of Company H. Andrews and his company left the ranch the next morning, reaching Fort Missoula at about noon on the 24th of November.

Andrews had left some of the company's equipment at the home of a man named Lemke. George Anderson, a trapper who lived on Lolo Creek, volunteered to take care of the goods in the three abandoned wagons until summer, when either Andrews or another officer from Fort Missoula would come and retrieve them.

The attempt to penetrate the Bitterroots from the east had failed. There would not be another. Lieutenant Overton, at the far end of a supply line anchored by Lieutenant Voorhies on the Lolo, must have known by now that he was about to fail as well.

General Carlin, retiring as commander of the Army of the Columbia, wrote to the Adjutant General of the Army in Washington, D.C., saying, "I respectfully request the Major General, Commanding, to instruct the commander of this department to continue the search until the lost party shall have been found or their fate known."

The request was granted. The adjutant general wrote in a longhand note that "The new commander Department Columbia is to be instructed to continue the search instituted in this department by General Carlin."

While camped at Pete King bar, Lieutenant Elliott discovered that Henry Ables, the guide he had hired at Kendrick, had misrepresented himself. Ables had told Elliott that he knew this country well, but after Elliott had questioned him at some length, he confessed that he didn't. The lieutenant decided he could not afford to keep this man in his crew. As he wrote later in his report, "At Pete King's creek, civilization ceases. There is nothing but the wilderness beyond, snow, ice, and an unknown river, coupled with cold, suffering and exposure." He wanted with him only men he could trust. When he sent Corporal Harris and the pack train back to Weippe on November 18, he sent Ables back too.

On this day also, a day of fair weather, Elliott began building his boats. Everybody helped—Freeman, LaMothe, Winn, Burke, and the enlisted men, Smart, Norton, and Norlin. They could work only as fast as Cunningham and McLain could saw the lumber, and they worked mostly in the rain. They shaped and nailed the boards according to Elliott's diagrams, and caulked the seams with rag strips soaked in hot pitch. By the end of the day on the 20th, the two boats were ready. Assigned to boat number one, the larger of the two, were LaMothe, Freeman, Norton, and Norlin, with LaMothe in charge. Manning boat two would be Burke, Winn and Smart, with Burke in charge. Elliott would help in either boat, according to the need.

They would start up the river the next morning.

On Sunday, November 19, the five members of the Carlin party finished a breakfast of coffee and bread, cleaned their utensils, and shouldered their packs. Three of the five picked up their rifles, ready to begin the day's march, and that is when the hunting ended for John Pierce. He unslung the rifle from his shoulder and hung it from the stub of a dead pine branch, saying he was too tired to carry it one step more.

The other four stood and quietly stared at the rifle hanging in the tree. To Spencer and Keeley, it meant nothing much; the little company still had two rifles, and there was practically no game to shoot anyhow. But to Carlin and Himmelwright, the meaning of it brought a crushing sadness. Nothing else that had gone wrong since the cook got sick was quite as wrenching as Pierce's simple gesture. Who would be the next to give up?

Keeley said finally that if he weren't carrying the ax, he'd take the rifle; it was a good one, and he'd be glad to have it. But he and Spencer agreed that they had more need of the ax, and Keeley couldn't carry both.

They left the rifle hanging there and began walking. The going wasn't quite as bad today. They found numerous game trails, prompting Himmelwright to ask, Where was the game? These small trails shot off in all directions, and Keeley was charged with deciding which ones to follow and for how far. There was much slipping and sliding; everything was wet, and they were frequently in snow. Keeley and Pierce had no hobnails left in their boots, and the boots themselves were all in such bad shape that Carlin, Pierce, and Spencer were by now suffering from foot sores that would not heal. They were not eating enough to sustain their energy or even their balance. They frequently fell, and dizziness on these wet slopes was a constant hazard.

In mid-afternoon they came across fresh signs of deer but saw none, nor any grouse. At about 4 o'clock they took a last look at Bald Mountain and started down to the river. Spencer, using the mountain as his reference point, estimated that they were about fifteen miles from a good trail that would take them to Wilson's ranch. They all got some encouragement from that, and from Spencer's announcement, a bit later, that they were now past the Black Canyon.

They reached the river and made camp near a small sand bar. In the rain and bitter cold they built two large fires in a futile attempt to keep warm. Their problem, Pierce said, was that they were not eating enough to maintain body heat. Carlin agreed, saying he and Keeley would try to catch some fish tomorrow with their homemade spoons. Spencer made enough bread for a few bites each, and after supper said there was flour for only one more meal.

They turned in early, but Carlin, unable to sleep because of weariness and the cold, got up again. He sat between the two fires on a piece of driftwood, trying to keep warm and wondering what his friends were doing in the outside world. It had stopped raining now, but the bitter wind still blew. As he sat there he noticed that one of the terriers, Idaho, also was suffering from the cold. She had approached as close to the fire as she could, and lay there, shivering, with her feet stretched out toward the flames. She was so thin that Carlin wondered how she had managed to keep up with them. She had rubbed off much of the hair on her legs against sharp rocks, and she was so weak she could barely move. Carlin wrote in his diary that as she was lying there shaking, her mate, Montana, "came and lay partly on top of her and partly on the outside of her so as to protect the side exposed to the cold. I do not recall ever having heard of a similar case of animal sympathy."

22 Lieutenant Overton and his troopers were sitting on their toboggans with their backs to the wind, eating rations and sipping tea, when a courier on snowshoes arrived with news from Lieutenant Voorhies. The search was ended on this front, the note said; he and Voorhies were to withdraw with their men and animals to Weippe and prepare to go to Elliott's assistance on the Clearwater. The note said that Voorhies would stay where he was, probably near Brown's Cabin, until Overton joined him, and they would return to Weippe together.

After reading the note aloud, Overton shoved it into a coat pocket, downed the last of the tea, and finished his lunch. The men repacked their utensils, turned the toboggans, and began pulling them back the way they had come. The going back would be easier. They would travel on a trail they had already broken, picking up the food and equipment cached along the way.

After two days on the trail, Overton's detachment reached the camp where Voorhies was standing by with hot food and a pack train. After another day's march, both parties were in Weippe. Boutelle, who had been waiting there, said they would all go immediately to Greer's Ferry on the Clearwater and from there to Kamiah and the Lochsa. He didn't know how much help Elliott might need in pushing his way up that wild river, or how good were his chances of success. He was pretty certain, he said, that if the rescuers could not get in by that route they would not get in at all. The search from the east had been abandoned, and now so had the search from the north. If they could not penetrate the Bitterroot country from the west, it would be all over until spring. Voorhies and Overton would go as far as they could with the wagons, then continue with the pack train as far up the Lochsa as necessary.

The next day, Captain Boutelle and Dr. Carter, with Overton's tiny outfit and Voorhies's wagons and twenty men, left for Greer's Ferry.

For breakfast on the 20th, Spencer baked the last of the bread. When breakfast was over it began to rain again. Nobody had got much sleep during the night and Himmelwright, who had got none, was almost out on his feet. Carlin suggested to Spencer that they remain here for a day and let Himmelwright rest. He said Abe had been averaging one hour of sleep a night for the past seven nights; he could not go on like this. But Spencer said they couldn't afford to waste a day, since they were out of food. They had some tea and coffee left, and for supper he was planning to serve the small piece of bacon he had been using to grease the baking pan.

Keeley started to chuckle. What was so funny, someone asked, but Keeley couldn't answer because he was shaking with laughter. Finally he rubbed the tears from his eyes and said to Spencer that the bacon weighed only two ounces. Two ounces split five ways was . . . he paused to calculate. Four tenths of an ounce each, Himmelwright said. Carlin threw an arm around Himmelwright's shoulder. Abe might be sleepy, he said, but the engineer could still figure.

Spencer said the walking would be much easier now that they were out of the Black Canyon, and they could do some fishing along the way. He didn't want to spend one day more on the trail than they had to. On that note all five shouldered their packs and started walking. Four tenths of an ounce, Keeley said to no one in particular. What a joke.

Spencer had been right; the way was easier today. They were able to stay close to the river most of the time instead of climbing up and down and around the cliffs as they did in the canyon. When they stopped to rest, which was often, Carlin and Keeley would cast for fish, but without much luck. Carlin caught none, and Keeley caught a one-pounder. Fine, Spencer said. They would have the fish for supper and save the bacon for tomorrow. During the day they found some frozen hawberries, which they picked and ate as they walked along. They stopped to make camp after covering about six miles, and Himmelwright went looking for deer. Although there were plenty of fresh tracks in the snow, he saw no game and returned to camp empty-handed.

They again put up a rough shelter of tree branches, and Spencer made a broth of their single fish after scratching together enough wood for a fire. Carlin noticed that his hunger pangs had subsided in the last couple of days. The others had noticed the same. Pierce said it was because their stomachs were becoming adjusted to the frugal cuisine.

What did he mean by frugal? Keeley wanted to know. He had just eaten a fifth of a pound of fish, almost.

And just think of tomorrow, Carlin said.

Don't get him started again, warned Spencer, but Keeley merely smiled and said, Yes, just think. Four tenths of an ounce of bacon fat! He was laughing again. Won't it be grand?

They ate the little chunk of bacon the next morning, each man sucking loudly on his four tenths of an ounce, and after breakfast Himmelwright found the strength to go hunting again for deer. He knew they were here; their tracks were everywhere in the snow. Keeley went down the river to a pool that looked promising, and there he caught three fish. Himmelwright returned to camp after half an hour, having seen nothing to shoot at. Carlin, Spencer, and Pierce were too weak and tired to move. After the men had eaten Keeley's three fish, however, they felt strong enough to begin walking slowly. It had begun to snow. A cold wind coming down from the Rockies blew the snow about, and as the flakes became bigger, the visibility grew worse. The footing along this route was not bad, but all five had trouble keeping their balance. They braced themselves on rocks and pieces of driftwood, and clung to tree branches to keep from falling.

After traveling in this way for about two hours, they came to a likely fishing hole, and Keeley and Carlin both tried their luck. Carlin noticed with surprise that he had almost no control of his arms. When he tried to throw out his spoon, it would fly every which way. Even so, he managed to catch four good-sized trout, and Keeley caught two. They built a fire and stewed the fish on the spot. The men were revived by their first decent meal in days, and the dogs made good use of the bones.

They had staggered down the river for only a mile today, but they agreed that was enough. They put up a shelter of boughs and driftwood, chose who would keep the fire going through the night, and went to bed.

Lieutenant Elliott did not like the looks of this weather. It was snowing and windy, as it had been ever since the boat building began. But the boats were ready, the crews were ready, and Elliott was eager to get on with it. He had finished breakfast and broken camp by 8:45, and by 9 o'clock he was ready to shove off.

The boats were to be propelled by poling except when that was not possible, and then they would be pulled up the river by men on shore. On this day, November 21, starting on the south side of the river, the crews towed the two boats upstream for a quarter of a mile. Then they crossed the river and towed upstream on the other side for almost two miles. It was hard, wet work. Boat number two, the smaller one, nearly swamped at one point, but Burke went over the side into water up to his waist and pushed the boat off the rocks. By noon, everybody was soaking wet and cold. The men on the bank, pulling the boats over the rapids, tried to find footing on slippery, squishy ground, and those in the boats scrambled with their poles to hold the craft against the current.

At one point, in mid-afternoon, three men were tugging on the line of boat number one, which had lodged against the downstream side of a large rock. When the man in the boat managed to push away from the rock, the boat sprang forward, the line went slack, and all three men on the towing team were thrown into the river. Their rubber boots filled with water and became as heavy as lead. At about four miles from the starting point they came to a series of rapids too rough to be crossed in the usual way. Elliott ordered both boats to land on the north shore. The men removed the boats' loads and carried them on their backs upriver and around the rapids. Then they pulled the empty boats through the rapids, some on the ropes and some on the bank with poles they used to nudge the boats around boulders. Once over the swift water, they replaced the loads and poled the two boats through pools in the river for another half mile. Then they landed the boats and made camp.

Lieutenant Elliott and Private Norlin had gone ahead and built a fire, so that when the boat crews arrived it was almost like a homecoming.

They had tents and plenty of food, and the bad weather proved no great problem. What concerned Elliott was the prospect of working these boats through the Black Canyon and all the way up the Lochsa to the warm springs, where he had been told the Carlin party was probably camped. John Gaffney had said, in their meeting at Weippe, that it would not be easy. Elliott respected Gaffney's opinion and was prepared to abandon the boats below the Black Canyon if necessary and go on foot to Jerry Johnson's place. If he ran across the Carlin party before going that far, all the better. If he could not locate Carlin anywhere on this river, he would have to return in defeat and report to the general that his son was still lost. It was depressing even to think about this, and he resolved that he would find young Carlin, either dead or alive, and bring him out.

Young Carlin, of course, was only one of five, as far as Elliott knew, and his assignment was to come out with all of them. But it was Carlin, the general's son, whom he had volunteered to rescue as a gift to his commander.

The five members of the Carlin party found two inches of new snow on the ground when they crawled out of their shelter on the morning of November 22. It was dark and cold and rainy, and nobody had much desire to do anything but rest here and try to keep warm. Carlin and Keeley tried fishing, but the fish weren't biting. They sat by the fire and drank some tea, and Himmelwright said it didn't make sense to walk any farther. They should stay here, try to find something to eat, and wait for someone to come to them. But who was going to come? Carlin wanted to know. Himmelwright said it was perfectly clear to him that anyone who wanted to find them would know where they were. Spencer agreed with Himmelwright. One person who surely knew where they were was his partner, Bill Wright. When they didn't come out on the Lolo Trail, he said, Wright would assume they were camping at the warm springs with Jerry Johnson. If he got to Johnson's place and found them gone, he would figure they were making their way down the river. That being the case, there ought to be a party coming up the river even now to find them.

Maybe, Carlin said, but he wouldn't count on it. He had been watching the river, and it seemed to him that it would now be possible to float all the way to Wilson's ranch on a raft—if they could find enough good driftwood to make one. Himmelwright said he had no heart for rafting, and anyway he didn't think they could make one. Pierce was inclined just to stay where they were until help came, if it ever did. Spencer's theory appealed to him, he said, and besides, his feet no longer were tracking very well. Even Keeley, the strongest of the bunch, was in no hurry to pick up his pack and start walking. But it was Keeley who said they couldn't sit here in the snow and wait for someone who might never come. Give it one more day on the trail, he told the others. Then, if they felt they could go no farther, they would stop, make a good camp, catch some fish, and rest until they had their strength back.

Keeley was right, Spencer said. One more day, and then decide what to do next. Carlin said he wanted to know how Abe felt, and Himmelwright said he would give it a try; he had almost passed out yesterday from weariness and lack of sleep. Then Carlin said that if Abe was up to it, so was he; Pierce said he would struggle through one more day.

They started walking through swirling snow, followed by the two terriers. It was hard going, and several times they had to climb up and around rock faces. At one point, almost overcome by fatigue, Carlin decided to throw away his gun but couldn't bring himself to do it; of all the material things he'd ever owned, this gun was closest to his heart. He sat on the ground, high on the hillside, wondering if he had the strength to get up again. The others had moved on ahead and Carlin realized that he was alone. Would they leave him here, he wondered, if he was too weak to follow? A great drowsiness suffused him, and he drifted with it, in and out of sleep. He went through alternating periods of dreaming and wakefulness, and he could not determine which was which. Was he really standing in the living room of the family home in Buffalo, and imagining himself on this hill above the river? Or was he sitting on the hillside and dreaming he was home?

Frightened by the confusion, Carlin picked up a handful of wet snow and rubbed it against his face. He was in the mountains of Idaho, all right, and he would not see Buffalo again. Or so it seemed, as he struggled to stand up.

Himmelwright, meanwhile, had raised his eyes to the west and noticed a change in the scenery. The mountains on both sides of the river had rolled back and the valley had widened. The vista was now more pastoral than wild. He tried to call Carlin's attention to the change, but got no answer. He turned and saw that Carlin was no longer behind him. Could he have fallen and tumbled down the hill? He decided he had better find out, and started walking back up the hillside he had just descended. Himmelwright had gone about twenty steps when his legs gave out and he had to sit down. He was still sitting there rubbing his thighs when Carlin came into view, carefully making his way down the hill. Carlin helped Himmelwright to his feet, saying that he himself had been in the same fix a few minutes ago. Together, leaning on one another, the two started walking toward a point that would give them a better view of the terrain to the west.

Elliott's two boats had been badly battered by the river and the rocks; they would have to be repaired. That could wait until morning, however. After a day in and out of the icy water, the men were cold and wet and hungry. They needed a good meal and a night's sleep, and they would be ready for another rough day tomorrow. Elliott was beginning to worry that the boats would not be of much use. Without instruments, he couldn't accurately gauge the fall of the river, but Burke and LaMothe, the boatmen, guessed it to be about twenty feet to the mile. That might be too much, Elliott thought; they would see.

After breakfast on the 22nd, Elliott and his crew began working on the boats. The green lumber had cracked and the planks had been split by continual thumping over rocks. The same rocks had knocked some of the caulking out of the seams and both boats were leaking. The crew worked in blowing snow and a cold wind. After the boats were deemed ready for the water again, they packed the camp and resumed the journey upriver.

By afternoon the men had worked boat number two, which was in the lead, up to a rocky point and moored it. Elliott told Burke that when the other boat arrived, both would have to cross to the other side to find good water. As they were talking, Winn's dog barked and Burke reached for his gun, expecting to see game. Instead, it was a small white dog that appeared above the rocks. Both Burke and Elliott climbed around the point that cut off the view up the river and saw a man coming toward them.

Elliott asked him who he was, and he said, "Spencer."

Carlin and Himmelwright, moving slowly and carefully, reached the bottom of the hill and were walking along a flat a bit above the river when they turned a point and saw two men hurrying toward them. Carlin assumed they were two of their own bunch and guessed that they had seen a deer and wanted one of them to shoot it. Himmelwright didn't think so. He thought someone must have fallen into the river. But when the other two came closer, Himmelwright recognized one of them. It was Fatty Norton of the Fourth Cavalry, with whom he had done some shooting in the past. The other man was Lieutenant Elliott.

The four walked back to the boat, some two hundred yards below, and there they found Spencer, Keeley, and Pierce as well as the boatmen, Burke, LaMothe, and Winn, and the enlisted men, Smart and Norlin. They had a fire going and oatmeal and bacon cooking.

Himmelwright, who took some pride in his ability to judge distance, asked Elliott how far they were from the Selway fork. About seven miles, Elliott said. Wonderful, Himmelwright thought; that was about what he had judged it to be. But Burke told him that other ranches had recently been established above Wilson's, and they were now only five miles from the nearest one.

Elliott said that Winn would go back as a courier with word of the rescue; the rescued men could send telegraph messages along with him if they wished. But first he wanted to know about the cook. All Spencer had said when they met was that they had lost Colegate. He got more details while questioning the others during dinner.

According to Elliott's later account of the conversation, he was told that Colegate "had failed to turn up on November 10th, twelve days before I met the others, and had not been seen since." Elliott said he wanted to go in search of Colegate, and he talked the matter over with Burke, LaMothe, and Winn. All three said they would go with him, but "the Carlin party insisted it was useless as the man was practically dying when they left him and probably died the first night. They said that they had left Colgate twelve days before; that it was impossible for me to get a boat through, and that if it snowed at all the trail would be impossible."

Elliott decided that a Colegate search would be futile, and he dispatched his courier, Winn, to the outside world. Winn set out that afternoon on foot with his dog. He would walk to the first ranch, get a horse to ride from there, and report to Captain Boutelle at Weippe.

23 Elliott had decided that if he was going to get all these people down the river, with their gear and provisions, two boats would not be enough. He would need a raft, and he set the three boatmen to building one. It would carry the bedding, tents, and provisions, along with the dogs, and the men not guiding the raft would ride in the boats.

On November 23, with the raft under construction, Elliott and a couple of the enlisted men scoured the riverside for game. They found none, and no fresh signs, although they searched as high as two thousand feet above the river. It snowed all that day, and by late afternoon the snow was some six inches deep at Elliott's camp.

Spencer had told Elliott that this was as far as his party could have gone. They could not have walked any farther without food and rest. Had the rescue party not found them, Spencer said, they would have made camp here, hoping to find some game. At the end of this day it was clear to Elliott that the Carlin party would have starved here or died of exposure, for there was no game. They would have eaten their two dogs, and after that there would have been nothing but a few fish, if they had the strength to catch them.

The lieutenant was also certain by now that it would have been foolish to go after Colegate. The snow that had fallen in the last two days, together with the ice forming on the edges of the river, convinced him of that. Even if they reached him they could only bury the body since there wasn't a chance in the world that he was still alive. He would ask Dr. Carter when he got back to Weippe, but in the meantime he was inclined to believe, with Carlin, that the cook had died that first night.

Two trappers had come up the river that day in a canoe with a winter's provisions, and had stopped to visit with the men who were building the raft. They hadn't thought the weather would be this bad so early, they said. They were hoping to follow the Lochsa into the Bitterroots, but this snow worried them, and the ice building up in the river discouraged them even more. After much conversation about snow, ice, and the river, and hearing what a hard time the hunters had had, the two decided they would follow the Lochsa no farther. Instead, they shoved off and headed downstream, saying they would spend the winter somewhere on the Selway fork.

During the three days it took to build the raft, Elliott kept Carlin and his companions warm and fed, and let them rest. He also exerted a strict discipline over what they ate. They had been on short rations for so long, he told them, that their stomachs had to be brought gradually back on line again. So they dined mainly on broths and oatmeal and a little bacon.

On November 25, in miserable weather, Elliott and his men broke camp. They roped and poled the boats down to where the raft was moored. The hunters, now rested and revived, walked the distance, and they all reached the raft at about the same time. Elliott's crew transferred the provisions from the boats to the raft, and at about 10 o'clock they started down the river. Elliott, Spencer, Pierce, and LaMothe rode in the larger of the two boats, and Norton, Keeley, Carlin, and Himmelwright took the smaller one. Burke and Freeman steered the raft, with Norlin, Smart, and the dogs as passengers. The water was fairly smooth, unlike the river above, but the current was strong enough to move the raft and the boats swiftly along. They passed the ruined sluice boxes of an abandoned placer mine, and shortly after that reached Pete King Creek, the end of civilization. They continued on, past the Selway fork, and at 1 o'clock, having covered some twelve miles, found the river blocked by the debris of winter.

It was a mixture of ice, snow, and slush about five hundred yards long, from bank to bank, and from three to ten feet thick. Elliott advised the Carlin party to get out of the boats and walk to Hinds's place, about two miles below. Elliott then examined the mess in front of him and decided that it might be possible to cut through it from downstream. He and his crew pulled boat number two by hand across the ice until they reached open water at the opposite end of the blockage. Then Elliott and Burke got in with paddles and sent the others back to bring down the other boat. Working hard with paddles and poles, the two managed to cut a narrow channel through the ice and snow. Then, with the help of the men in boat number one, they cut around a block of the stuff about forty feet square, isolating it from the mass. Once freed, the block started floating downstream. As they watched it go, Elliott and Burke heard the ice above them crack, and when they turned they saw that the whole mass was beginning to move. Both crews paddled quickly to shore and pulled the boats up on the bank. After about an hour of grinding and turning on itself, the center of the ice floe moved by and floated downstream, and the raft was able to get through. The raft and both boats resumed the journey, and at 4 o'clock reached Hinds's place at Smith Creek. The hunters were already there, eating dinner and playing cards, when they arrived.

Elliott returned to Hinds the tools he had borrowed earlier, and the whole party remained there Saturday night and Sunday. Elliott reported later to his headquarters that Hinds "treated the lost hunters and my men with the greatest kindness, sheltering them in his home, and giving them the best that he had of every-thing. The worn out men were much benefited by the rest."

J.T. Winn, the courier who had taken word of the rescue to Captain Boutelle in Weippe, returned to Smith Creek Sunday night, the 26th, with a dispatch for Lieutenant Elliott. Boutelle advised Elliott that he should continue on to the North Fork, and said he would meet him at Greer's Ferry.

Elliott and his crew plus the Carlin party left Smith Creek, reluctantly, at 8 o'clock Monday morning. They rafted and boated down the Middle Fork of the Clearwater to Butcher's Bar, and there they put ashore two people, Smart and Winn, who were to pick up four horses and take them to Greer's Ferry. They were to wait there for the boats to arrive, and then take the boatmen, Freeman, Burke, and Winn, back up the river to where they had been when Elliott first found them. Smart would leave them there and return alone to Weippe and thence to Kendrick.

The rest of the travelers, in boats and raft, continued down the Clearwater, through occasionally bad water and worse weather. On the way the raft struck a rock, slid sideways to the current, and hung up at a sharp angle. The load shifted and everything got thoroughly wet, including the rations, before the men were able to free the raft and get it to shore. The men in the boats, meanwhile, kept going down the river to Sutler's Creek, near the village of Kooskia, where there was a post office that received mail by courier once a week. The postmaster had apples for sale, and the travelers bought some. After passing Kooskia the river widened still more between hills almost bare of timber. The boaters had to stop twice to work their way around dangerous rapids, and reached Kamiah at 2 o'clock. There was an Indian trader's store here, and while waiting for the raft they bought butter, cheese, and milk. When the raft arrived, they all floated on down for three more miles and camped at the mouth of a canyon. It was a good campsite, on level ground with plenty of dry driftwood for the fire. Most of the men were wet, all were cold, and after a hot supper under canvas shelters, the travelers turned in. It had rained or snowed all day.

After starting again the next morning, November 28, they encountered frequent rapids and boulders, and at one point Elliott told the hunters to get out of the boats and walk around some particularly dangerous whitewater. At this place boat number two, carrying Keeley and Norton, hung up on a rock but spun around and slipped off without damage to the boat or the cargo.

Later that day the occupants of boat number one—LaMothe, Elliott, Carlin, and Pierce—had a narrow escape. The boat bounced into the bottom of a rapid and then, in swift water, was carried out of its course and thrown against a boulder. It hung there for a moment, then turned on its side and started to fill. The weight of the water caused the boat to slide down the face of the rock, and the boatmen were able to paddle it to shore with a foot of water rocking around in the bottom. The two boats and the raft reached Greer's Ferry that morning at 11 o'clock after four and a half hours on the river.

Captain Boutelle, Dr. Carter, and Lieutenant Voorhies were at the landing to meet them, and for Carlin and Voorhies it was a joyous reunion. Elliott's men and the hunters dried themselves and rested, and Elliott took a moment to confer with Carter. He described Colegate's symptoms to Carter and explained in detail how Colegate had behaved on the day the party left him.

Carter said the cook's symptoms were the kind to be expected in a man who had gone that long with a severe urinating problem.

The poison collecting in the body had overwhelmed his kidneys. If he hadn't died that first night, he would almost certainly be dead by now, Carter said, but at least he would have died without pain. His behavior was typical of a person in the last stages of edema, he said, and at that point he would have lost all awareness of his surroundings, of his predicament, even of his own reeking body. Carter assured Elliott that any effort to save Colegate would have been fruitless, and he should stop being concerned about it.

After an hour at John Greer's ferry, Elliott's party got back into the boats and raft, and headed downriver to the North Fork. They arrived there at 3 o'clock after a fairly easy run of eighteen miles. There they made camp and cut up the raft for firewood. It had been intermittently raining and snowing for ten days, and no one in the party could see any sign of a letup.

On that day in Kendrick, General Carlin was sitting in his room at the St. Elmo Hotel, evidently in a sour mood. He was writing a letter to Colonel Thomas Ward, at the general's former headquarters in Vancouver Barracks, and in it he complained about a number of things. He had got word that Elliott had found his son, but had heard nothing since. He was angry at William Wright, saying Wright was overcharging for his services. And he criticized the behavior of Corporal Harris, the soldier from G Troop who had brought Elliott's pack train back to Weippe.

He told Ward that Wright was demanding three hundred dollars for his services and for the gun he had lost in the river. He had asked Colonel Burt to investigate the matter "and decide what I ought to pay Wright, if anything, and offered to pay him twice what I consider such services worth ordinarily, for the time actually employed in the trip to the Clear Water—that is, ten dollars a day—and to pay for the gun dropped in the water. He will get his gun next summer, I suppose, if he should consider it worth getting. I lost a gun in a stream like that many years ago, when upset from a canoe in Minnesota—and it was found some months later by an Indian, and uninjured. I believe, however, most sincerely, that Wright did not care a particle for the lost men or his partner Spencer (guide), but intended to play the game for all it was worth, in money . . ."

He wrote that Corporal Harris had left for Weippe that day, presumably to meet Elliott's party, and added:

> As a sample of the discipline and courtesy in the 4th Cavalry I will mention that I met Corporal Harris and Private Lefter [of Overton's outfit] at the depot on arriving yesterday. They stood with their hats on and hands in their pockets, and answered such question as I asked them. Afterward, Corporal Harris was in this hotel sitting in a chair, hat on and feet cocked up, and when I spoke to him and sought further information, he remained sitting and kept his hat on, never rising, saluting, or removing his hat. There being a crowd of people around, looking on and listening, I didn't care to take notice of these actions, but it shows how utterly the Regiment is lacking in discipline....Retired, as I am now, and never expecting to be with troops again, I do not care to take any action in the matter, but it would be well for the proper authorities to look into the condition of that Regiment and to correct it immediately.

As far as the general knew at this time, neither Overton nor Voorhies ever got as far as the Lolo Trail. General Carlin, in his letter to Colonel Ward, wrote that "Tom Beall and Frank White [the guides]. . . had abandoned Overton—as you learned from Boutelle—at least that Beall had done so." And Harris had told the general that Voorhies did not get even as far as Weippe, although he must have got beyond Weippe, according to his note to Overton. Boutelle, who was in command of the whole operation, had ordered Voorhies to take his men to Greer's Ferry and lend what assistance might be needed to Lieutenant Elliott. And that is where Voorhies was, along with Boutelle and Dr. Carter, as the general was writing the letter in his Kendrick hotel room.

The next day, November 29, two ranchers came by in a four-horse covered wagon on their way to Kendrick, and the Carlin party bought passage as far as Snell's mill, some eight miles distant. They spent that night there, in the house of a man named Gainer. When they were here before, on September 19, they had slept in Mr. Snell's barn. While here this time Carlin bought some venison, pork, and fresh vegetables from Gainer and sent them down to the North Fork by an expressman. It would make Thanksgiving dinner for Lieutenant Elliott and his men, Carlin said, and it was certainly the least he could do.

From here it was only fourteen miles to Kendrick. Pierce said he could hardly believe it. There had been so many nights when he had lain in his blankets listening to the river and thinking he might never see Kendrick again. Spencer's chief reaction was that they were all damn lucky. And he wondered if his partner, Wright, had tried to get in from Missoula, and what might have happened to him. Himmelwright by now had got his energy and his high spirits back, and was looking forward to greeting his mother and friends in Spokane.

Keeley was still with the Carlin party but no longer of it. Once off the river he began thinking of Himmelwright, Carlin, and Pierce as the New York men, the way the locals did. They were no longer joined in the same endeavor, facing the same perils, dealing with the same hardships. Bumping along in the wagon enroute to Snell's mill, Keeley thought that what he had been through was worth more than two hundred and fifty dollars. It was a thought that would not go away.

<hr />

The bag of venison, pork, and fresh vegetables that Carlin had dispatched by courier from Snell's mill arrived at Elliott's camp at 4:30 on the 29th. To men who had eaten no meat for three weeks, this present "from the rescued to the rescuers," as Elliott put it, was a gift beyond measure. The party remained in camp on the North Fork all day, enduring an incessant rain.

The next day Elliott cooked a Thanksgiving meal for his men, and at 2 o'clock, Sergeant Smart and J.T. Winn arrived from Smith Creek in time for dinner. Captain Boutelle and Dr. Carter showed up at 4:30 and Lieutenant Overton at 5. Elliott wrote that "all were cheered by our big fire and warm dinner and reception. The night was cold and rainy."

24 On November 30, after an overnight stay at Gainer's house, Carlin and his four companions left on horseback for Kendrick, warmly clad in Army overcoats supplied by Lieutenant Elliott. Six inches of snow had fallen during the night and it was cold, but the sky was clear for a change. The travelers were back in familiar territory—Keeley also had been here before—and the road was good. Now that they were out of the wilderness, they could talk of plans. Spencer would accompany the hunters to Spokane and take the train from there to Missoula. He and the others had

been given a rough description of the efforts made by the various search parties, and Spencer was eager to get Bill Wright's version of the work on the Montana side. Carlin, Himmelwright, and Pierce had many things to catch up on as soon as they got back to New York. Keeley probably would stick around Kendrick for a while, he said, or he might go to Spokane; he wasn't really sure what he would do. He did have it in his mind to talk with Carlin about their financial arrangement, he said. He was not happy with the deal they had made, but they didn't need to go into that now.

Why not go into it now, Carlin asked. What was the matter with their deal?

Keeley said that what he had gone through in getting them down the river was worth more than two hundred and fifty dollars.

This surprised and angered Carlin. What was Keeley getting at, he wanted to know. Who got whom down the river? They had all shared in the effort, and no one of them could take the credit.

Keeley reminded Carlin that during their conversation in Jerry Johnson's cabin, Carlin had offered to buy Keeley's grub and also pay him two hundred and fifty dollars for his help in running the rafts down the Lochsa. Well, he said, as it turned out they didn't run the rafts down the Lochsa; they walked down and had one terrible time of it, and if it hadn't been for Keeley they might not have made it.

Spencer angled his horse over to where Carlin and Keeley were riding side by side and said to both of them that maybe this conversation could wait.

That was fine with him, Keeley said. He was only saying that he and Carlin should talk about this some more; they didn't have to do it right now.

This did not soothe Carlin. He had sensed that Keeley was going to make trouble, and he didn't need that, either now or later. They had agreed on the deal, he told Keeley, and Keeley had accepted it.

They didn't shake hands on it, Keeley said.

Carlin couldn't remember whether they had or not, and he didn't care.

Keeley said he had no problems with anybody, he just didn't like to be taken advantage of.

Nobody was taking advantage of anybody, Carlin snapped.

Carlin's voice was rising, and Himmelwright said they should drop the subject. A deal was a deal, he said. If Keeley didn't like the deal he could have said so before now.

Keeley said nothing. Carlin slowed his horse enough to let Keeley's get ahead, and hoped the subject was closed. Nothing more was said of it that day, but the conversation had cast a cloud over this otherwise pleasant journey.

The road, which had been fine most of the way, became almost impassable in places after it dipped down from the plateau to the valley of Bear Creek some three miles from Kendrick. The autumn rains had washed out portions that had been built along the hillside, making the going hard in spots. But the riders got over it and into Kendrick, arriving there in time for Thanksgiving dinner at the St. Elmo Hotel.

The general had been in Kendrick for several days, and he and a dozen other soldiers and townspeople rushed into the street as soon as word came that the rescued hunters had arrived. As they dismounted, the general shook hands all around, saying he was pleased to meet Ben Keeley and wanted to hear a full report on the adventure as soon as possible. The St. Elmo's stable boy came around to take care of the horses, and everybody else went inside in a hubbub of laughter and back-slapping.

It had been seventy-five days—ten and a half weeks—since they rode away from here, full of anticipation and high spirits. Thank God, Himmelwright said to himself as he signed the hotel register. They were back at last.

Lieutenant Elliott, together with Captain Boutelle and Dr. Carter, left the North Fork camp on horseback at 8 o'clock on December 1, in the rain. Overton, Voorhies, and the enlisted men were to follow later in the day with the pack train and wagons. As the three riders ascended to the heights above the river, the rain changed to snow, and as they dropped down again toward Bear Creek, they were once more riding through rain.

A mud slide had covered the road near the bottom of the gulch and appeared to have displaced a narrow bridge there. Elliott told the other two men to ride on ahead; he wanted to stop here and check the bridge, to make sure it would be safe for the pack trains and wagons that would be crossing after dark. He left his horse standing in the road and walked to the crossing. He kneeled down to get a better look. At that moment his horse walked up behind him, gave him a nudge, and Elliott slipped into the creek. The rushing water pushed him feet first under the bridge, and he was about to be swept away when his left foot lodged against a rock. With all the strength he could muster, Elliott managed to straighten his left leg, then grab a wooden beam under the bridge and pull himself out.

He was now angry, tired, and soaking wet. He spoke roughly to his horse, mounted, and rode into Kendrick, arriving in the dusk and rain at 4:30. Voorhies and Overton arrived an hour and a half later with the pack train and wagons.

The next day, December 2, the detachments were broken up and the men sent back to their respective stations. Voorhies returned with his outfit to Fort Walla Walla and Elliott and Overton to Vancouver Barracks.

Captain Boutelle and Dr. Carter, traveling separately, also entrained for Vancouver, and Boutelle a few days later forwarded Elliott's report of his activities to the commandant of the Army of the Columbia. With it he sent this endorsement:

> There can be little doubt that the lost hunters are indebted to Lieut. Elliott for their lives, as when found they had been without food or blankets for several days and were too weak to have traveled much farther. Mr. Carlin's words to me, in his account of the adventure, were "I had walked my last day."
>
> From a standing tree, with few tools and the assistance of one mechanic [John Freeman, presumably], Lieut. Elliott, in four days, constructed two boats capable of enduring any journey from the head waters of the Clearwater to the mouth of the Columbia river. This I believe a feat unparalleled in military service.
>
> I recommend that the attention of the War Department be invited to the heroic conduct of Lieut. Elliott and the party of soldiers and citizens under his command in the relief expedition to the end that their services be mentioned in orders from Headquarters of the Army, and also that the service be brought to the attention of the Life Saving Bureau of the Treasury Department.

On December 1, as Elliott, Boutelle, and Carter were leaving the North Fork camp, the Carlin party, together with the general, all left Kendrick by train for Spokane. Keeley had decided to go along also, saying there was nothing for him to do in Kendrick. No one had mentioned Keeley's altered attitude to the general, and Keeley had said nothing since yesterday about his discontent. When the train reached Spokane at 2 o'clock, the men were met by Himmelwright's mother and by Carlin's wife and mother, all of whom had been brought to the city as guests of the general.

It was a grand reunion, and the hunters were surprised to find that their arrival had been anticipated by a great many unrelated people who had been following the search in the papers. Himmelwright realized, with mixed feelings, that they had become famous. Several members of the happy throng at the railway station mistook a fellow citizen for a member of the Carlin party and whisked him off to a free hotel dinner before realizing their error. At one point a newspaper reporter interrupted the celebration by managing to get Himmelwright aside long enough for a brief interview.

The reporter quickly made the mistake of referring to "the lost hunters," and that riled Himmelwright.

They were never lost, he said, and he resented any insinuation that they were. There was no time, he said, when they did not know exactly their location. He said that before they met Elliott they had estimated the distance to the forks at ten miles, whereas it turned out to be only eight. And that was pretty damn close considering this was after ten days of travel on foot in the worst possible conditions.

Carlin, overhearing this, excused himself from others in the party and went to Himmelwright's side. He realized that Abe, the engineer, was taking the "lost" business personally; he didn't want anyone in the bunch to create bad feelings between them and the newspaper.

Carlin suggested to the reporter that the interview be postponed for a while, after which he would be happy to give the *Spokane Review* all the information it desired. This was not a good time, he said, because of the pressure of other business. He and the reporter made arrangements to meet here in three hours, and the reporter left. Carlin then told Himmelwright that it would be better if just one person spoke to the newspapers on behalf of the group, and Himmelwright said that was fine with him; he didn't like giving interviews and had not planned to give this one.

That settled, everyone trooped to the Hotel Spokane to relax in preparation for a festive dinner. For Carlin, however, there was to be no rest. A bellboy came to his room with a note saying there was somebody in the lobby who wished to speak to him. He said he would be right down, and the bellboy left. Carlin was pretty sure he knew who it was. He changed his shirt, combed his hair, and went downstairs to meet Fannie Colegate and her son, Charles.

25 George Colegate's widow, Fannie, and his son, Charles, were standing in the lobby of the Hotel Spokane with three of their neighbors from Post Falls when the well-dressed young man in the trim mustache stepped nimbly down the stairs and strode toward them. He was Will Carlin, he said. Was this George Colegate's family?

Charles introduced himself and his mother and the three men who were with them. After that, for an awkward moment, nobody said anything. The other five stared at Carlin, waiting for him to speak. Finally, Carlin said that he supposed they were here to ask about George.

More silence and a nodding of heads.

Good, Carlin said. He welcomed the opportunity to explain to them what had happened out there in the mountains, and in fact he was planning to meet with the family the next day in Post Falls. But since they were here, he would be glad to speak with them now.

However, he said, this lobby was not the place; he would ask the desk clerk if there was a room they could use. He did, and the clerk directed him to a private dining room just off the lobby—the same room where the Carlin party had dined on the night before going to Kendrick.

Carlin pulled some chairs into a semi-circle and everyone sat down. Carlin wished fervently that somebody would say something. No one but he had spoken since Charles made the introductions. And still, no one did. They all just looked at him, in a way that was neither friendly nor hostile—the look of people waiting to hear a dark suspicion verified, a tragic event exhumed.

Well, Carlin thought, he would tell them what they wanted to know—or didn't want to know, as the case might be.

He said he was very sorry that he and his party had lost Mr. Colegate, but that they had done everything they could do to keep him alive and comfortable until they could do no more. He told them what he had told the cook: That he did not look well enough for this trip and that he should not go with them. And he told them what the cook had told him: That he was just tired and would be fine, and—most important—that he had his doctor's permission to go.

It irritated Carlin that he had to seem so defensive; there was no reason for him to feel guilty.

Finally, Fannie Colegate spoke. But what happened? she wanted to know. And where did they bury the body?

There was no body to bury, Carlin said. Mr. Colegate was still alive when they saw him last.

One of the men asked Carlin to explain this, and Carlin realized he could not explain it in any way that would satisfy these people. But he would try. He would start at the beginning and give them the whole upsetting story.

He described his first conversation with Colegate and all the subsequent ones. He told them how many times he or Spencer had asked Colegate what was wrong with him, and how many times Colegate had said it was just weariness, or stomach cramps, or this or that. He told them how Colegate had finally confessed the truth, explaining that he hadn't brought his "instruments" because he hated to use them. He described Colegate's gradual decline and explained how others took over his duties, how they kept fires burning to keep him warm, how they cared for him in every possible way. He described the terrible hazards of the Lochsa and the fateful moment when it became clear that they could go no farther on rafts.

Carlin was describing the meeting at which they decided they would have to walk out, with Colegate or without him, when one of the neighbors interrupted. He pointed out that there were five of them and only one of him. Couldn't they have found some way to pack him out? Carlin assured him it would have been impossible. They all remembered Colegate as a small man, he said, but the illness had swollen his body so much that by this time he probably weighed two hundred pounds. And he described the steep terrain that confronted them.

Fannie wanted to know why someone couldn't have stayed with her husband rather than leave him to die alone, and Carlin said that would have been useless because Colegate at this point was beyond further help; he was in a stupor and didn't know what was happening. He was so far gone that he didn't care whether they left him or not. And no one knew how long that person would have to remain with Colegate before he died, consuming precious food. And then that person would have had to walk out alone.

One of the men reminded him that he had earlier said he was certain Colegate died that first night. Surely they could have stayed one more night, then given him a decent burial.

Carlin was feeling sweaty, defensive, and increasingly help-less. He could feel their accusing eyes on him. Why did they keep this room so warm? Damn it, he said, they had done everything they could for Colegate despite the fact that Colegate was the cause of their trouble. He must control his anger, he told himself, but he went on. If Colegate had been honest with them he would be alive today, and they wouldn't be having this conversation now.

Fannie Colegate was dabbing at her eyes and Charles's face had reddened. One of the men wanted to know why they had not brought Colegate out when he first became ill. Because Colegate kept insisting he was all right, Carlin replied. But he clearly was not all right, the man said. And Carlin, becoming snappish, said that by that time it was too late. They were snowed in.

One of the men asked Carlin why the guide had let that hap-pen. Carlin said the snow storms had caught them all by surprise; everybody knew the mountains were safe until the middle of Octo-ber, and they had tried to come out before then. But they could not come out on horses, he said, and Colegate was too sick to walk. Their only hope of getting Colegate out was to take him down the river. If they hadn't had him to care for, they could have got out easily on snowshoes.

Carlin described again how they had cared for Colegate, how they had nursed him, fed him, tended fires all night for him, car-ried him on and off the raft, and always made him as comfortable as they could. But the time came, he said, when they had to leave Colegate in order to save themselves. They had their own families to think about.

The men who had come with Fannie and Charles seemed to have the most trouble understanding the decision to leave this sick man to die alone in the mountains. Carlin could not seem to con-vince them that he and his companions had no choice. They had to save themselves, he kept insisting; they owed it to their families. Why should six men die because one of them had got them all into trouble unnecessarily?

Carlin immediately regretted that outburst. He knew he must not lose his temper, but this inquisition after all he had been through was unfair. He resented having to defend himself this way. The meeting had gone on too long; members of the hotel staff were now moving around in the room, preparing it for dinner. He would have to find some way to bring it to an end, as pleasantly as possible.

He stood up, and the others did the same. He reached into his jacket pocket and pulled out his billfold. He opened it and took out twenty-five dollars in bills and handed them to Charles. He was sorry he couldn't pay more for Mr. Colegate's services, he said, but he was practically flat broke after all of his expenses.

Fannie Colegate uttered a small gasp, and Charles tried to give the money back, thrusting the bills toward Carlin, but one of the neighbors grabbed his wrist. It was time to go, he said. Charles and the three men gathered around Fannie and ushered her out of the room, across the lobby, and through the front door.

Carlin stood quietly, watching them go, and started climbing slowly up the stairs. On the landing he met the general coming down and told him that the Post Falls people had just left the hotel. General Carlin, guessing that the meeting had not gone well, said he would try to catch them before they got away and offer to take them to lunch.

Young Carlin washed his face and went to Himmelwright's room to tell him about the visit with the Colegate family. Abe was lying on the bed, reading that day's issue of the *Spokane Review*. Carlin got one look at the newspaper and remembered that he had promised the reporter an interview at about this time. He told Himmelwright he would talk to him later and hurried back downstairs. He picked up a copy of the *Review* that had been left on one of the chairs and sat down with it to wait for the reporter. Catching up on the news wasn't much fun. The financial panic that had bloodied Wall Street was closing businesses, driving people off their farms, and fomenting political unrest across the country. The Northern Pacific Railway was in receivership. You could buy a beer for a nickel in Missoula, if you had a nickel, and Seattle was flooding. Carlin, already depressed by his visit with the Colegate family, decided he didn't need any more bad news and put the paper down. He was sitting and studying the wallpaper behind the registration desk when the *Review*'s reporter arrived. The young man came into the lobby and went to the desk clerk, who pointed to Carlin. The reporter walked briskly to where Carlin sat, introduced himself, and pulled a chair up beside his.

Carlin told the reporter he was pressed for time—he had a dinner engagement that evening—and he hoped they could get this done quickly.

The reporter, who said his name was Roberts, whipped out a notebook and pencil, saying that was fine with him. All he wanted to know, he said, was what happened after the Carlin party left Kendrick. Carlin told him that he and his companions had gone from Kendrick to Brown's cabin, then to Bald Mountain, down to the Lochsa, and from there had built a couple of rafts and floated down the river....

The reporter interrupted, asking for more details. Carlin, encouraged, warmed to his subject and gave the reporter an interview so rich in detail that the story filled four columns in the next day's paper.

When Carlin came to the matter of leaving Colegate behind, Roberts quoted him as saying, "The whole question was talked over seriously. We saw how it was that to stay behind meant death, while it was even doubtful if we could be saved in going ahead. We said that we would start out and that whoever fell behind should bear his own misfortune. All that was explained to the old man early one morning. He seemed to have only a general idea of what was going on. Once he said to me, 'Well Carlin, I guess I'll be the first one to fall.' All of us were in a deplorable fix. We divided our grub, discarded all our blankets and arms, except a dozen rounds of ammunition each and two guns. Then we made the start. The old man was scarcely walking. He just moved, that was all. That was the last we saw of him."

After the interview, Carlin returned to his room, combed his hair and washed his face, and went looking for his father. He found him in the hotel bar, with Himmelwright and Pierce. How was lunch? he asked the general. It was civil, the general said. The Colegates and their neighbors had accepted his invitation, but they clearly were not satisfied with what they had been told. And he said no one should be surprised at that. The four men had time only for a quick drink of whiskey before they were to meet the women in the private dining room—which was as overheated as before, young Carlin found.

That night's dinner, which was to have been a celebration, was instead a rather dismal affair. Retirement did not suit the general, as he made clear to everybody. Himmelwright's mother made a few playful suggestions as to how the general, a single man now, should spend his time, but the laughter was strained. Carlin and Himmelwright had hoped that Keeley would have the grace not to attend, but he was there, hovering over the evening like a storm cloud, saying little. Young Carlin's meeting with the Colegate family had given him a headache, and his interview with reporter Roberts had left him feeling he had said too much. When it came time for the general to offer a toast, he did his best. To the stalwart adventurers, he said, who had survived the rigors of a hostile wilderness in the true spirit of the pioneers....Glasses were raised and emptied, but there were no cheers or huzzahs. The ghost of George Colegate had laid its bloated hand on the party and snuffed out the candles.

Mrs. Himmelwright said the boys must be tired; she certainly was, and the party broke up. Spencer and Keeley went into the bar for a nightcap and the others went to their rooms. Himmelwright stopped by Carlin's room before going to bed, to ask whether it should bother them that Spencer and Keeley were drinking together downstairs.

No, Carlin said, they needn't worry about it. Spencer was a solid fellow and he would be on their side. Just go to bed, Carlin said, and get some sleep.

━━━⊱✦⊰━━━

Spencer had no wish to be a part of this conversation, but Keeley had him trapped and wouldn't stop talking. The general had offered a reward for the rescue of the Carlin party, and Keeley wanted it. He seemed to think that Spencer could be talked into supporting his demand. He and Spencer had more in common, he pointed out, than either of them had with the New York men. They were both mercenaries, hired to handle specific chores, whereas the New Yorkers were friends and playboys, a couple of social layers above the two of them. Didn't Spencer realize that if it hadn't been for him and Keeley the others could never have made it down the river? Spencer had to lead them into the hunting grounds and Spencer and Keeley had to lead them out. That meant that they were more deserving of that reward—he'd heard it was two thousand, five hundred dollars—than anyone.

He would put in for the reward, Keeley said, and if Spencer testified to Keeley's services, he could have part of it. They would share fifty-fifty, straight across, Keeley said.

Spencer considered the whole idea absurd, but he didn't say so. Instead, he told Keeley he didn't want to get involved in Keeley's scheme because he wanted to stay on Carlin's good side. Carlin and Himmelwright had talked about coming back in the spring to pick up their trophies, and if they did he wanted to be the guide.

Besides, Spencer said, Himmelwright, Carlin, and Pierce would all campaign against Keeley if it came to that. Keeley didn't think so. He had been the strong back on the journey down the Lochsa, and he had given them good advice; they just hadn't taken it. For instance, he said, if they had used the rafts the way he wanted to, instead of stopping every five minutes to explore the river, they would have saved several days of travel.

Keeley took another sip of his whiskey.

And speaking of rafts, he went on, they were a rotten idea to begin with. They should have taken his advice and pulled Colegate up to the Lolo Trail on a sled.

Have it your way, Spencer said, but leave me out of it. He finished his drink, gave Keeley a slap on the back, and left the bar.

The next morning Carlin decided he would look up Dr. Webb. Yesterday's visit with the Colegates had served as a warning of troubles to come if he didn't take steps now to protect himself. He found the doctor's address and went there with Himmelwright. Webb was eager to find out how George Colegate's illness had progressed. He had spent weeks wondering what was happening to his patient, and now the answers were sitting here in his office. He was delighted to see them, he said.

Carlin and Himmelwright told Webb that Colegate had claimed at first that he was simply tired, then that he was having stomach cramps, and finally, after they had been on the trail for eight days, that he had a urinary blockage. They said he had swelling in the hands and wrists, then in the legs; that the legs had become gangrenous, and that toward the end Colegate was utterly helpless.

The classic symptoms of uremic poisoning, Webb said, or dropsy, as some called it. It was what he would have expected, knowing the patient's history.

Carlin asked Webb if he would mind writing a statement giving his professional opinion that Colegate was a doomed man when he left Post Falls without the instruments needed to sustain him. Webb agreed to do so, and more. However, he had patients in the waiting room. He would have to see them first, and as soon as he was free he would write out a statement and have it delivered to Carlin at the hotel. That would be fine, Carlin said, a bit disappointed at the delay. He and Himmelwright returned to the hotel, and that evening this note arrived from Dr. Webb:

> Mr. Colegate came to me from Post Falls last summer and I placed him in the Sacred Heart Hospital, where he remained about three weeks and then returned to Idaho. Early last fall he again came to me to be examined and said, if he was well enough, he would start on a hunting trip as cook. Mr. Colegate was troubled with an enlarged prostate and chronic inflammation of the bladder and had been for twenty years compelled to use catheters to relieve the bladder. I told him he could make the trip but to continue the use of the catheters, and from the history of the case and symptoms described by the Carlin party, I am satisfied Colegate's illness would have resulted fatally under any circumstances, and when he was left behind in the condition described, he would not have survived twenty-four hours.
>
> W. Q. Webb
> Spokane, Wash., December 4, 1893.

26 Ben Keeley, as good as his word, took General Carlin aside within days and told him he had heard about the reward and thought that he should have it.

The general at first thought Keeley was joking. Then he found himself wondering if Keeley was sane. He was serious, Keeley said. He insisted that he had the money coming because of his successful effort to get the Carlin party to a point where Elliott could find them. They could never have made it that far without him, he said.

General Carlin began to laugh. Keeley was not the rescuer, he said; he was one of the rescued. Keeley, becoming angry, told the general he was prepared to sue for the money, but the general brushed him off. Keeley stormed away and the general told young Carlin later it was the first good laugh he'd had in a long time. It was pretty funny, all right, Will said, but he was not laughing. Keeley had now been humiliated by both of them, since Will had refused him any more money. He was in a mood to cause trouble.

It quickly became clear that Keeley was not the Carlin party's only problem. Others were questioning the decision to walk away from the dying Colegate, and in Post Falls, Colegate's home town, the grumbling was especially loud. The *Spokane Review*, in a dispatch from Post Falls, reported that "it was felt that one man might well desert four [*sic*] in extremity, since he could not hope to care for so many, but that four able-bodied men should not have deserted one tottering companion."

Other newspapers reported much the same sentiment, and it worried Carlin and Himmelwright. They decided to submit a report in writing to the *Spokane Review* in an attempt to rebut some of the harshest criticism. In a long statement signed by both of them, they recounted their concerns about Colegate's health and his insistence that he would be all right, and described in detail their efforts to make him comfortable.

(At one point in the treatise, they wrote that Jerry Johnson "was willing to sell out and go down the river with us at an exorbitant price," if they wished to leave Colegate in his cabin for the winter. They didn't accept the offer, they wrote, because Colegate was too helpless to cook for himself, or bring in his own firewood, and he would not survive. This offer is not mentioned elsewhere by either Carlin or Himmelwright, and could hardly have been a serious one. Johnson considered rafting the Lochsa roughly the same as suicide, as he made clear to the Carlin party as the rafts were being built.)

They said again that they had gone down the river only for Colegate's sake; they could not take him with them over the Lolo trail on foot. They included Dr. Webb's statement and another by Dr. C.S. Penfield supporting Webb's conclusions. They came to the defense of Lieutenant Elliott, who was being criticized for not going in search of Colegate after finding the Carlin party. Elliott was eager to go, they said, and so were his men, but Carlin and Himmelwright convinced him that the effort could not succeed. After describing the hazards of such a mission, they added:

> We therefore feel convinced that an effort to reach Colegate would certainly have resulted in a failure, and might have caused the loss of brave and valuable men, while all that could have been accomplished by so dangerous an expedition would have been to bury a man whose body they might have been unable to find. We know Lieutenant Elliott's course was the only proper and reasonable one under the circumstances.

That *apologia* appeared in the *Spokane Review* on December 5. On the 6th, the New York men checked out of their hotel and boarded a train for home.

Their farewell statement had done little to quell the storm. The *Lewiston Tribune*, noting that Carlin planned to write a book about his adventure, declared the book "will necessarily be incomplete and unsatisfactory since it will not be able to describe the chief feature of the expedition: how George Colgate died. No human mind will ever know how death came to that poor fellow...the book will be flat and unfinished. It is also a matter of grave question whether Mr. Carlin's book will describe the actions of George Colgate when told that he was condemned to solitary death, or what he said when Mr. Carlin's party not only abandoned the old man to die alone but also deprived him of every atom of food or nourishment that could have sustained him until relief might arrive."

The defense of Lieutenant Elliott by Carlin and Himmelwright apparently had no effect on the *Tribune*'s Weippe correspondent. The reporter, noting with pride that the Weippe post office had served as headquarters of the relief party, wrote:

> The fact that the expedition could proceed no further after finding Carlin and his three comrades is too ridiculous to be entertained by any person of ordinary intelligence. Had they failed to find young Carlin when they did the expedition could and would have proceeded on its way. But Carlin was found and the expedition could go no further. The fact that one man is inferior to another was never more clearly demonstrated than in the present instance, and while the General was successful in finding his son his soldiers have covered themselves with infamy and have retired from the scene of action disgraced and dishonored.

The sentiments of the Weippe reporter were widely shared. As one newspaper put it: "Had it been young Carlin or one of his friends who had been deserted, instead of the party's cook, there is no doubt that Elliott would have reached him with his command even though he would have to tunnel through forty feet of snow."

The *Spokane Review* was more generous toward the Carlin party than either the *Tribune* or most of the other papers around the country. Referring in an editorial to the abandonment of Colegate, the *Review* said that "Unquestionably the act was not heroic. It was selfish in a measure....With the snowy wilderness around them, face to face with danger and playing at desperate odds with death, the Carlin party took a philosophical view of their duty and requirements....So they put away sentiment and sacrificed something to their instinct of self-preservation." And it added that most men, in similar straits, probably would have acted just as these men did.

Elliott did not get off so easy. The editorial writer asked, "When [he] met the wanderers, why did he fail to dispatch a detail of his party in search of the abandoned man? Here was a case where nothing should have been left to doubt."

Blame fell about equally upon Carlin and Himmelwright for abandoning Colegate, and upon Elliott for letting them talk him out of continuing the search. Some people observed that the two trappers who were going into the Bitterroots might have found Colegate if they had not been told by Elliott's raft builders that the Lochsa was too dangerous.

Some old-timers, in letters to the papers, maintained that Carlin and Himmelwright were exaggerating their hardships; those river bottoms were relatively warm and anyone with outdoor skills could safely winter there. And William Wright, the Montana guide, had expected there would be little or no snow on the Lochsa. Others pointed out that this was not an ordinary winter, and there were later reports of ten feet of snow at Jerry Johnson's cabin.

Keeley continued adding fuel to the fire. He visited Post Falls during the week following the party's arrival in Spokane, claiming that the Carlin-Himmelwright version of events was wrong. He said that while the rafts were under construction both of these men spent their time hunting, and that Colegate, instead of being in a stupor at the time they left him, was feeling better and looking forward to a happy homecoming. Keeley told the widow that on the morning of the abandonment, the five able-bodied men divided all the food among themselves and marched off without any further care of the ailing camp cook.

Fannie Colegate, already upset by what she considered a flippant brush-off by young Carlin, became more angry and so did her neighbors. They organized an entertainment program at the hall of the Grand Army of the Republic to raise money for the Colegate family. Keeley attended, and his story was much discussed during an indignation meeting that preceded the program. He had said he was seeking the reward money and would sue if he didn't get it. According to the reporter who covered the meeting for the *Review*, the people attending took this to mean that he was not an unbiased source of information; they agreed they should not treat his story as gospel.

After a long discussion that was "earnest and orderly," the group reached its conclusion and adopted the following resolution:

> That we extend to the family of George T. Colegate, in their terrible bereavement, the heartfelt sympathy of this community.
> That we hold William E. Carlin and A.L.A. Himmelwright responsible for the management of the Carlin party.
> That we express our thanks to William E. Carlin and A.L.A. Himmelwright for the care and patience shown toward George Colegate—according to their published account—up to the hour when he was left behind.
> That we deplore the long delay on the river bank—which the construction of rafts does not explain—whereby time and food were wasted that should have been used, for the sake of the sick companion, in prompt and careful retreat.
> That we condemn the abandonment of George Colegate, while confessedly within a few hours of his death, and leaving him on his feet staggering in the snow without shelter, without fire, and without the presence of a loyal comrade to close his eyes and note the location of his body, as an act of hideous barbarity.
> That in the light of their own published statements and such other information as we can obtain, we denounce William E. Carlin and A.L.A. Himmelwright as unfit to associate with sportsmen, wanting the elements of manhood, and in their treatment of George Colegate's widow, wholly void of the considerate spirit and generosity of gentlemen.

Over its report on the Post Fall meeting, the *Spokane Review* carried this headline:

LEFT ALONE TO DIE

Survivors of the Carlin Party
Accused of Cowardice

FOR DESERTING COLGATE

Citizens of Post Falls Pass Resolutions
Condemning the Hunters.

WIDOW AND FAMILY DESTITUTE

Keeley showed up a few days later in Missoula. There, he said he had wanted to leave some of the food with Colegate but that young Carlin, who had bought the grub from him, would not permit it. Keeley said also that after the five men had walked away from Colegate, he went back and gave the sick man his revolver and a cartridge belt. Even after they realized the fix they were in, Keeley said, the New York men couldn't be roused out of their blankets before 10 o'clock in the morning, and he added that they had offered no help building the rafts—suggesting that he and Spencer had done it alone. Furthermore, he declared, they could have made it all the way out on the rafts had the New Yorkers not lost their nerve.

Keeley's interview appeared in the *Missoulian* under this page one headline:

OH! MAN'S
INHUMANITY!

Ben Keeley's Dreadful Tale
of the Desertion

A TIN CUP, MATCHES, AND SALT

A Harrowing Narrative Which
Reveals the Dark Secret of
the Trip into the
Bitter Roots

Throughout all this, nothing was heard from John Pierce. Carlin's brother-in-law gave no interviews, and after the party's arrival at the Spokane railroad depot he dropped out of sight.

Spencer, however, *was* heard from, and more than once. In newspaper interviews he defended Carlin's decision to leave Colegate behind, but he insisted the tragedy could have been avoided. If Carlin had heeded his advice in the first week of October, they could have got out by way of the Lolo trail on horses. But he said Carlin and Himmelwright were enjoying the hunt too much and would not leave. When Jerry Johnson warned them that they should get out while they could, he said, Carlin complained that the old gent wanted all the hunting for himself.

Spencer's description of the parting with Colegate differed from those of Carlin and Himmelwright. Carlin, in his interview with Roberts, said that after they decided to start walking, they had an early-morning conversation with Colegate.

"He seemed to have only a general idea of what was going on. Once he said to me: 'Well, Carlin, I guess I'll be the first one to fall.' All of us were in a deplorable fix. We divided our grub, discarded all our blankets and arms, except a dozen rounds of ammunition each and two guns. Thus we made the start. The old man was scarcely walking. He just moved, that was all. That was the last we saw of him."

In their joint statement published in the *Review* on December 5, Carlin and Himmelwright wrote that "after making him comfortable with a blanket and equipping him with matches, salt, etc., as we were ourselves, we began our journey afoot. When last seen Colegate was slowly and aimlessly moving toward us. He did not speak a word that we remember after he crossed the river with us where we abandoned the rafts."

Spencer was quoted as saying the men divided their food evenly with Colegate, "and then we knelt beside him and in fervent prayer we bade him goodbye....We made a fire, placed wood within his reach, and came away, Colegate moaning, and amid his sobs making us promise to tell his family he died like a man. He begged all of us that we should go and save ourselves, and so we left."

In a later statement, Spencer seemed to contradict himself: "The reason that we did not leave Colegate what might seem to have been his rightful share of the little company's provender was that we did not think it would be of any assistance to him as he was too weak to have any use of it, and we couldn't well afford to spare him any of our grub."

Throughout that winter, newspapers across the country batted the story around, sometimes lobbing it off the court. On December 16, the *New York World* printed an account provided by a brakeman for the Northern Pacific Railroad who said that two trappers had found Colegate staggering around in a heavy snowstorm, dazed and nearly dead. He said they had nursed him back to health and then had taken him to Lewiston.

The story took a chilling twist on December 27 when a boatman dragging driftwood out of the Snake River some ninety miles downstream from Greer found a bottle with a note in it that suggested the abandoned cook was still alive. It was written in pencil and this is what it said, according to *The New York Times* of December 30, 1893:

> Bitter Root Mountains, Nov. 27.
> I am alive and well. Tell them to come and get me as soon as any one finds this. I am fifty miles from civilization, as near as I can tell. I am George Colgate, one of the lost Carlin party. My legs are better. I can walk some. Come soon. Take this to Kendrick, Idaho, and you will be liberally rewarded. My name is George Colgate, from Post Falls. This bottle came by me one day and I caught it, and write these words to take me out. Direct to the St. Elmo Hotel, Kendrick, Idaho.
> GEORGE COLGATE
> Goodbye, wife and children.

If the sick man had written that note he would have been alive and rational fifteen days after the rest of the party walked away from him. But if the signature on the note was as reported, Colegate couldn't have written it because he didn't spell his name that way.

The New York Times, having received this dispatch from Moscow, Idaho, asked Himmelwright to comment. Himmelwright said the note had to be a fraud because even if Colegate had lived that long, where would he have got the bottle? The only person upriver from him was Jerry Johnson, and the only bottle Johnson had he had given to Carlin and Himmelwright for carrying gun oil. And even if he had found a bottle, Himmelwright said, Colegate had no pencil to write with. This note was Keeley's doing, Himmelwright told the *Times.*

According to the reporter in Moscow, the note was taken straight-away to Kendrick, where the writing was compared with

Colegate's signature on the register of the St. Elmo Hotel. It was a match, the reporter wrote, but that would be hard to prove now. Neither the note nor the hotel register has survived the fires and floods that wracked the town of Kendrick around the turn of the century.

27 General Carlin decided to settle in Spokane. It made sense to him to spend his retirement in a region where he had friends and where he was known. The Army of the Columbia was under a new commander now, but the old one still had ties to the command, had good friends still serving in the various forts and detachments of the region, and still was welcomed wherever military officers gathered for food, drink, or reminiscence.

He had suggested to young Carlin that possibly he and Cora might like to live in Spokane also, but Will was burning over the continued sniping, as he called it, by people who accused him of abandoning a dying comrade. The newspapers insisted on keeping the issue alive, or so it seemed to him. But if he thought he could escape the heat by returning to the East, he was mistaken. The eastern press was no more kind than the papers of the Pacific Northwest.

The *New York World* published Keeley's version of the episode, including his statement that Carlin had been implacable in his decision to leave Colegate behind even though he, Keeley, had tried to talk him out of it; and that Keeley had returned to Colegate after the others were marching away and given the cook a revolver and ammunition belt plus one of his blankets. Carlin demanded equal space, and in late December the *World* published his statement denying most of what Keeley had said. The decision to leave Colegate was not his alone, he insisted, and he said among other things that Keeley had not given Colegate anything; Colegate himself had picked a blanket at random off the pile that had been discarded, he said, and Himmelwright had tied it onto him.

The crossfire became so heavy in the eastern press that Himmelwright wrote a thirty-point defense of himself and Carlin and circulated it among their friends. Like their previous statements in the *World,* the *Spokane Review,* the *Missoulian* and other papers, it was mainly a denial of Keeley's charges. Himmelwright put the blame for their problems firmly on Colegate and insisted he and Carlin had done what anyone in a similar fix would have done. He ended it this way: "Finally, I assert that were all the details known, and the many trying situations of the party thoroughly understood, our actions during the entire trip would be proved to be not only justifiable, but honorable and praiseworthy."

As this was written, friends of the Colegate family in Post Falls were talking of organizing a party to go in search of the body. Their resolution condemning the Carlin party for its treatment of the camp cook had helped the family in its bereavement, but it had been in the end an empty gesture. There were some in Post Falls who felt a need to act. They held meetings at which some cited Keeley's claim that Carlin and Himmelwright had exaggerated the dangers of winter travel on the Lochsa. Some continued to insist that Elliott could have gone up the river and found Colegate if Carlin hadn't talked him out of it. On word that a note bearing Colegate's signature had been found in a bottle in the Snake River, the meetings took on fresh urgency. They produced no action, however, until Charles Colegate volunteered to put on his boots and go, if some others would go with him.

That was in January, 1894. In February, in the dead of winter and despite warnings that they could not possibly succeed, Charles and three of his father's friends—William Martin, M. Shelton, and Jack Rexford—left for Kendrick en route to Weippe and the Lochsa.

They carried provisions for twenty days and managed to make their way on foot up the river to a point some distance above the camp where the Carlin party was thought to have abandoned its rafts.

They saw no sign of George Colegate or any of his goods. Not a blanket, not a shred of clothing, nothing. The rigors of the trail, pushing through deep snow under heavy packs, frequently over steep hillsides, had reduced them to near helplessness.

One evening, trying to keep warm, they built a fire beside a cedar snag and got into their blankets. During the night the snag fell and struck Bill Martin as he slept. It broke Martin's collar bone, tore away flesh and skin, and nearly killed him. The others threw together a rude shelter of boughs and for a week they took care of Martin, a former sheriff of Kootenai County. When it seemed that they could safely move him, they fashioned a rough litter and carried him on it back down the river. They packed him for thirty-five miles to the first cabin, a prospector's shack, and continued to carry him from shelter to shelter until they were met by a party sent out to find them.

It did not escape notice, especially in Post Falls, that two men and a boy had done for their comrade what five men had not been able to do for George Colegate.

In March, two members of another four-man party drowned in an attempt to get up the Lochsa and find either Colegate or his body. And in May, Carlin and Himmelwright, with the help of the Anaconda, Montana, *Standard,* hired Spencer and Wright, and a man named George Ogden, to go in search of Colegate's remains.

The searchers were to hike in from Missoula and go first to Jerry Johnson's cabin. They would arrange to pick up the hunting trophies and camp gear the Carlin party had left there in November. Then they were to hike down the Lochsa as far as necessary to find some sign of Colegate. The three men left Missoula on May 21 with two pack animals and reached Jerry Johnson's cabin on June 7. Johnson had spent the winter alone except for his dog, Tootsey, and was almost out of food. He told Spencer that the horses, his three and Carlin's ten, had died during the winter and that he had been almost a prisoner in his cabin for two and half months, trapped by snow. The snow on the flat beside his cabin had been ten feet deep, he said. And Spencer, having come off the divide over packed snow deeper than that, believed him.

Spencer and Wright found the antlers, scalps, and camp equipment in good condition and proceeded down the river in search of some signs of Colegate's fate. After three days they reached the place where the Carlin party had made its last camp. This was where Keeley and Himmelwright had chopped down the pine tree so it would fall across the river, and where the party had abandoned its rafts. This was where the other five men had left Colegate and started out on foot for civilization. They saw the remains of a tent and a blanket caught on driftwood in the river. They found more blankets in the sand several feet from the water, and farther downstream they found the unopened bedroll that must have been Colegate's. Still farther down, a half mile or so, they found part of a corduroy coat sleeve, also presumably Colegate's, dragging in the water.

They continued down the Lochsa for several miles but found nothing more and returned to Jerry Johnson's cabin. After resting there for two days, Spencer and Ogden packed the Carlin party's trophies and camp gear and left for Missoula. Wright, who had been bruised and battered on the trail, decided to remain with Jerry Johnson for a few days to rest and heal.

Meanwhile, the *Missoulian*, possibly unaware that the *Standard* had a party already on the scene, hired Ben Keeley to make a search for George Colegate. Thus it was that as Keeley and his party were starting in to the upper Lochsa they met Spencer and Ogden coming out. Spencer told Keeley that he was wasting his time and the *Missoulian*'s money because there was nothing on the Lochsa to be found. But Keeley pushed on anyhow. When he reached Jerry Johnson's cabin, Wright told him what he already had heard from Spencer: That he was wasting his time because Wright and his party had been over that ground and collected everything there. Keeley apparently did continue on down the river, only to discover that Spencer had been right.

In Spencer's report to his sponsors, he said it seemed unlikely that Colegate had gone any distance from the place where the others had left him. His bedroll had not been opened, and that meant that he probably was not fully conscious during his last hours—meaning, in turn, that he probably had died painlessly. Spencer said also that high water in the early spring must have carried the body downstream, and that was why they couldn't find it.

When summer came, the Army sent several units into the field to survey and map areas of the inland Northwest. Among these was a detachment under Lieutenant Charles P. Elliott assigned—probably not by coincidence—to the Clearwater River region. Elliott went in by way of the Lolo Trail, then down the switchbacks that the Carlin party had earlier descended to Jerry Johnson's well-trampled back yard. The troops paused there long enough to build a canvas boat and floated down the Lochsa to the point where the Carlin party had abandoned its rafts.

From here, Elliott began a meticulous search of the shore on both sides of the river, looking for clues to Colegate's presence. Finally, on an afternoon in August, one of his men noticed a pile of something on the north bank that seemed out of place in that setting. It was all that remained of George Colegate: A mangled left thigh and leg, with scraps of clothing attached.

The spot was eight miles below the camp where Colegate had last been seen.

As soon as the newspapers reported Elliott's find, the whole controversy boiled up again. How could he have traveled eight miles if he had died that first night? Some speculated that Colegate must have staggered all that way in spite of his illness—a sign that he had been needlessly abandoned. Some said it must have been animals. In most minds, the remains—all there was after the animals had scattered the rest—had simply been carried downstream during spring thaw.

Elliott and his men carried the bones back up the river to the warm springs, near where the Carlin party had built the rafts, and buried them. Then they piled some rocks on the grave to mark it, and one of the troops burned Colegate's name (misspelled) into a piece of wood as a monument.

Fifteen years later, in 1909, a Northern Pacific railroad survey crew happened upon the grave and Charles Harrison photographed it. The crew's report of the location subsequently got lost, and the grave location remained unknown until 1924, when a U.S. Forest Service employee, camping in the area, went looking for it. Ralph Space found a mound of rocks not far from the warm springs but couldn't be sure these were the rocks that Elliott's party had piled on Colegate's grave. In 1956, the *Spokesman-Review,* successor to the old *Spokane Review*, published an article about the Carlin hunting party. Charles Harrison read the piece, then looked up the old 1909 photograph and mailed it to the newspaper, which published it.

Ralph Space, by then the supervisor of the Clearwater National Forest, happened to see the picture. It looked to him a lot like the pile of rocks he had seen on the Lochsa, and he wrote to Harrison, asking if Harrison would take him to the site. Harrison did, and Space was able to confirm that he had indeed found Colegate's grave on that camping trip thirty-two years earlier.

There is a Forest Service marker there now, visible from U.S. Highway 12. When the author of this account last drove past the spot, in the summer of 1993, there were fresh flowers, a coffee can full, brightening the shoulder of the road.

Epilogue

General Carlin settled in Spokane, made his home at the Spokane Club, and invested in downtown real estate. He died on October 4, 1903, near Livingston, Montana, while riding a Northern Pacific train from Spokane to his boyhood home in Carrollton, Illinois, where he planned to visit his sister. According to his obituary in the *Spokesman-Review*, he was in apparent good health when he got into his berth on Saturday night, October 3. He became ill early the next morning and quickly died. The body was taken to a funeral home in Livingston, and his only son, Will, was sent for. The general was seventy-four years old.

Will Carlin died at his home on New York's Fifth Avenue on March 19, 1928, at the age of sixty-two. His obituary in *The Times* devotes a single sentence to the event for which he is remembered in the Clearwater country, and makes no mention of George Colegate or his fate. Perhaps this is not surprising; Carlin was much better known in New York as a naturalist, photographer, and firearms authority than as the leader of the so-called "Carlin party" of 1893.

Martin Spencer remained in Spokane also, and Abe Himmelwright returned to a successful civil engineering practice in New York. What happened to Ben Keeley, the fractious one, or John Pierce, the quiet one, the author does not know.

Did the two terriers, Idaho and Montana, get back to their home on the upper St. Joe? The author assumes that they did. George Colegate's Post Falls neighbors would have made sure of that since Colegate had borrowed them from Fred Palmer and would have wanted them returned.

Charles Colegate married a Post Falls girl, Grace Delameter, on July 14, 1897. He died four years later of typhoid fever, leaving his wife and a daughter, Elsena. The Kootenai County census of

1900 lists his occupation as engineer. His obituary in *The Silver Blade* of Rathdrum, Idaho, suggests that there was still some rancor remaining from the Carlin party's treatment of the elder Colegate eight years earlier: "His father, George Colegate, it will be remembered, accompanied the Carlin hunting party to the Clearwater country in the fall of '93, acting in the capacity of cook. There he fell sick and was foully deserted and left to perish among the rugged mountains, while the cowardly curs comprising the Carlin party sneaked into civilization and reported that they had been unable to bring Mr. Colegate out with them."

Fannie Colegate, George's widow, remained single until 1914, when she married Martin Wold of Coeur d'Alene.

The highway built along the north bank of the Lochsa in the 1950s and 1960s, U.S. 12, skirts the flat where Jerry Johnson's cabin once stood and provides easy access to the lower warm springs where the Carlin party did much of its hunting. The highway has made the warm springs so popular in recent years that authorities have sometimes had to establish hours of use—partly to settle disputes between nude bathers and families with children.

After more than a hundred years, much about the Colegate episode remains tantalizingly unclear. For example, some readers must wonder why the guide, Spencer, allowed the hunters to prevail in several crucial decisions that he argued against; after all, they had hired him because he knew this country better than they did. Perhaps the employer-employee relationship that existed in the 1890s gave them that privilege. There is a not-so-subtle indication of separation by social class in a book that Himmelwright wrote later, under a pseudonym, in which he refers consistently to his companions (and himself) by their first names, and to the hired hands by their last. Here's *In the Heart of the Bitterroot Mountains*, page 93: "Spencer and Keeley went down the river to look for suitable timber for the rafts. Will was laid up in camp with a bad boil on the ankle of his right foot, and Abe had a sore neck from a wrench he had received while out hunting a few days before. Colgate grew gradually worse."

Why, in Heaven's name, did Charles Colegate and three others strike out in the middle of winter on a search that was almost certain to be fruitless? Couldn't it have waited until spring? Perhaps the public outrage in the small town of Post Falls was such that it couldn't. George Colegate clearly was well-liked; he was a justice of the peace, or had been, and he had many friends. Those friends were angry at the New York men, protective of Fannie and the children, and determined, one can guess, not to be found wanting when there was something to be done. To seize the day, they had to go before any others did, and so they went—and returned broken down, but with honor. They didn't find a body to bury, but in the extremity of their bad luck they accomplished something more: They showed everyone who noticed how you dealt in these mountains with a stricken comrade.

Should Lieutenant Elliott have gone in search of Colegate after making the Carlin party safe and comfortable? The lieutenant may have asked himself the same question as he surveyed the cook's remains on that August afternoon eight months later, lying several miles from the spot where he'd been left. But in November, Elliott's judgment, based on what he had been told by Carlin and unclouded by the desperation that propelled the Post Falls search party, can hardly be faulted. It would have been foolhardy to risk his troops and his civilian volunteers on a search for a man he presumed was already dead.

Only George Colegate could answer the most enduring question of all: Why he went into the mountains without his catheters, against the advice of his doctor, and why he refused to go back to Kendrick in order to save himself. The simple answer may be the one he gave Carlin and Pierce when they pressed him for it. He hated to use the instruments, he said, because it hurt every time, and he thought he could get by. And when Spencer offered to take him out, he told Spencer he would go when the rest of them did, and not until. Perhaps it made no difference. By this time it may already have been too late to get out on horseback.

The most damning question raised by the Post Falls neighbors during Carlin's briefing in the hotel dining room was this: If the New York men were so sure that Colegate did not survive the first night of his abandonment, why couldn't they have stayed with him one more day and buried the body? It seemed to the Post Falls people, and to many others, that perhaps the hunters were not so sure after all that Colegate died that night. And to the hunters themselves, it must later have seemed clear that it would have been much better to leave a dead man behind than one who was alive and standing up. Yet the fact remains that the calculation which determined their course of action—that they didn't have enough food for another day in camp—was correct. When the rescuers found them, they had nothing left to eat.

It can also be said, in the hunters' defense, that if they had lived in Weippe instead of New York state, and if they had done precisely what these hunters did, not so much would have been made of it. The old rancher who met them at Brown's cabin, on learning that they were Easterners, assumed that they must be greenhorns. Himmelwright especially was aware of the stigma; it accounts for his laborious defense of his own and Carlin's wilderness expertise (see Appendix C). Some of the old-timers who claimed a superior knowledge of the Bitterroots also said the weather didn't get bad in the valley of the Lochsa. The winter of 1893 proved even the locals wrong.

According to Himmelwright's book (page 176), the expedition met disaster for two reasons: The early fall of snow, and Colegate's disability. "Had either of these misfortunes befallen the party singly, there probably would have been no more serious consequences than a little inconvenience or exposure for members of the party; but both occurring simultaneously, the party found every resource by which the one misfortune could be averted, handicapped or rendered impracticable by the other." Earlier in the book (page 72), however, Himmelwright reports that on October 2, "Spencer expressed fears that we might be snowed in, but no one deemed the danger from that source sufficiently serious to devote a day to climbing to the top of the burnt ridge to investigate the matter....[On October 6] Spencer began to urge our return, and John, who did not care to hunt in the rain, vigorously seconded the motion. Abe insisted that Indian Summer and milder weather must yet come before the winter would set in, and that the return in the rain and snow would be undertaken under the very worst conditions for Colgate." So they continued to hunt until finally heading for the ridge on the 10th, only to be turned back by deep snow.

Spencer had every reason to believe it was going to be a bad winter. He suspected it as early as mid-September, after checking weather reports; he understood the warning of the rancher at Brown's cabin, that they had better not stay long in the mountains—a warning confirmed by Jerry Johnson and by both Larson and Houghton. But Spencer could not convince Carlin and Himmelwright of the need to move until it was too late. That is the flaw in Himmelwright's defense of the party's actions.

Deepening snow on the Lolo Trail might have made it impossible to get out even as early as the 2nd of October, but neither Carlin nor Himmelwright could have known that. They didn't leave when Spencer urged it because they wanted more hunting. Himmelwright himself makes that clear, and in doing so demolishes his own claim that the circumstances gave them no choices.

In the end, however, it was Colegate who assured his own death by hiding from the others the source of his illness. Himmelwright, seeking to explain this behavior, suggests that perhaps it could be traced to "the effects of his long-standing ailment, which in twenty years may have impaired his faculties." That's a generous and forgiving assessment, but it may be as good as any.

Appendix A
Young Mr. Carlin's Book

The Lewiston Tribune *in 1893 published a weekly column called "Etches and Sketches," unsigned but apparently written by the editor. This is "Etches and Sketches" for December 7, 1893.*

Young Mr. Carlin says he is going to write a book. In it he will describe the incidents and amusing features of his trip into the mountains in the fall of '93. The book will probably be for private circulation only among the friends and acquaintances of this young man who has had fame thrust upon him, for the great world no more cares for him now that he is no longer lost. The book will necessarily be incomplete and unsatisfactory since it will not be able to describe the chief feature of the expedition: how George Colgate died. No human mind will ever know how death came to that poor fellow; whether the snow and ice literally froze the life spark out of his feeble frame; whether the gnashings of hunger snapped the life-chord in twain; whether forest wolves scented the helpless body and kind in their cruelty ended his earthly anguish, or whether the divine spark lingered on and on, hoping, hoping ever, until perhaps the spirit fled in an ecstacy of deluded expectation; without such morbid yet important detail as to how and when—why we all know—the tragedy occurred, the book will be flat and unfinished. It is also a matter of grave question whether Mr. Carlin's book will describe the actions of George Colgate when told that he was condemned to solitary death, or what he said when Mr. Carlin's party not only abandoned the old man to die alone but also deprived him of every atom of food or nourishment that could have sustained him until relief might arrive.

We know what young Mr. Carlin would have said and done if he had been forsaken under similar circumstances—or at least we know what he did say and do when the guide volunteered to leave the party after making them safe and reasonably comfortable while he went in search of rescue for them. At that point young Mr. Carlin objected stoutly and refused to be left without a guide even though he and his friends were absolutely safe and certain of rescue. No, he would rather die, provided his companions died too, than to live forty-eight hours in comparative comfort but bereft of a guide. So we can easily imagine that young Mr. Carlin would have made Clearwater canyon howl if the suggestion had been made to leave him there alone, sick and disabled, while his stout and able-bodied comrades proceeded homeward and took his last crust wherewith to feed their contemptible carcasses. In this connection the *Spokane Review* feebly glosses over the inhumanity of Carlin and his party under the plea that the old man was almost dead anyhow, but proceeds to scorify Lieut. Elliott for not continuing on to Colgate's rescue. But Elliott was told by Carlin's gang that the old man was by that time dead and if not, he ought to be. And so he ought to be, for Carlin certainly put all the facilities within easy reach, and if he did not die it was through some miscarriage of Carlin's arrangements which he could neither forsee [*sic*]nor prevent. An interesting feature of the forthcoming book will be a full account of the pathetic scene wherein young Carlin decided that he durst not attempt to rescue a superior camera for which he had paid—or promised—$85; how he eventually resigned himself to break it and take therefrom the films which—let angels rejoice—he saved. But the collection of films is also incomplete for it contains for the wife and six children of George Colgate no views of the culminating tragedy of Clearwater canyon.

Appendix B
Ben Keeley's Narrative

In this page-one story, the Weekly Missoulian *of December 20, 1893, prints Ben Keeley's version of the travail in the Bitterroots, and in the process makes clear whose side it is on.*

———————

The startling account published in yesterday's *Missoulian* of the abandonment of poor George Colgate to a horrible death on the banks of the Clearwater River in the Bitterroot mountains, by his comrades of the Carlin-Himmelwright hunting party, on or about the 13th day of November, is probably one of the most heart-rending and, at the same time, inconceivable stories within the scope of ordinary imagination. That five men in the full possession of their senses should desert a comrade and leave him in such dire distress as was the unfortunate Colgate, seems improbable; that the first opportunity thereafter presented to send relief to their abandoned comrade should be allowed to pass over without even serious consideration seems almost barbarous. Yet these are facts that are rapidly being brought in connection with the desertion of George T. Colgate, a former respected citizen of the pretty little village of Post Falls, Idaho, and for which, William E. Carlin, a young New Yorker, the son of General William P. Carlin, but recently retired from active service in the United States army and his companion, A.L.A. Himmelwright, also of New York, are in the main responsible. The story told in these columns last evening is more than corroborated by Ben Keeley, the trapper himself. Mr. Keeley arrived in Missoula yesterday and upon being broached by a *Missoulian* representative declared himself more than willing to narrate the circumstances attendant upon the desertion of Colgate upon the banks of the Clearwater, by the party of which he, himself, was a member. Mr.

Keeley is a young appearing man though slightly more than 40 years of age of rugged build and apparently just the man to attempt a trip so full of hardships as was experienced by the little band of beleagured [*sic*]hunters. In narrating his story Mr. Keeley made no attempt whatever to shield himself from any blame that might be laid at his own door on account of the unfortunate business, other than to say that he had placed himself in the service of Carlin and Himmelwright and that he was bound to abide by their instructions during the journey to civilization.

THE TRAPPER'S STORY

"It was sometime during the month of October," said Keeley, "I cannot give the exact date, for I did not carry a calendar with me, when I went into the mountains, to trap for the winter, that Martin Spencer, the guide of young Carlin's party, came to my cabin and stated that he and his charges had too long delayed their exit from the Bitterroots and that he thought they were in a bad fix. The main body of the party shortly after came up and Carlin and Himmelwright questioned me very closely regarding my knowledge of the country and ability to construct and handle a raft in mountain streams. Being satisfied with the information they thus acquired, they proposed to purchase my share of the provisions in the cabin occupied by Jerry Johnson and myself and to engage me at a liberal figure to assist them in making their escape by means of the Clearwater. This proposition I quickly accepted, being induced largely to do so by the fact that my mountain partner and myself were on anything but good terms and I was glad of an opportunity to get out of putting in the long winter with him. I noticed at this time that George Colgate, who accompanied the Carlin party, was a very sick man and called attention to the fact that the trip ahead of us was an exceptionally difficult one and that it would be almost impossible for a man in his condition to successfully accomplish it. There was some talk of leaving the poor fellow behind with Johnson, in the cabin, but the latter was surly and we feared he would refuse the suffering man even the necessities of life and so we decided to take him along with us. We traveled a distance of about three miles when we struck the river, and as timber was plentiful concluded to at once set about the construction of two rafts."

THE ABANDONMENT OF COLGATE.

"It was then that Carlin and Himmelwright exhibited their actual indifference to their surroundings and the necessity of hurrying along as rapidly as possible, particularly on Colgate's account," continued the trapper. "They were both exceedingly particular that the rafts should be constructed in a certain way, but instead of assisting in the work they put in their time hunting and fishing and eating like beavers, not withstanding that our provisions were rapidly becoming exhausted. Pierce assisted Spencer and myself in building the rafts but the work was necessarily slow and I think we consumed about fourteen days in this task. Colgate, however, was much improved by this time and we looked forward to but little trouble on his account. On the third of November, according to Carlin's diary, we divided the provisions between the two rafts and started down. On the first day out the head raft was caught in a whirlpool and submerged, Colgate being thrown into the cold waters of the river, but was promptly pulled out and the journey continued. All went well until the 13th, when we landed, and on reconnoitering found that the stream was no longer navigable and that the tedious, perilous trip along the rocky and almost impassable banks of the river must be at once commenced. It was necessary, however, to cross the stream and we were obliged to fell a large tree and crawl across on its trunk and branches. Colgate, though striving manfully, was very weak and almost unable to walk, the plunge into the river a few days before having had a very serious effect on him. Young Carlin was very impatient. More through his own selfishness than through any other cause, our provisions were nearly exhausted and it certainly did appear that we should all go hungry before reaching civilization, and Carlin's orders were to make all haste. We talked the matter over with Colgate before crossing the river and told him it was a case of every man for himself. The poor old fellow begged us not to desert him, but young Carlin was inexorable and turning on his heel ordered us to proceed. I gave the poor old man my blanket, an old army covering, and Carlin handed him a tin cup, some matches and salt. Colgate had his own fishing tackle.

BUT NOT A MOUTHFUL OF FOOD

was left with him. It was cruel and cowardly I suppose, and our action will, no doubt, be thoroughly condemned by all sportsmen, but such were the orders from those in charge of the party and Spencer and myself were powerless to prevent it. After crossing the river I turned and looked at the unfortunate Colgate for the last time.* Not a word escaped his lips, but the look of horror that crossed the old man's weather-beaten face as he realized his awful position, will remain in my memory until my dying day. The journey from then on until we met with Lieutenant Elliott's party has already been fully and correctly told. We had been entirely out of provisions for two days and all were weak and considerably played out, particularly Carlin, who could not have lasted much longer."

ELLIOTT'S NEGLECT OF DUTY.

"It was on Wednesday, the 22nd of November, that we were met by Lieutenant Elliott's command. We had therefore traveled nine days after abandoning Colgate, but we had not accomplished any great distance in that time, some days but scarcely a mile being covered. The desertion of Colgate was fully explained to Elliott at that time, and there was some talk of sending back a relief party in quest of him. I told Elliott that it was a difficult and dangerous trip up the river, and young Carlin finally persuaded him to abandon the idea. There was no snow whatever along the route we had just traveled and it was certainly possible, but a very dangerous undertaking, to attempt the trip back to the rocky bank where we had left poor Colgate to perish, and I am confident that had it been young Carlin, or one of his friends, who had been thus deserted, that the attempt at rescue would have been promptly made. However, young Carlin carried his point and after resting for a couple of days we journeyed into Kendrick and subsequently, in company with General Carlin, reached Spokane. A few days later Mrs. Colgate, heartbroken and barely able to stand up under her sad bereavement, arrived in that city to learn the story of her husband's untimely end from the lips of his associates and was received by the general, his son and

---

*Keeley is saying the others left Colegate on the south bank when they crossed the river to the north bank in order to walk out. All the rest seem to agree that Colegate was with them when they crossed the river.

Himmelwright in an almost insolent manner and summarily disposed of with a few paltry dollars that they figured was due Colgate for services rendered on the trip. The poor woman's pathetic appeal for justice was pitiful in the extreme and I hurried on to her home at Post Falls and without reserve, told her all the harrowing circumstances surrounding the desertion of her husband far up in the Bitterroot mountains and far beyond the reach of loving hands or human assistance. After leaving Post Falls I came straight to Missoula, arriving here this morning."

A TRAGIC COINCIDENCE

Mr. Keeley left yesterday afternoon going to the ranch of a friend, Mr. Wilkinson, on the Lo Lo, with whom he will reside this winter as it is now too late in the season for him to return to the mountains and follow his avocation. In connection with that visit arises a singular incident, which the trapper related just as he was taking the train and which in effect was as follows: "A little more than a year ago," he said, "I assisted Mr. Wilkinson in locating the ranch on the Lo Lo where he now resides with his family and with whom I am going to visit. Shortly after I arrived there I saw the necessity of a foot-bridge across the stream and, taking an axe, felled a monster tree which, by careful calculation completely straddled the water just in the position I wanted it. It was a monster log, nearly five feet across, and little did I dream when cutting it, that it would, a year later, prove the stepping stone to the graves of the two unfortunate ladies—mesdames Hartley and Hickernell—who last spring met their death in the icy waters of the turbulent Lo Lo by falling from that log. Last month, in the wooded labyrinths of the Clearwater I felled another tree; a tree which led another party to safety, but at the base of which poor Colgate remained to give up his life. When I cut that tree, visions of the tragedy on the Lo Lo arose before me and the crash of the falling pine appeared as the death knell of the poor fellow we left behind. Yes, it was a singular coincidence—the cutting of those two trees—each act being attended with a tragic result."

Appendix C
The Case for the Defense

Abraham L.A. Himmelwright, stung by criticism in both the western and the eastern press, wrote this statement in defense of himself and William E. Carlin shortly after returning to his home in New York City. He intended it for private distribution among his and Carlin's friends and acquaintances. He mailed a copy of the statement to J. O. Maxon of Lewiston, Idaho, and Maxon gave it to the Lewiston Tribune, *which printed it on July 12, 1894.*

The Carlin hunting party, of which I was a member, has been grossly misrepresented and unjustly censured on account of their action toward George Colgate, a member of the party.

In the absence of authoritative accounts of the trip, the press and the public have preferred to accept the sensational story of Ben Keeley, the trapper, as true. Waiving the fact that correct information was wanting regarding the region through which the party was struggling, without any knowledge of the danger which menaced them, and without the remotest idea of the circumstances that led them to adopt the course they did, the party is judged and condemned, forthwith, and accused of the most selfish and mercenary motives.

So effective did the story of Ben Keeley prove that in several western towns public feeling was aroused in indignation to fever heat and found expression in the adoption of resolutions condemning and denouncing Mr. Carlin and myself in the most scathing terms.

Nor is this all. With the most consummate bigotry and injustice, the kind and efficient Lieut. Charles P. Elliott, who generously volunteered his services to come to our relief, is drawn into the net of popular criticism, where he is basely ridiculed and roundly denounced for not continuing the search for Colgate after meeting the rest of the party. Whether such a search was possible or advisable under the circumstances, was not at all considered.

The story of Ben Keeley has since been proved to be false and malicious by the testimony of all the rest of the party; but the damage it has done and the injustice it has wrought, can never be wholly eradicated.

It would be useless to attempt to go into details within the scope of a communication such as this is intended to be; and an endeavor to describe the situation, with all the attending circumstances, would in all probability prove futile. Persons who have never been in the wildest regions of the far northwest or similar places in South America or elsewhere, can form no idea of the vast and almost impenetrable "Seas of Mountains" that actually exist; nor can anyone who has never undertaken a "hard trip" into such mountainous districts comprehend the many real difficulties and hardships that are invariably encountered. For these reasons it is a difficult matter for the uninitiated to imagine any circumstances whatever which would justify the actions of a party in leaving one of their number behind. There are, besides, certain facts relative to George Colgate, which from a sense of propriety, and a due regard for the feelings of his family, cannot be made public.

Contrary to popular impression, Mr. Carlin and myself are accustomed to the hardships and fatigue incident to such a trip as ours would have been under ordinary circumstances. Most of Mr. Carlin's life since 1871 has been spent on the frontier and in the northwest. He has been a member of numberless hunting parties and has accompanied government exploring expeditions which penetrated into the Lake Cheelan and Okanagan districts of northern Washington, which are known to be among the roughest and most inaccessible regions of the civilized world. Our guide, Mr. Spencer, practically lives in the mountains as he has acted in the capacity of guide for many years. As to myself, in the practice of my profession as a civil engineer, in the employ of the Northern Pacific railroad, I have, on one occasion spent a whole winter in the Coeur d'Alene mountains of northern Idaho, with a party of 22 men, 40 miles from the nearest railroad station, and 16 miles from the nearest ranch. We lived in tents and brought in our supplies by pack train. The snow varied from two to four feet deep, occasionally stopping our pack train for considerable periods, but never inter-fering with the progress of our work, except for one day.

Taking these facts into consideration we were eminently well fitted by training and experience to undertake just such a trip as we proposed. We are also, we trust, justified in claiming that we have a fair idea of what it is possible for a man or a party of men to do under circumstances and conditions which might ordinarily be developed during a hunting trip of that kind. Consequently our opinions on the subject should be, at least, accredited worthy of consideration. Based upon our knowledge of the existing circum-stances and conditions at the time, I make the following assertions:

1st—That George Colgate's illness was due to his leaving be-hind, in the first instance, certain instruments which for ten years had been indispensable to him.*

2d—That he persistently journeyed day after day on horse-back into the woods, for eight days without acquainting any of us of the fact that he had left his appliances behind, when he must have been cognizant of that fact during the first day out from Kendrick.

3d—That on the eighth day he became exhausted when within a short distance of our camping place, and only when importuned by Mr. Carlin did he divulge the truth, informing Mr. Carlin then for the first time that he had been using such instruments for years.

4th—That in his then weak condition he could not have stood the fatigue of a return trip.

5th—That it rained incessantly for thirteen consecutive days after we made camp. This was snow on the mountains where the trail was located, and it was not considered advisable to send him back with the guide during that time.

6th—That on the fourteenth day we curtailed our hunt and made an honest attempt to return by trail.

7th—That when but two-thirds of the way up to where the main trail was, we encountered two and a half feet of soft snow, which indicated, according to our guide's knowledge, four feet of snow or more on the main, or Lo Lo trail.

8th—That to have continued homeward on that route under existing conditions would in all probability have necessitated the

---

*Colegate may have told Himmelwright it was ten years, but Colegate's doctor, in the note he wrote at Carlin's request, said it was twenty.

abandonment of our horses and Colgate in the snow, as he was so incapacitated by his illness that he was unable to walk, and practically helpless.

9th—That because we thought there was a probability of getting Colgate out by floating him down the Clearwater river on a raft, we decided to forego all other considerations, return to our camp on the river, buy out a trapper who had provided himself with a winter supply of provisions, and engage him to assist in building the rafts and accompany us out to civilization.

10th—That notwithstanding the most careful nursing and attention to his requirements, Colgate grew steadily worse and worse.

11th—That examinations of the trail on the 18th and 30th of October by Spencer showed that a crust had formed on the deep snow, so that the rest of the party during that interval could have gotten out of the woods on snow-shoes over the trail—a safe and known route.

12th—That every possible alternative and resource for getting Colgate out safely was investigated, but no other course was practicable than to attempt a passage down the river.

13th—That while we expected to make the passage down the river in about five days or a week, we took fifteen days' provisions with us as a safeguard, and supposing we did not require more, we gave the balance of the provisions which we had purchased to Jerry Johnson, a prospector (the partner of Ben Keeley, who on account of our agreement with Keeley, was compelled to live alone in a rude cabin all winter).

14th—That unexpected difficulties and hardships were encountered and, at the end of eight days, when a point 25 miles down the river had been reached, the river-bed was found to be so full of boulders that further rafting with the object of transporting Colgate safely was an impossibility.

15th—That when Mr. Carlin informed Colgate that we would all have to walk down the river in order to get back to civilization, he received the information with apparent unconcern, showing that he was incapable of realizing the situation.

16th—That Colgate's condition at that time was such that he was incapable of appreciating further kindness or attention from us, and that it was absolutely impossible to take him with us on foot.

17th—That he made no remarks concerning his family, nor paid any attention to us when he saw us make ready to go away on foot, and made no motions or outcry when he saw us disappear one by one down the river, with our packs on our backs.

18th—That we are almost certain that the man died without pain, and without a full return to consciousness that same night, and that had we remained with him and cared for him he would not have appreciated it, and might have lingered in a stupor or unconscious for possibly a day or two during which nearly a third of our remaining provisions would have been consumed and the chance of ultimately saving ourselves greatly lessened.

19th—That while we hoped to accomplish an average of four miles a day on foot, we had according to our estimate 45 miles to travel with only seven days' provisions, along a route where there was practically no game. We saw we would be out of food for a number of days at the latter part of our foot journey under the most favorable circumstances, and we knew that the dreaded Black canyon was before us.

20th—That three and a half days of difficult climbing were spent in going through the canyon which is no more than eight miles in length.

21st—That at the end of ten days after having journeyed about 28 miles, and having been without food for two days, we fortunately met Lieut. Elliott's rescuing party.

22d—Had it not been for the fortunate meeting with Lieutenant Elliott's party, it is yet a mooted question whether all or any of the party would have survived.

23d—That snow fell the day after we met Elliott, and ice floes were forming in the river at that time. These, coupled with other conditions would have made a trip up the river and through the canyon in search of Colgate at that season of the year extremely hazardous, if at all possible and in any case it would have been impossible to bring out Colgate's body. In view of the dangerous nature of such a trip, and the fact that the burial of the body, if found, would be all the expedition could accomplish, Lieutenant Elliott wisely decided with us, that the result would not warrant the jeopardizing of the lives of the valuable men who readily volunteered to go.

24th—That on our return to Spokane we met the widow and eldest son of George Colgate, and Mr. Carlin spent nearly four hours with them, explaining all the circumstances relative to Mr. Colgate. At the noon hour Gen. Carlin invited them to lunch at the Hotel Spokane, which invitation they accepted.

25th—That having lost our entire outfit, and paid out considerable sums of money to Ben Keeley, and for rewards, and the expenses of large relief expeditions—all of which expense was indirectly caused by Colgate himself—we were, in consequence, reduced in funds so as to be unable to assist his family financially beyond their actual necessities at that time.

26th—That we all strenuously advised against sending out searching parties at that season of the year, and that Mr. Carlin volunteered his services and assistance in the spring, when parties could undertake such a trip with safety and with a reasonable hope of success.

27th—That the circumstances under which a letter was reported to have been written by Colgate and sent down the river in a bottle, are such as to preclude the possibility of its being genuine.

28th—That we note with regret that people ignorant of the roughness and dangers of the region have recklessly gone in search of Colgate's body. From our knowledge and situation we know that at this unfavored season of the year the success of such expeditions is next to impossible, and we sincerely hope that none of the parties will come to grief.

29th—In conclusion, I assert that we did our whole duty toward George Colgate as a friend and companion; that for him we sacrificed the fears and anxieties of our relatives and friends, our outfit, as well as large sums of money, and jeopardized our own lives to the very last extremity in a vain endeavor to get him back to civilization; and that we left him only when circumstances made it a folly to remain longer with him.

30th—Finally, I assert that were all the details known, and the many trying situations of the party thoroughly understood, our actions during the entire trip would be proved to be not only justifiable, but honorable and praiseworthy.

A.L.A. HIMMELWRIGHT,
41 Park Row, New York City,
Jan. 16th, 1894.

Appendix D
Accounts and Expenditures

Vancouver Barracks, Washington.
November 20th, 1893.

The Adjutant General of the Army,
Washington, D. C.

Sir:

In consequence of a party of young men, including my son, Wm. E. Carlin, having been snowed in or otherwise prevented from getting out of the Clearwater country, Idaho and knowing that they are and have been in the greatest possible peril, and destitute, I have ordered several small parties to go in search of them and have required the officers in charge of these expeditions to hire guides, Indians and other men to assist, and to make purchases of articles necessary in the search not kept on hand in the quartermaster's department—snow-shoes, toboggans, &c.

I respectfully request that all this be laid before the Secretary of War for his information, and with the request that all expenditures on account of this service be sanctioned and approved by him.

Very respectfully,
William P. Carlin
Brigadier General,
Commanding.

General Carlin had great difficulty with this request. The quartermaster general, R.N. Batchelder, held him accountable for $1,108.85 "for the purchase of snow-shoes, toboggans, moccasins, rubber boots, etc., reimbursement of expenses, services of boat-men, packers, guides and couriers and hire of transportation at excessive rates." And Batchelder's recommendation to the secretary of war was that "General Carlin be held responsible."

The acting judge advocate general concurred in the recommendation of the quartermaster general, "for the reason that it does not appear that [General Carlin] had any authority to authorize the expenditures."

The Army commander, Major General J.M. Schofield, came down on neither side in his recommendation to the Secretary of War:

> ...If it is considered within the limits of administrative discretion to approve the purchases made in this case I recommend that it be done. If not, I respectfully suggest that the matter be brought to the attention of Congress, so that a Bill providing the necessary relief may be passed.
>
> In respect to the purely official question of responsibility for the purchases made, of course the Commanding General who ordered them is the responsible authority.

The Secretary of War, Daniel S. Lamont, ruled on November 3, 1894, that "The recommendation of the Quartermaster General as concurred in by the Acting Judge Advocate General that General Carlin be held responsible is approved."

The general carried his case to Congress, and in February, 1896, the House Committee on Military Affairs approved a bill relieving General Carlin of the debt.

Lieutenant Elliott had less trouble:

Vancouver Barracks, Washington,
January 6th, 1894.

The Assistant Adjutant General
Department of the Columbia
Vancouver Barracks, Washington.

Sir:

I have the honor to make the following report to accompany application for authority to drop rations issued to civilians and lost hunters. On November 8th, 1893, I was ordered by the Department Commander to proceed with a detachment to the Clearwater country and use every possible effort to rescue a party of hunters reported to be starving in the Bitter Root Mountains. Pursuant to said orders I employed such civilian guides, boatmen and snow packers as were absolutely necessary to ensure the success of the expedition. These men were engaged enroute and there was no way of subsisting them except on the rations which I had taken with me or purchased nor had they money to pay for subsistence. The five lost hunters were starving when I met them and consumed at least double the ordinary ration during the seven days that they were with me. There was also great waste due to snow, rain and river water, in camp on the boats and on the raft, which at one time was entirely submerged.

The civilians and number of days for rations were: Henry Ables, ten (10) days. James Strangers, five (5) days. Norbert La Mothe, nineteen (19) days. James T. Winn, fifteen (15) days. Rory Burke, fourteen (14) days. John Freeman, fourteen (14) days. Seventy-seven (77) rations.

The subsistence stores purchased were: 200# potatoes, 100# beans, 8½# dried apples, 50# bacon, 100# flour, 5# tea, 25# coffee, 25# sugar, 16½# dried apricots, 10# soap, 10# rice, 20# oatmeal, 12 cans condensed milk, 10# dried fruit, mixed.

The milk, oatmeal and rice was given to starving hunters.

When I left my last camp at North Fork Ferry, Clearwater River, all that was left of my supplies were one sack of red beans, swollen and unfit for use, and one sack of dried fruit swollen sour and unfit. These I abandoned as it was useless to take them further.

Very respectfully,
Your obedient servant,
Charles P. Elliott,
1st Lieut. 4th Cavalry

Washington, March 30, 1894.
The Commanding General
Department of the Columbia,
Vancouver Barracks, Washington.

Sir:

Referring to your recommendation of the 11th of January last, upon letter from 1st Lieut. C.P. Elliott, 4th Cavalry...I have the honor to inform you that the Acting Secretary of War has approved the recommendation of the Commissary General of Subsistence, U.S.A., that the expenditure of money for subsistence supplies, and the issues made, together with such losses as occurred on the expedition referred to be allowed in the accounts and returns of Lieutenant C.P. Elliott, 4th Cavalry.

Very Respectfully,
H.C. Conlein
Asst. Adjutant General.

Sources

Books

Himmelwright, A.L.A. *In the Heart of the Bitterroot Mountains*. New York: G.P. Putnam's Sons, 1895.

    Himmelwright wrote this "authorized account" of the 1893 hunting expedition under the pen name Heclawa. It is based in part on the diary William E. Carlin kept while in camp and on the trail, and provides most of what we know about the Carlin party's journey from Spokane to the Lochsa and return. Some have put it down as a self-serving defense of the party's behavior toward the camp cook, George Colegate. If so, it's understandable; Himmelwright wrote it while he was defending himself and his companions against a storm of criticism. More surprising is the book's general tone: Much of it is a testament to the pleasures of wilderness travel, as though this particular trek had not ended in tragedy. Himmelwright begins the book with a hymn to the beauty of untrammeled Nature and its solace for the troubled soul, and ends it with a discourse on the proper powder loads for hunting big game. The book includes a long excerpt from the journals of Lewis and Clark relating to their travels in the Clearwater region. A 1993 reprint by Mountain Meadow Press contains most of the 1895 edition but omits the Lewis and Clark section while adding some new material.

Dryden, Cecil. *The Clearwater of Idaho*. New York: Carlton Press, 1975.

    The chapter on the Colegate incident (page 234) briefly reviews the events of the fall of 1893, leaving the reader to decide whether the Carlin party acted as any other group would under the circumstances or whether the hunters broke "the immutable law of the trail."

Space, Ralph. *The Clearwater Story*. Missoula: U.S. Department of Agriculture/ U.S. Forest Service, 1964.

    The author, as a Forest Service ranger, had walked over much of the Lochsa area and knew it well. In this account he describes the terrain, names the places important to the story of the Carlin party, and recounts his efforts to find George Colegate's grave. He places the end of the rafting at Lost Creek, and Elliott's meeting with the hunters at Canyon Creek.

Kendrick-Juliaetta Centennial Committee. *A Centennial History of the Kendrick-Juliaetta Area*. Published by the committee in 1990.

    This book is the source of the material about Kendrick in chapter two.

Articles

Cerveny, George R. "Human Spirit Broke Down; When 1893 Hunters Left Cook in Idaho Wilds to Die." *The Pacific Northwesterner* (Summer, 1975).

Cerveny, whose aunt married George Colegate's oldest son, Charles, reviews events leading up to the abandonment of the camp cook, and then sums up the case against the New York men as a prosecutor might. He sees the tragedy as a failure of the human spirit and blames that failure largely on the Easterners' romantic notions about a healing, loving nature as opposed to "a decadent, soul-destroying civilization."

Christopherson, Edmund. "Tragic Trek." *Montana, The Magazine of Western History* (Autumn, 1956).

This article reviews not only the Carlin party's trials in the Bitterroots but the swirling controversy that followed the party's rescue from the wilderness. Christopherson makes clear his contempt of the hunters for what he calls "an almost unheard-of breach of etiquette among true westerners." The article, quoting the Walla Walla *Statesman,* is the source of the statement that Carlin gave Charles Colegate $25 for his father's services.

Joe Baily. "The Tragic Story of the Carlin Hunting Party." Spokane *Spokesman-Review* (February 19, 1956).

Baily's account, based largely on the Himmelwright book, hits the high points of the story and then suggests that the readers decide whether the New York men had broken the law of the trail or simply done what they had to do. Baily seems to believe that Colegate did write the note found in a bottle in the Snake River in December, 1893; and that the dying man did manage to struggle from the place where the hunters left him to the spot eight miles downriver where Elliott found his remains.

Letters and Reports

Official correspondence of the United States Army.

These files, housed in the National Archives, include Lieutenant Charles P. Elliott's detailed report of his attempt to reach the lost hunters from the west; Captain George Andrews's report of his campaign to rescue them from Fort Missoula to the east; and letters of Brigadier General William P. Carlin, commandant at Vancouver Barracks, who launched the rescue effort.

Newspapers

Most of the newspapers that contributed material for this narrative are identified in the text. Contemporary news accounts are useful, but the newspapers of the 1890s made less distinction between news and opinion than those of today. They also tended to put quotation marks around statements that clearly had been paraphrased, leading modern readers to suppose that people actually talked that way in 1893. People may have spoken more carefully then than most of us do today, but no one can believe that the words attributed to Ben Keeley by the *Weekly Missoulian* (Appendix B) actually came out of his mouth.